CONSTANCE MARKIEVICZ
IRISH REVOLUTIONARY

For John and Maureen Haverty

CONSTANCE MARKIEVICZ

IRISH REVOLUTIONARY

Anne Haverty

THE LILLIPUT PRESS
DUBLIN

First published in 1988 by
Pandora Press, London, as
Constance Markievicz: An Independent Life

This edition published by
THE LILLIPUT PRESS
62–63 Sitric Road, Arbour Hill,
Dublin 7, Ireland
www.lilliputpress.ie

A CIP record for this title is available
from The British Library.

ISBN 978 1 84351 672 9

Set in 10 pt on 13 pt Sabon by Marsha Swan
Printed in Spain by GraphyCems

CONTENTS

ILLUSTRATIONS

The following are found between pages 126 and 127.

INTRODUCTION

WHILE THE REVIEWS for the original edition of this life of Constance Markievicz were good, they were more muted than first-time authors are prone to expect. In particular, reviewers seemed to express a discernible note of resistance towards the subject. This should not have been altogether surprising. The Troubles in the North were still continuing and the new revisionist project in Irish historiography was at its height. Enthusiasm for nationalism and its heroes was on a downward slide.

But it was the attitude to Markievicz herself that I found puzzling. The first woman ever elected to parliament, the first woman to be a minister in government, the woman without whose corps of well-trained erstwhile boy scouts the events of 1916 might not have happened, without whom surely it could not have lasted as long as it did – why was she absent from the list? Why was she almost unmentioned in school history books? Why did she not figure among those who had influenced the making of the Republic? This was also after the feminist movement of the 1970s had helped to broaden perceptions and expectations of the place of women in society. We would soon elect a woman president. And here was a woman who, share though she might along with the famous ones an ideology that was now deeply unpopular, was surely a standard-bearer for equality, social and political engagement and not least courage.

That first edition was one of a series of lives of Irish women, published by Pandora, a feminist press. I chose Markievicz because among the possible subjects offered to me she was the one I knew least about. The others included women such as Maud Gonne, Lady Gregory and the Parnell sisters and, like almost everybody else, I knew about them mainly because of their connection with more famous men. Markievicz, as I was soon pleased to discover, was a stand-alone. Of course she was influenced by those around her and influenced them in turn. But she was more than a muse or an enabler or a facilitator, the preferred roles for women to play. She chose her influences, chose her associates. She was self-driven and self-confident enough to be able to be selfless. This was the heyday of giving up your advantages for your convictions. And she gave up quite a lot. In her writing she could express gracefully and blithely her ardent way of seeing things. Her humanity and sensibility is immanent in almost everything she writes. I found her admirable and hugely likeable. And revisiting her twenty odd years later, I still do.

In her own time she was admired and loved by a great many; was appreciated enough by the poor of Dublin to be chosen again and again as their representative, to be given a last farewell by them in their thousands. But then too Markievicz had her detractors, notably Sean O'Casey and Sean O'Faolain. It was O'Faolain, her first biographer, who perhaps did her most damage. Her friend, Helena Molony, described his book, published in the thirties, as 'bad, inaccurate, catty and misleading' and as a result she was 'in great danger of being misunderstood'. The keynote of her character, Molony said, was 'simplicity and sincerity'. Maud Gonne was angered by O'Casey's and O'Faolain's 'sneers at her'. Markievicz, Gonne said, 'was a great woman and I always think she does not get the credit she should'.

But it's the cattiness that can seem to prevail. In our time Markievicz is also someone many love to hate. Some of the reasons why are fairly obvious. To be able to cast aside what most of us value so much – privilege, money, position – can cause discomfort or resentment. Her fervour and disregard for the conventions offend the prudent and the sensible. And for all the advances in equality, for a woman to be as assertive as she was is strangely even less acceptable now than it was then.

Maybe for these reasons much is made, as I say in the text, by present-day detractors of the allegation that it was she who shot a constable in St Stephen's Green on the Easter Monday of 1916. The only source for this allegation, apart from rumour – and rumours were flying about anyone and anything in that dramatic week – is the account of a Miss Geraldene Fitzgerald. This came to light since the the first publication of my book and since it is so often cited against her and could be said to have passed into public lore it bears investigation.

Fitzgerald's account is in the Dublin Castle files (kept in the British National Archives at Kew) marked 'Evidence Against Countess Markievicz' and stamped 14 July 1917. It purports to be from her diary, 'kindly supplied' to the taker of the evidence by her mother who lived in Birr, County Offaly. Consisting, however, only of two typewritten pages this cannot be verified. In fact it reads more like a deposition, taken down by someone tasked with gathering incriminating evidence.

Constable Lahiff was shot, according to the Dublin Metropolitan Police report, at about 12 am – Fitzgerald, who was training to be a public health nurse, says that on that day she was in High Street at 12.30 am. On her way home to St Stephen's Green past Christ Church she took a longer route to avoid Jacob's where the Sinn Féiners were in possession, and spoke to several people about the events. Making her way to the Jubilee Nurses' Home on the south side of the Green adjacent to Harcourt Street, she was 'greatly astonished to see the Sinn Féiners in the Park, digging trenches inside the railings while others of them were ready with rifles to fire on anyone in military or police uniforms who passed that way'. She sat down to dinner in the dining room with some colleagues. It would now be approaching 1 pm if not later:

> Dinner! Such a meal. We were just seated and were taking our soup when we heard the most awful firing outside the house. We jumped up immediately and rushed to the front room to see what was happening. What we saw was this. All the men with their rifles fixed towards Harcourt Street. A lady in green uniform, the same as most of the men were wearing (breeches, slouch hat with green feathers etc) the feathers were the only feminine feature in her appearance, holding a revolver in one hand and a cigarette in the other, was standing on the footpath giving orders to the men. We recognised her as the Countess Markievicz – such a specimen of womanhood. There were other women, similarly attired, inside the Park, walking about and bringing drinks of water to the men. We had only been looking out for a few moments when we saw a policeman walking down the path from Harcourt Street. He had only gone a short way when we heard a shot and then saw him fall forward on his face. The 'Countess' ran

triumphantly into the Green, saying 'I got him' and some of the rebels shook her by the hand and seemed to congratulate her.

Apart from the crucial matters of the timing and the location of the shooting (Constable Lahiff was shot at the Fusiliers' Gate facing Grafton Street), which differ so greatly from all other accounts, including the official account, there are other very questionable aspects to this testimony. It was a warm day and the windows in the front-facing room may well have been open. But even so the likelihood of a remark carrying from inside the Green and across a wide stretch of road noisy with the activities of the revolutionaries, onlookers, and the traffic that was still going up and down, is small. Also, Constance was experienced with guns and it's difficult to imagine her exulting like an untried markswoman in the accuracy of her shot when it was at such short range. The room adjoining the dining room would almost certainly have been on the ground floor, a vantage from which it would not have been possible to see into the Green. And there is the matter of those other women Fitzgerald claims to have seen 'similarly attired'. Among the women revolutionaries only Margaret Skinnider may, apart from Constance, have worn breeches. Even the very assertive and rebellious Helena Molony wore a skirt. If indeed there were others 'similarly attired' could the witness be sure the person she saw was the Countess?

It's difficult to know what to make of this account or to say what Geraldene Fitzgerald may or may not have seen – except that it seems at the very least fanciful and based more on a year's worth of rumours than on reality. None of it would stand up in a court of law; which is probably why it did not appear on Markievicz's charge sheet when she was tried in 1920. Only the obstinately mischievous, to put it kindly, can continue to cite it.

As well as Geraldene Fitzgerald's 'diary', I am glad to have been able to make use of more recent publications. The archives of the Bureau of Military History, accessible online, are a trove of information through personal reminiscences, all the more intriguing for often contradicting each other. Among the books, Patrick Quigley's *The Polish Irishman* provides much-needed new information about Casimir and Stanislas (Stasko) Markievicz.

Anne Haverty
Dublin, April 2016

ACKNOWLEDGMENTS

THE WRITING OF this biography has depended on the help of good friends and benevolent acquaintances. I want first to thank Gemma O'Connor who suggested that I embark on it, and who was alway there with advice and books; Josslyn Gore-Booth who was more than generous with the papers in his possession relating to his great-aunt; and Aideen Gore-Booth who welcomed me to Lissadell.

There were several people who gave me information, ideas, time, encouragement and books. I am especially grateful to Seamus Scully who spent a lifetime compiling an archive devoted to the Gore-Booth sisters; to Caitriona Crowe, Frank Callanan, Sean MacBride, Richard Hayes and Maud Long; also Lucille Redmond, Margaret Robertson, Francis Stuart, Peter Haugh, Colm Tóibín, Mary Campbell, Patricia Boylan, Jim Ryan, Brian Lynch, Tim O'Grady, Taisy Grimes and Sheena Joughin; the Loughlins at Annaghmakerrig and my sister Geraldine Haverty. My gratitude is due to the staffs of the National Library, the National Museum, the Library of Trinity College Dublin, the British Museum and the Irish Astrological Society for their assistance and consideration.

Above all I want to thank dear Tony (Anthony Cronin); and for his invaluable help with this edition, Simon Beesley.

CONSTANCE MARKIEVICZ
IRISH REVOLUTIONARY

ONE

LISSADELL: CHILDHOOD
AND FAMILY LIFE

IN DUBLIN, where the streets have solidly Irish names and most of the public monuments commemorate Irish people, the exotic name of Markievicz stands out, even if attached to relatively modest things – a block of municipal flats, a leisure centre, a small bust in St Stephen's Green. Constance, Countess Markievicz, might have liked the flats, built in the austere economical style of the 1930s, to be more beautiful than they are but she would be proud to have them as a memorial. She spent much of her life earning the entitlement to be associated with the people of the city. Countess Markievicz got her title and foreign name from her marriage. She was actually Irish, a Gore-Booth from Co. Sligo.

As Constance Georgina Gore-Booth, she enjoyed every advantage the late nineteenth century could offer a girl. She belonged to a wealthy, aristocratic and kind family. She was clever, talented and beautiful, and enjoyed a wild, somewhat eccentric Irish upbringing as one of the spoilt darlings of a big country house on the romantic west coast. Born in London on 4 February 1868 at 7 Buckingham Gate, a family town house close to Buckingham Palace, she was the first child of Henry Gore-Booth, then aged twenty-five and heir to the baronetcy of Lissadell in Co. Sligo, and Georgina, *née* Hill, of Tickhill Castle in Yorkshire, whose grandfather was Lord Scarborough. Soon after her birth Constance was brought home to Ireland, to the house known locally as Lissadell Court. Her brother Josslyn was born in the following year, her sisters Eva and Mabel in 1870 and 1874 respectively, and another brother Mordaunt in 1876.

Lissadell is a classically beautiful and rather forbidding house. The approach from the main gate is by a winding avenue, two and a half miles long, that climbs and falls along the light Sligo coastline with the shore of Drumcliff Bay on one side and dark silent woods on the other and rises at its end to reveal the formidable grey stone building in low-lying parkland. Built by her grandfather, Sir Robert Gore-Booth, to replace a less impressive house, this structure was some thirty years old when Constance was brought here.

Lissadell expressed Sir Robert's self-image as a great land-owner, his effectiveness, his interest in the arts and something of an indefinable quality that might be called innocence. It had forty-eight rooms and was the first country house in Ireland to be lit by gas from a gasometer. Francis Goodwin of London who designed it was well known for his churches and public buildings and gave it a gaunt and ecclesiastical feel that may not have been intended. He – or Sir Robert – was probably inspired by the neoclassicism of Thomas Hope whose ideas appealed to rarefied tastes. The splendour of the house that resulted was modified by its austerity and idiosyncracy. The starkness of the exterior was alleviated by a bow on the south face and an unusual and grand *porte-cochère* as the main entrance on the north. Inside, there was the imposing geometry of neoclassicism and the coldness of marble. In the great hall, black Kilkenny marble was used for floor, columns and staircase. The principal rooms had chimney pieces of Italian marble sculpted in the style of the Egyptian revival, one of the rarest and most esoteric versions of neoclassicism.

The most striking feature at Lissadell, however, is the manner in which the family rooms, the dining room, drawing rooms etc., had the status of ante-rooms, pushed aside to right and left by a long and lofty gallery that possesses the heart of the house. The gallery was top-lit, its roof supported by thick white pillars, square columns running down one side, Ionic down the other. It contained an organ and Sir Robert's collection of pictures, many of them Old Masters brought back from his European Grand Tour. These included a Rape of Lucretia, a St John the Baptist that was possibly a Caravaggio, and touchingly sentimental depictions of the Irish peasantry by Joseph Haverty, the noted nineteenth-century artist, hung in Florentine frames.

Lissadell was a house that easily accommodated reflection, solitude and high aspirations. It was also of course a hive of activity, its many charming sunny rooms, with their views of the sea, bustling with children, live-in relations and servants, noisy with animals and the comings and goings of farmworkers, stable grooms, herdsmen, coachmen and gardeners. Constance claimed to have not been particularly fond of the house but that was perhaps a necessary ideological stance. What she and Eva did love however, and were to write and speak of at length in the years to come, was the countryside around it:

> We lived on a beautiful, enchanted Western coast where we grew up intimate with the soft mists and the coloured mountains and where each morning you woke to the sound of the wild birds, the sad wintry cry of starvation that came like a keen from the throat of the phill-abin driven from its haunts by the storm winds ... Behind the big gray barrack-like house, ranges of mountains lay like a great row of sphinxes against the sky and shut us out from Ireland. Trees and glades sloped down to the bay, across which Knocknarea rose, crowned by the great queen's cairn. The bay slipped into the Atlantic, somewhere behind black cliffs, and the Atlantic was the end of the world.[1]

That part of Sligo, bounded by the great mountains, Ben Bulben and Knocknarea that rise like whales out of the sea, had an ethereal beauty. Salty fields and rich graceful vegetation washed in the volatile Atlantic light, birches rustling in the ocean breezes, a peasantry who, though poor, were imaginative and credulous – it was in this place that the poet Yeats gathered the stories of magic and legend that he wrote down in his book *The Celtic Twilight*, a place which provided him with images and metaphors for his poems that marked the beginning of the Gaelic resurgence.

On Ben Bulben, it was said, lay the door to the land of the Faery; and on its slopes Diarmuid, the tragic hero of the story of Diarmuid and Gráinne, met his death in a tussle with a boar. Under the cairn on the summit of Knocknarea was buried great Queen Maeve of Connacht who fought Cúchulainn of Ulster.

These unearthly figures, seen by day and by night, were both admired and feared. Yeats tells how his uncle's housekeeper saw Maeve, 'the finest woman you ever saw travelling right across from the mountain straight towards her, dressed in white with a sword by her side and a dagger lifted up in her hand and her feet and arms bare'.[2]

Lissadell (in Irish, *Lios A' Daill*, the Fort of the Blind) itself has its story, one grounded in history more than legend. It was owned before the English conquest by the O'Dalys, hereditary poets who were free of tribute, or rent, because of their profession. In 1213 an O'Daly killed with an axe the tax collector of his territorial chief. He had to flee to Scotland but was eventually restored to favour and to Lissadell by writing poems in praise of his chief. The area also has its share of remains from the time of the great monasteries. In 574, St Columcille (Columba) founded at Drumcliff his monastery that was to last for almost a thousand years and its ruined round tower and carved high cross still stand on the road to Sligo from Lissadell.

The peasantry that gave Yeats his stories were of the people who provided much of the income of Lissadell. Sir Henry, Constance's father, also had considerable property in Manchester but he owned almost 32,000 acres of the county of Sligo. From the letting of this land he received a yearly income of £15,000, an amount that in today's terms would be equivalent to something like £750,000. About half of this land lay around Lissadell, the other half lay about twenty miles to the south and included the town of Ballymote, bought by Sir Robert in 1833 from Lord Orkney.

The tenant families who paid rent directly to Sir Henry and whose lives were, theoretically at least, in his control, numbered about one thousand. There were many more who paid indirectly through renting from one of Sir Henry's larger tenant farmers such as Mr Barber, a model tenant who leased 450 acres and then sublet at a profit. Many of the smaller tenants were desperately poor. Some 300, paying less than £4 a year, rented a portion of land ranging from a few roods to a few acres that could provide a living of only bare subsistence. In a newspaper article many years later Constance described with revolutionary fervour the social structure of the Sligo countryside of her childhood:

> You saw the landlords in their big demesnessnes, mostly of Norman or Saxon stock, walled in and aloof, an alien class, sprung from an alien race. ... The prosperous farmers were mostly Protestant ... and hidden away among rocks in the mountain sides or soaking in the slime and ooze of the boglands or beside the Atlantic shore where the grass is blasted yellow by the salt wind you find the dispossessed people of the old Gaelic race in their miserable cabins.[3]

The landlord system was an aspect of Irish life that was becoming ever more contentious during Constance's youth. The majority of landlords were descendants of those successive waves of soldier-adventurers who came during the sixteenth and seventeenth centuries to subdue Ireland on behalf of the Crown. The more prominent and effective among them were granted land in return for their services, land from which the native Irish were turned out and then re-admitted as tenants. The first ancestor of Constance's to set up in Ireland was a Paul Gore, who rode in the Elizabethan campaigns in which the conquest of Ireland became conclusive. He was granted the nucleus of the Lissadell estate and was made a Baronet of Ireland in 1621. The second great push came fifty years later when Cromwell's bloody campaign uprooted the Irish and allowed English settlers to establish themselves throughout the country. The resistance of the Irish was sporadic and ineffective but it was to remain as an aggravation for generations to come.

The new proprietors saw themselves as brave and enterprising colonists and Ireland as a colony to be exploited. And the colonized regarded them with bitterness, resentment and a hostility that flickered into insurrection at irregular intervals. There was certainly hatred on both sides, at least initially. With the self-justification typical of colonialism everywhere, the English found the Irish uncivilized – and indeed they were not civilized in the English sense – and indolent. Their favourite prescription for peace and prosperity was to be rid of them entirely and to populate the land with a loyal and industrious peasantry from Scotland. To the Irish, their English conquerors were upstarts, foreigners and the cause of their servility and poverty.

The situation was exacerbated by the identification of both sides with opposing religions. In England, the Reformation and the establishment of the new Protestant Church were then burning issues while the Irish generally remained immune to the controversy and maintained the old Catholicism. Along with the Protestant settlers came a Protestant clergy. As a means of subjugation, the Penal Laws – a set of punitive measures including economic sanctions – were introduced, which reduced the Catholic population to the status of non-citizens. To the Irish, Protestantism came to be associated with coercion and privilege and Catholicism symbolic of a private revolt, a badge of pride and independence in the face of defeat. By 1775, 95 per cent of the land was owned by Protestants.

By the early nineteenth century turbulence had subsided into the apathy of an agrarian subsistence economy. The potato had been introduced; and its use became widespread since a plot of ground under this crop could feed twice as many people as the same plot under corn. This tenant population increased dramatically through the first half of the century while more and more of them lived in a state of distress, which contemporary travellers and observers found shameful and abhorrent. The hostile relation between landlord and tenant was by now largely replaced by a mutual tolerance and contempt. Whether landlordism was the principal reason for the endemic poverty is still open to question. The poorest tenants certainly – and they numbered at least a quarter of the whole – were obliged to hand over as rent any cash earned from the sale of animals or grain; and much of this money was either spent abroad or sent to landlords who lived abroad. About one-third of Irish landlords were absentees. Because of this, and because most of the people had little or no disposable income, Ireland was notoriously under-capitalized. Irish industry was at first proscribed, then never actively encouraged. Ireland never experienced an Industrial Revolution.

The population problem was solved quickly and brutally by the great mid-century crisis, the Famine. The destruction by blight of the potato crop in the years 1845–50 was more widespread and unrelenting than failures that had occurred before. Native resources were too meagre to avert starvation and the government, with the ambiguity characteristic of its dealings with Ireland, failed to act decisively. One million people died of starvation in those years and one million more left Ireland, most of them for America, in the wave of mass emigration that followed. Some millions more would emigrate within the next half-century. In 1841 the population numbered more than eight million. By the end of the century, it would be half that.

Constance was born into the relatively prosperous period of the post-Famine. The horrors of the Famine may have left a psychic scar but the physical effects were beneficial to those who remained. There were fewer people. Holdings could be larger where the landlord did not prefer to graze cattle on land cleared of tenantry. The prices of farm animals and farm products such as butter rose steeply from the 1850s to the 1870s so rents were easier to pay. Landlords, however, were becoming uneasily aware that their autonomy and the system under which they flourished was for the first time open to question. The analysis offered by the Radical, James F. Lawlor, before the Famine – 'It is a question between a people and a class ... a people of eight million and a class of eight thousand. They or we must quit the country or they or we are doomed...'[4] – had invaded respectable English political circles in the shape of Gladstone and some Liberal allies. It was a Liberal government that had suffered the embarrassment of Famine on British territory and on Britain's doorstep and succeeding generations of Liberals sought to lay the blame on the irresponsibility and wanton speculation of landlordism.

In an electoral speech at Wigan in 1868, the year of Constance's birth, Gladstone, the future Prime Minister, spoke of the Irish aristocracy as

> some tall tree of noxious growth, lifting its head to Heaven and poisoning the atmosphere of the land so far as its shadow can extend. It is still there, gentlemen, but now at last the day has come when, as we hope, the axe has been laid to the root. It is deeply cut round and round. It nods and quivers from base to base. There lacks, gentlemen, but one stroke more – the stroke of these Elections. It will then, once and for all, topple to its fall, and on that day the heart of Ireland will leap for joy.[5]

The iron seemed to have entered too into the soul of the peasantry. The Land League, a movement formed to win greater control of the land they farmed, enjoyed the support of the mass of the people. By 1881 even a benevolent landlord like Sir Henry Gore-Booth, Constance's father, complained that his tenantry was less trustful, friendly and pleasant to meet, even if they were not positively ill disposed. Despite appearances however, the Irish tenantry was not innately radical. Its disaffection was primarily a result of what it regarded as the alien nationality of the landlords.

The identity of the landlord class and its position in Irish life was indeed ambiguous. The French writer de Tocqueville wrote that the Irish aristocracy 'wanted to remain separated from the people and to be still English. It has driven itself into imitating the English aristocracy without possessing either its skill or its resources and its own sin is proving its ruin.'[6] Although there were notable exceptions, the Irish aristocracy saw itself as the representative of England in Ireland. It knew only English culture, spoke with English aristocratic vowels, sent, if it could afford it, its children to England to be educated, its daughters to be presented at the English court and its younger sons to the English army, navy and church. Since the Irish people had never given their mandate to English rule, the harmonious relationship between the English landlord and his tenant was never reproduced in Ireland. Landlord and tenant shared neither the same church nor, in many parts of the country, the same language. Though they might behave as badly or, in some cases, worse than their Protestant counterparts, the few 'Irish' or Catholic landlords, known as the Old Irish, enjoyed a traditional loyalty that pre-dated the coming of the English. 'In the minds of the Irish people they were different,' wrote David Thomson in *Woodbrook*. 'Their rights of possession were not questioned and their relationships with workmen and tenants were more intimate.'[7]

Constance's father had a considerable standing among his peers. Sir Henry was not among the wealthiest – there were a few men such as the Duke of Leinster who owned well over a hundred thousand acres – but he missed by only a couple of thousand acres the status of being the second-largest landowner in the County of Sligo. His income placed him well above the level of most of the neighbouring gentry. And at a time when landlordism was under siege on several fronts he could be held up as an example of the justice of this system of land tenure. His tenants might well have thought that if they must have a landlord, they were fortunate in having Sir Henry Gore-Booth.

If his nearest neighbours, a Mr Gethin and Mrs Huddleston, who between them owned about three thousand acres at Ballyconnell, illustrated the worst aspects of Irish landlordism, Sir Henry, in the conduct of his estate, illustrated the best. Mr Gethin and Mrs Huddleston were absentee to the extent that they were not known by sight to their tenants. Sir Henry and his family lived on their estate and when his father's agent died in 1871, Sir Henry took over its management using a thorough system of accounts and book-keeping that was undertaken on few Irish estates.[8]

The rents he charged, averaging 12s. to 15s. per acre, were lower than those approved by the Griffith Valuation. The Ballyconnell tenants paid 40s. per acre for land that was no better. Sir Henry oversaw an equitable and efficient distribution of land and organized the tenants to construct roads. He gave assistance with drainage and provided lime and slates for houses. At Ballyconnell, a man who improved his land by making a watercourse had to pay more rent, and all tenants paid 4/2d. more in the pound for the right to gather seaweed, which they used as fertilizer, from the foreshore. The people living in wretched conditions whom Constance remembered may have been the Ballyconnell tenants who ran out of potatoes by March and lived from then until summer on Indian meal bought on credit, to be paid for by 'an extra take of fish or the produce of a cow or a crop of oats'.

At such a level of subsistence, finding the money to pay the rent was obviously a crippling burden. It was essential to pay it because a tenant could face eviction from his home and the loss of his livelihood if he did not. In the Famine years, the distress was augmented by the eviction of starving and desperate people from their holdings for non-payment. In the 1870s when the number of evictions rose again, there were only six evictions on the Lissadell estate, all, according to Sir Henry, of 'idlers who would neither work or pay'.

Sir Henry's attitude towards his tenants and the conduct of his estate was paternalistic, like a Victorian father's towards his children. He was concerned for their welfare, did whatever was in his power to relieve the distress that many of them were regularly subject to, distrusted their capacity to handle their affairs and regretted their profligacy. He expected them not to question his authority or position. And it is unlikely that he himself ever questioned it.

Constance was familiar with most of her father's tenants because, before the advent of the bicycle, urban bureaucracy in Sligo, and disposable cash, Lissadell was the centre of their world. Many of them supplemented the income from their little holdings with employment on its farm, woods and gardens; and they came to the house not only at half-yearly intervals to pay the rent but to consult Sir Henry about their personal affairs:

> Few owners [wrote a correspondent of *The Times* who inquired into the Irish land question] have such intimate knowledge of their tenantry, holdings and necessities. The people come to him as adviser and friend, as an arbiter in family feuds and as their depositor for wills and marriage settlements. He has a curious carefully kept record of the troubles, disputes and condition of his poor neighbours.

But Sir Henry was typical of most landlords in that he regarded his tenants as essentially a nuisance. 'The pity is,' he told the *Times*, 'that half the population of these townlands could not be deported and their holdings doubled in size.' While he neglected to consider the material and psychological ill effects of tenant status, his exasperation is understandable since under the prevailing system, such small farms could not be economic. When the system changed, as it did in due course, the tenants set about consolidating their holdings as fast as any landlord could wish. Unlike many landlords, he was too humane to engage in the common practice of what was effectively deportation through offering to the people meagre inducements to emigrate, such as the fare to America and a small sum for necessities for the voyage. There was said to be a skeleton in the family cupboard that, it was believed, made the Gore-Booths conscientious.

In the 1830s when Sir Henry's father, Sir Robert Gore-Booth, bought the town of Ballymote, he also bought a piece of land of about 800 acres, called the Seven Cartrons, and decided to farm it more profitably by grazing cattle on it. It was necessary therefore to induce the fifty-two families who lived there to quit. According to local lore, they were given £2 passage money and £4 in compensation and placed on a chartered ship called the *Pomania*, which was so unseaworthy that she foundered before she had sailed beyond Sligo Bay and was still in sight of land. Drowned bodies, it was said, were washed ashore at Lissadell and Raughley from where they had set out. A ballad still heard in Sligo tells of the purported tragedy:

> The ship she was a rotten one,
> The truth to you I tell;
> They struck her on the Corraun Rock
> Right under Lissadell ...
> Our rent was paid
> We were not afraid
> That from home we'd have to go.
> We were forced to yield
> And quit the field
> And board the *Pomano*.[9]

There is evidence, however, that while the *Pomania* did sail from Raughley on 31 May with the tenant families on board she arrived safely in Quebec on 6 June, returning to Kingstown on 29 August. The writer of the ballad seems to be conflating this emigration with that of the notorious coffin ships during the Famine a decade later as a political ploy.

The Lissadell estate afforded a lifestyle that was delightful in its Victorian insouciance. Amusements were taken seriously and accomplishments cultivated. There was a ready supply of servants to hand and Lissadell had its full complement. In Constance's childhood, the household included her grandfather, Sir Robert Gore-Booth, her maternal grandmother, Lady Emily Hill, and Aunt Augusta, her father's sister. Sir Robert died in 1876, the year in which Constance's younger brother, Mordaunt, was born. Lady Hill, to whom Eva had been very close, died in 1879.

Although he was a careful steward of his estate and, as President of the Sligo Agricultural Society and Chairman of the Sligo Leitrim and Northern Counties Railways embedded in regional development, Sir Henry was at heart a 'huntin', shootin' and fishin'' man. But his exploits were not confined to his own and his neighbours' fields. He had a lifelong enthusiasm for the Far North and in the years before the Pole had been reached, he was one of those intrepid explorers who made pioneering expeditions in the icy waters of the Arctic. As a young man, he spent his summers yachting and fishing for salmon off Norway and his activities did not cease after he married. There is a family story that Lady Gore-Booth had the artificial lake in the grounds constructed as an attempt to keep him at home. In 1873 he went in a friend's yacht as far as Spitzbergen; and in 1879 he explored the polar cap as far north as 780.241 when he voyaged in the Barents and Kara Seas under Captain A.H. Markham who would later go farthest north in the nineteenth century. Not long after this, he bought his own yacht and named her *Kara*. In 1882, fulfilling a promise he had made to the explorer Leigh Smith, he sailed to his aid through uncharted Arctic waters, successfully rescuing him. There is said to be a tiny isle in the Arctic Ocean called Gore-Booth Island. The exotic fauna he hunted accreted at Lissadell in glass cases: birds, great salmon, a bear with which Mr Kilgallon, the butler who travelled with him, engaged in a life-or-death struggle, and trophies such as walrus tusks and a whale's skull.

Constance's female relatives also had strong personalities. Her mother, Lady Gore-Booth, bore five children, managed the estate when Sir Henry was away, liked to entertain, and involved herself in philanthropic work such as her patronage of a lace-making school for the local women. Aunt Augusta, known as Wee Ga because of her very small stature, had a formidable will and was intensely interested in horses. Constance was greatly loved and approved of as a child in part because she inherited to a lavish extent the best qualities of these people. She resembled her mother in looks and had her self-assurance. She had Augusta's love of horses and surpassed even her noted talent at riding. From her father, she got a skill and daring with guns and animals, a tendency to go far with whatever occupied her, to commit herself, and perhaps an ambition to be extraordinary, to test herself in some area that was not domestic.

She was loved especially because she was happy. She was healthy, energetic, clever and apparently uncomplicated. She put her siblings in the shade. Josslyn was a serious and conscientious boy while Con was quick-witted, quick in movement, the one with the japey schoolboy sense of humour. Eva, the future poet, was rather timid and fragile, an introspective, more inaccessible child. That the sisters were so different did not prevent the development of an almost symbiotic friendship between them. They complemented each other and Eva was to be Con's closest, most affectionate and constant friend throughout her complicated life. Mabel and Mordaunt, who were much younger, had little impact on Constance.

An Anglo-Irish family (by the end of the nineteenth century, the word 'Anglo-Irish' was coming into vogue to describe those, usually of 'planter' descent, whose Irishness was ambiguous – before that they were known simply as Irish) could be quite isolated within its demesne. But Sligo was among the most planted of Irish counties and there were plenty of neighbours to visit and to hunt and shoot with. A family of cousins, the Wynnes, lived nearby at Hazelwood, a splendid eighteenth-century Palladian house. There were other relations not far distant. In the summer, there was a languid beach life of boating, fishing and shrimping. Swimming was not yet done, at least by the female sex, although the Morris family, many miles away in Connemara, was famous for having one of the new bathing machines. In winter, there was the hunting and shooting. The extensive stables were close to the sands where Constance, as a very young child, would ride her pony Storeen at full speed and on side-saddle. Her father taught her to ride and later to shoot, and she was among the zestful shooting parties who went after pheasant and woodcock in the mountain plantation on Ben Bulben and in the waterlogged boglands, or stalking the deer Sir Henry had introduced. These were occasions when Constance would display a quite extraordinary courage, daring, and enthusiasm for danger.

There were major events: the visits to Sligo town, sometimes on horseback when the Gore-Booth family rode the ten miles there, greeted on the road with the deference that fitted their station. Sligo was not one of those depressed and somnolent Irish towns that came alive only on fair day. Among its population of 11,000, it had its share of ragged children; but 500 ships called then at its port every year and it had a thriving middle class, professional and merchant families like W.B. Yeats' relations, the Pollexfens, who enjoyed an active social life. There were yachting regattas and a rowing club, which specialized in races – although gentry like the Gore-Booths remained aloof from these traders' activities. In August there was the journey to Dublin by train for the Horse Show. The Horse Show was the annual outing and social event for a gentry that worshipped the horse. Horses were bought and sold, there were riding and jumping competitions for all ages, side-shows, displays of the ladies' philanthropic classes in handicrafts, and for the adults, balls and parties and gossip.

The girls' education was provided by a series of governesses, the last of which, a Miss Noel, always called Squidge, commanded the undying affection of Constance and Eva. Squidge had intellectual interests. Before she came, they were taught only the usual female accomplishments of music, poetry, sketching and French, but no classics or history, and nothing to fit them for a career. Precocious, spoilt Con, whose interests lay primarily in the outdoors, was probably a trial to these women. But with anyone who suffered or needed help, she redeemed herself with an aristocratic impulse to kindness. There are stories that have a slightly uneasy ring of the princess among the poor about them but which hold some truth: how she sat up night after night with a stable groom who was ill; how, coming down to the kitchen one day, she saw a woman who was pregnant washing clothes, pushed her away from the tub and washed them herself; how she and Eva were liable to give away the clothes they were wearing to poor girls they met on the road – Eva her coat, Constance her shoes.

Both Eva and Constance endeared themselves to the country people – who were always called that, never 'peasants', except as an insult. Eva is credited with being as skilful a horsewoman as Constance, and when they were out riding across the country-side, they used to alight at the cabins and regale their inhabitants with tales of the feats to which they had pushed their ponies. The country people, with what many considered their regrettably retro-spective cast of mind, told the children stories of the fairies and the queen who was seen on the mountain, stories of emigration and 'the men of '98' (the men of the rebellion of 1798, of which Wolfe Tone was the most famous). They probably kept to themselves the stories of the Fenians and the Rising of 1867 because those events were too close to the present, too close to the divide that stood between them and the children from the Big House. The children's heroes were men who grappled with bears and pushed farther the frontiers of the Empire. The heroes of the people were men who fought against the Empire and for something called freedom, in the hopeless little risings that broke out in Ireland from time to time. The most recent of these was the Fenian conspiracy of 1867, which ended in a damp squib and the usual arrests and executions.

One sedentary occupation to which Con gladly applied herself as a child was sketching. Artistic inclinations ran in the Gore-Booth family. The book of sketches her grandfather made on his 'grand tour' in the 1830s lay around at Lissadell. And as further inspiration there were the pictures hanging high up in the gallery depicting wonderful and mysterious scenes. She drew horses, endlessly, and, later, the country people in characteristic attitudes. She watched with interest the process by which the women made dyes for their homespuns from wild plants and flowers. Constance could regard nature with a practical, exploitative eye whereas Eva's gaze was meditative. Though Con's outspoken, indiscreet personality could seem lovably bumptious, her empathy with her sensitive, reserved younger sister suggested it had a more complex dimension.

In 1880 when Constance was twelve and Eva ten, the then almost unknown artist, Sarah Purser was invited to Lissadell to paint some portraits of the family. Sarah Purser had just returned from a six-month stint as an art student in Paris, learning the trade by which she intended to make her living. Although rather plain and an ageing *jeune fille* she was admired and respected by the brilliant, scornful Maria Bashkirtseff. Bashkirtseff envied even Sarah's poverty and wrote of her as a philosopher 'with whom you can have discussions on Kant, on life, on the Ego and on death, which make you reflect for yourself and imprint on the mind what you have read or heard'.[10]

The Lissadell commission was clearly very important for Sarah Purser because, through a network of Gore-Booth relations, she soon 'went through the British aristocracy like the measles',[11] and became one of the wealthiest and most popular artists in Dublin. She remarked later how lovely a child Constance was, 'how idolized and spoilt and always so good-hearted in her absurdities', and how her mother invested great hopes in her. But, a rather no-nonsense lady, she preferred Eva who was reserved and not given to self-dramatization. Miss Purser's portrait of the two children positioned them in that era straddling the nineteenth and twentieth centuries, which they would both essentially inhabit. They are posed in the open air amongst the trees of Lissadell in an impressionist iridescence of blues and greens. Constance is wearing a hat, her expression wilful and dreamy at the same time, while Eva nestles in the grass at her feet, her averted profile angelic.

A year before the children had been exposed to a darker side of life. The late 1870s were years of poor harvests because of bad weather, and low prices due to competition in agricultural products from Holland, France and Scandinavia. The summer of 1879 saw incessant rain and cold and the potatoes rotted in the ground. The spectre of the Famine rose again. Many of the Gore-Booth tenants faced starvation. Sir Henry toured his lands and arranged for the poorest of his tenants to go into the workhouse of which he was a guardian, without suffering the forfeiture of their plots and cabins, which a contemporary regulation required. Lady Gore-Booth and the older children set up a food distribution centre at Lissadell, an event, it was said, 'unique of its kind in Ireland at the time.'[12] A measure of the extreme poverty of the people even then, as well of the benevolence of Constance's family, is that straw was carted from the haggard at Lissadell to the houses of those who had no beds. It was in that year that Sir Henry gave 40 per cent reduction in their rents to his Ballymote tenants.

In a very graphic sense, politics lay all about Lissadell. Less inchoately, the rumbles of politicians could also be heard near at hand if one chose to hear them. The crusade, known as the Land War, to change the system of land tenure in favour of the peasantry was in full swing, in tandem with the Home Rule movement, which was seeking to have returned to Dublin the parliament it had lost in 1801. Gladstone seemed more extreme in his attitude to inherited wealth and privilege every day. There was a branch of the Land League in Sligo and a mass meeting was held in 1880 on Lissadell land.

Occasionally, an estate agent or landlord was shot. Even 'good' Sir Henry received in 1882 a couple of the ubiquitous threatening letters sent by one of the peasant secret societies common in nine-teenth-century Ireland. But agitation and ill-spelt histrionic missives could still be ignored or treated with derision or irony. Politics, according to Constance, was never talked about at Lissadell. The attitude prevailed there that it was the bad landlords who gave a good system a bad name. Of course, acceptance of the status quo was not regarded as 'politics'. Only reformism was considered 'political'. Indeed, landlords liked to believe or pretend that nothing was happening and their tenants were loyal, and it was thought bad form to bring up the subject in conversation. 'There were,' it was written of the time, 'euphemisms for receiving threatening letters, for being shot at, and other euphemisms for running away.'[13] What made landlords complain loudly was that their hunting might be stopped or curtailed, or that their tenants were shooting their game. At mid adolescence, this may too have been Constance's main concern and the extent of her political consciousness.

NOTES

1. *Eire*, 18 August 1923.
2. *The Celtic Twilight*, W.B. Yeats (Colin Smythe, London, 1981) p. 81.
3. *Eire*, 18 August 1923.
4. *James Fintan Lawlor, Collected Writings*, ed. L. Fogarty (The Talbot Press, Dublin, 1947) p. 62–3.
5. *Gladstone*, P. Magnus (John Murray, London, 1954) p. 193.
6. *Journeys to England and Ireland*, Alexis de Tocqueville (Anchor, New York) pp. 152–3.
7. *Woodbrook*, David Thomson (Penguin, London, 1976) p. 80.
8. Article in *The Times* on the Irish land question on 7 March 1881 described the Gore-Booth estate as an example of good management.
9. *Sligo, Simbad's Yellow Shore*, T.A. Finnegan (Keohane, Sligo, 1977) p. 80.
10. *Journals of Maria Bashkirtseff*, trans. Mathilde Blind (Virago, London 1985) p. 515.
11. *Daughters of Erin* by Elizabeth Coxhead (Secker & Warburg, London, 1965) p. 131.
12. *The Times*, 7 March 1881.
13. From an unpublished novel by Hon. Mary Ponsonby, sister of Horace Plunkett, quoted in *Kilcooley* by W.G. Neely (Universities Press, Belfast, 1983) p. 119.

TWO

THE DEBUTANTE:
LONDON AND DUBLIN

CONSTANCE GORE-BOOTH grew up to be singular, although the manner in which she expressed her singularity was as yet banal. She seemed set fair to be a shining example of the classic type of wild Anglo-Irish girl, hard-riding, jolly, tomboyish. She was beautiful, slender but robust, with thick waist-length brown hair and classic features that her high-spirited vitality made distinctive. Her friends were the hunting crowd. In the winter there was a meet of the Sligo Harriers every Tuesday and Friday and Con rode with them from when she was fourteen. Her superior horsemanship was quickly recognized. The *Sligo Independent*, a local newspaper that reported the meets, regularly carried glowing accounts of Miss Gore's deeds: 'Her performance must be regarded as simply marvellous. ... Her gallant and daring horsemanship, as she led the field almost from the start, was the subject of universal admiration.'[1] It was Wee Ga who gave Constance the hunter she called Max after a hero she knew from her reading in German literature and their partnership was eulogized by a Mr Rowlette, neighbour and Master of the Sligo Hunt Club:

Miss Gore and Max came to be regarded by the regular followers of the hunt as being so much in a class of their own as to be altogether outside the ordinary realm of competition. I have known a number of hunting people whom I regarded as very courageous riders, who would risk anything anywhere, but they sensed where real danger lay, and would always have to force themselves to risk a bad fall if the occasion warranted. But Miss Gore-Booth never had to force herself – for she enjoyed the risk. ... In all the years I knew her I never saw her take a bad toss. She was not only fearless but attracted by danger.[2]

The young poet William Butler Yeats used to visit his relatives, the Pollexfens, in Sligo town and was wistfully aware of the sort of lives the country families led. He would see from the carriage 'the grey stone walls of Lissadell among the trees' but would never venture inside its walls: 'We were merchant people of the town, no matter how rich we grew, no matter how many thousands a year our mills or our ships brought in, we could never be county nor indeed had we any desire to be so.'[3] He was very aware of the beauty of Miss Gore-Booth and of her extravagant behaviour, for instance, her riding down an old shopkeeper who deliberately blocked her path during a hunt.

Constance Gore-Booth all through my late boyhood had been romantic to me and more than once as I looked over to the green wall and roof I would repeat to myself Milton's lines 'Bosomed deep in tufted trees / Where some lofty beauty lives / The cynosure of neighbouring eyes'. She had often passed me on horseback going or coming from the hunt and was the acknowledged beauty of the country. I heard now and then of some tomboyish feat or of her reckless riding but the general impression was that she was respected and admired.

It is he who has left us the most illuminating picture of how she was then:

> When long ago I saw her ride
> Under Ben Bulben to the meet
> The beauty of her countryside
> With all youth's lonely wildness stirred,
> She seemed to have grown clean and sweet
> Like any rock-bred, sea-borne bird:

Sea-borne, or balanced on the air
When first it sprang out of the nest
Upon some lofty rock to stare
Upon the cloudy canopy...[4]

Yeats saw in her an unspoilt innocence; and saw too how this well-made girl was integrated into the landscape that was hers, as Miss Gore-Booth, in a very real sense. His image of the wild bird suggests also that he saw in Constance even then a solitary, questing quality. It was not that she was aloof or expressed this in any overt way. She had the confident carrying voice of her class. Her outspoken, direct, even indiscreet manner could be off-putting. There was an early governess who used to confide her love life to Con and Eva in the schoolroom, and Con would later relate in her clear voice these secrets to her mother and whatever guests she was entertaining in the drawing-room, who would listen in an embarrassed if fascinated silence.

Once, an important male guest foisted his unwelcome atten-tions on her and, at the crowded dinner table one evening, placed his hand on her knee. Constance picked it off, held it up in the air for everyone to see and announced, 'Just look at what I have found in my lap.' She loved fun and laughter but she was a joker rather than a humorist. She could apply herself with huge dedication to constructing elaborate tricks to play on people. Those designed for people she didn't like, such as the poor foolish governess, could be cruel, while those meant for people she did like tended to be magnanimous. The tandem, fitted out with an unfixed board for a seat that pitched the traveller out on rough ground, was kept for the pompous; the apparition of the 'Fairy Princess' for a peasant family.

Her journal of 1893, when she was twenty-five, illustrates her propensity for the theatrical: 'My grand joke comes off. Armed with an old ass, a child (Mickey Mashey) and much broken crockery we arrange the tableau on the high road ...'[5] The ass was saddled with creels the bottoms of which could be opened with a lever; and when two young men staying at the house came along the road, they found a weeping woman and her child whose distress was so persuasive that they gave her money to replace the broken china. She went in for disguises. The 'Fairy Princess' masquerade took place on a May eve when the 'little people' visit human folk. Mr Rowlette tells how Constance and Mabel in wonderful array, Constance's hair 'illumined from its hidden depths by myriads of fairy lights struck by the rising moon from countless facets of multicoloured glass,'[6] knocked at the door of a remote cottage, chosen because there were a lot of young children in the house. They were admitted; they danced, played some obscure musical instrument and frightened the smaller children. Later, Con was jubilant because the man of the house, who had leant with composure against the dresser throughout, said she was 'a real nate tight woman'. Some of her tricks, meant to teach a lesson to friends who showed a lack of feeling for poor people, suggest an unformed political awareness. Got up as a beggar, she accosted one of these young men on the road and when he berated her rudely, she embarrassed him by revealing her true identity. It may not be fanciful to see in these episodes an impulse to protest against the complacencies of her class.

There were diversions in which all the Gore-Booths participated: cricket on the lawn, jaunts to Knocknarea and other scenic spots, and drawing-room theatricals. Putting on plays for each other and for guests was a popular entertainment among the leisured classes. Constance annotated and kept for years a book called *Twenty Minutes* by Harriet Childe Pemberton, which consisted of a set of drawing-room dialogues. The family also wrote pieces to perform as we can see from a farce in rhyming couplets, written by Eva. It was called 'The Daughter of Eve or Alphonso's Bride' and contained some whimsical but astute political allusions. They called themselves The Company of Angels. Papa (Sir Henry) acted as stage manager while Mama and Wee Ga made up an orchestra of violin and piano. Occasionally, they brought a production into Sligo for some charity entertainment.

Constance's life at this time, however, was not devoted – although there was no practical reason why it should not have been – entirely to fun and games. There was her drawing and her painting about which she was already nurturing serious ambitions. She was reading French and German literature and, motivated by Squidge, the last of her governesses, she was assiduous in learning long passages in those languages. All her life she could recite lines from poets such as Heine and Goethe. She considered Squidge to be very scholarly and knowledgeable.

In 1886 at the age of eighteen, Constance was given a kind of 'finishing'. She was sent to Italy for six months. Squidge, who had probably accompanied other young ladies abroad, was her chaperone. Constance, who thought Squidge knew everything, found her 'almost as good as a guide-book'.[7] In Florence, as discerning tourists, they avoided the 'small and select colony' of English people. They stayed in a *pension* in the Piazza Cavour and became so familiar with the city that, thirty-five years later, Constance could write to Eva from prison of how she would like to see the front of the Duomo again and view the sunset from San Miniato, and how she kept the memory of that and San Marco and the Campanile 'clearer than anything else' all these years. 'I did so love it long ago,' she wrote. 'I remember catching butterflies wildly across hedges and ditches at Fiesole and distressed Squidge quite unable to follow ...'[8]

It was doubtless not only at Fiesole that she made such demands on poor old Squidge's stamina. Squidge's great admiration was for the extreme and apocalyptic Savanarola. Constance however, could 'never quite forgive him his bonfires of vanities. So much beauty must have been burnt.' That she found Squidge so congenial suggests Con had unusual and unconventional proclivities, which promised to cause difficulties in the marriage market of the London Season that she was to attend in the following year. There were already difficulties in fact because it seems that Constance was secretly engaged at this time. The young man was called Phil Percival, properly Philip Dudley Percival of Templehouse. Con would have known him from the hunting field and from house visits. The young man had no fortune however – which accounts for the secrecy of their engagement – and had to go to Australia to make one. In his absence the infatuation died and she broke their agreement. Philip Dudley Percival later married Muriel Wynne of Hazelwood, Constance's first cousin.

The year in which Constance came out, 1887, was also the year of the Queen's Jubilee, an event that came round every ten years and always aroused a variety of emotions and reactions in Ireland. In Sligo, Con attended a meeting of local ladies over which Lady Gore-Booth presided, to discuss a collection for a jubilee gift, which would represent their love for and allegiance to the monarch. A month later, Constance herself was presented at the Court of Queen Victoria, at three o'clock on the afternoon of 17 March, St Patrick's Day, by the Countess of Erroll who was a cousin of her mother's and a lady-in-waiting to the Queen. Victoria was in her customary black festooned with pearls and her numerous Orders. Constance wore the regulation dress of the debutante: made of white satin with a train three yards long, long white gloves and an arrangement of feathers in her hair. Then she spent four months out and about, at the society dinners, parties, balls, and occasions that made up the 'Season'. She was seen at Ascot in 'a pale blue gown draped with old lace'[9] and somewhere else in a red dress with black satin stripes, surmounted by a black hat with three ostrich feathers, which sounds very *belle époque*.

The entry into the coteries of London society by a girl who had spent her life on the west coast of Ireland was smoothed by being related to such families as the Dunravens, the Zetlands, the Scarboroughs, and the Westminsters. Lady Fingall, who was a friend of Constance's and had met Lord Fingall during her first Season, took to the social round with great enthusiasm. She wrote of the delights of the Season at that time, how there were 'flowers everywhere and sunshine and jingling hansoms. There were Sunday Parades in the park, where people walked up and down after Church, met their friends and talked to them. The women were beautifully dressed. It was the time of big hats and full rustling silk dresses.'[10]

Lady Fingall hated riding so, unlike most of the debs, would not have started her day with a ride on Rotten Row. Constance, on the other hand, would, and no doubt collected friends as she went along, but she may not have enjoyed other aspects of the Season. Her pose, in a photograph taken at the time, suggests an awkwardness, perhaps a sense of displacement. A girl like Constance would certainly have found it hard to have to present herself as the demure yet covertly intent husband-seeking young Victorian lady that convention demanded.

At home, she had left Eva pursuing her reading of Dante with Squidge and long summer days of going about barefoot and riding over the countryside with her hair blowing free. London must have seemed stuffy and its endless social engagements tedious by comparison. She had exchanged the simple life for one of artifice. While face make-up was never worn – it was considered scandalous and too reminiscent of the stage – bodies were submitted to lavish embellishments. It was the era of the bustle. There were hair pads, side pads, front pads and back pads. 'Sitting out' rather than dancing was encouraged at parties. To spy her daughter sitting out with an eligible man gave a mother great cause for complacency and a ball had little chance of success if enough sitting-out places had not been provided through the skilful placing of Japanese screens, large palms and gilt chairs in nooks and corners.

Constance was gregarious but she was also more serious, more straightforward and more willful than the average English deb, so the atmosphere of coyness and intrigue must have bored her. It was also quite competitive. This may have been the first time that she, who enjoyed a position of such distinction in Sligo, found herself among great numbers of girls who were her social equals and to whom the honours of battle were the bouquets sent round by one's beaux to wear to the ball. Constance's objections, if any, were not strenuous, however. Lady Fingall wrote that she was 'much loved and admired'. She was 'a wild beautiful girl and all the young men wanted to dance with her. She was lovely and gay and she was the life and soul of any party.'[11] The Gore-Booths returned to Dublin for the week of the Horse Show in August, went to the grand garden party at the Viceregal Lodge in the Phoenix Park, and to other dances and dinners. There was a respite then for a month or two at home in Lissadell before the hunting season started in November. This, broken by the Christmas festivities, lasted until March when the Dublin Season began, a shorter, less grand, more democratic version of London's.

The Dublin Season was centred in Dublin Castle, the seat of administration, which was also the hub of the social life of the capital. The Viceregal Court, which was the Castle in its social guise, was one of those anomalies of English rule that was, in its way, delightful. Dublin had lost its own parliament in 1801 but the office of Viceroy and his court remained, with all the pomp, splendour and ceremony of the Court of St James at Buckingham

Palace. The Viceroy, also known as the Lord Lieutenant, provided his own horse, plate, glass etc. so successive viceroys tended to vie with each other in putting up a good show. There was a hierarchy of officials to assist him: Chamberlain, Vice-Chamberlain, Comptroller, State Steward, Master of the Horse, Gentleman Usher and many more. The Season opened with the Lord Lieutenant's levee and ended with the St Patrick's Night Ball on 17 March, a great social occasion for the city because even the professional classes could attend.

Real life pressed very close to the Castle walls. Lady Fingall wrote: 'We can hear the music as we put last touches to our hair and our frocks in one of the bedrooms upstairs. The windows of that room look out on an appalling slum, a fact characteristic of the life of those days. But the windows are curtained and one need not lift the curtains.'

The grandest of the Castle set then went off to London for its Season. Eva came out the following year and for several years she and Con, and in due course, Mabel, did the glittering round of balls and parties where one met eligible young men. If Constance received proposals of marriage, which is not unlikely because all of Ireland 'was said to be in love with her to a man', she did not accept.

Con's physical courage is also remembered. Once, in London, she and a friend were driving to the theatre when they passed two drunken men, fighting. She jumped from the carriage, and threw herself between them as she appealed to passers-by to help her stop the brawl. She is also said to have made the graceful if hackneyed gesture of pressing the money she had won at bridge into the hands of vagrants she came upon in the early hours of the morning sleeping on benches on the Bayswater Road.

In 1889 Lord Zetland was appointed Viceroy and as his Vicereine, Lady Zetland, was a cousin of Lady Gore-Booth's, the family were regular visitors at the Viceregal Lodge. Both the Zetlands were said to be charming but both were afflicted with shyness and short sight. The Vicereine was staying at Lissadell when Parnell came to Sligo in 1891 as part of his last tragic campaign to retain his position as leader of the Irish Party.

For ten years, this autocratic, handsome and enigmatic landlord, Charles Stewart Parnell, had been the leader of the Irish

Home Rule Party and the force behind the Land League agitation. By brilliantly opportunistic parliamentary tactics, he had made the Irish question the burning issue of English politics. In spite of his aloof manner and uncommunicative nature, the people adored him. He had survived charges of complicity in terrorism to forge an alliance with the Liberals who seemed about to make Home Rule a reality when he was named as co-respondent in a divorce case and thrown over by Gladstone and the Liberals. The Irish Bishops then denounced him and there followed an acrimonious struggle for the leadership of the Irish Party, which Parnell lost.

Refusing to accept the verdict of his colleagues, Parnell appealed to the people and fought several bitterly contested by-elections, against candidates nominated by the party. He went to Sligo to support the candidature of a follower of his who was, in the event, defeated. Lissadell would no doubt have preferred to ignore the arrival of this politician, a Home Ruler and enemy of landed privilege, regarded in their circle as a troublemaker and rabble-rouser. But Constance and Eva rode secretly to his meagerly attended meeting at the Town Hall. Their sympathies would certainly have been with Parnell as a man, pale, disdainful and defiant. But whether their political ideas coincided with his is another manner. In fact, some remarks Constance wrote in her journal a couple of years later suggest she still gave politics little thought.

This journal she kept in the years 1892 and 1893 provides a vivid picture of her life, and here and there gives an insight into those elements in her character that were to shape her future. She was finding her circumstances increasingly irksome. She was twenty-four, unmarried, and still living at home. This was clearly exasperating to her mother for whom success where a girl was concerned consisted of a successful marriage. She had been hoping for a great success for Constance.

On the first day of 1892 Constance was very happy. 'May the whole year be as happy as today,' she wrote. A shooting party at Lissadell included Lord Dunraven, a cousin, and Wilfred Ashley, a neighbour, later to become Lord Templemore, for whom Con was developing a special affection. Wilfred left on 3 January. 'Such a dull lonely feeling waking up and knowing the friend is gone. What is it that makes me so fond of him, something deep down somewhere in both of us that meets and meets.' Two nights running, Eva had toothache and Con sat up with her, stroking her face for 'many hours' and trying to persuade her to take some spirits for the pain.

A week later Wilfred returned for a house performance of a play called *Pilot Rosalie* and threw Con into confusion. She wrote that after the performance, 'nobody was real, nobody themselves, nothing but shams, acting and falseness' and she was 'in the blues most thoroughly having mortally offended W. ... He threw me over for a dance. I was very X and he went off to the billiard room with Joss.' Next day, they 'avoid each other with determination and make a boast of it'. He made it up when they were out shooting by offering her a piece of chocolate. On her birthday, 4 February, they went fishing together on the lake in the collapsible boat 'with scores of cushions and rugs. We rowed into the mud to steady ourselves and fixed our little ship steady by sticking an oar into the mud and ate our frugal meal *tête a tête*. It was an idyll.'

W. stayed on longer than was intended because he had sprained his ankle. But, sadly for Constance, he left on 6 February. 'It is so good for one to have someone to look after ... seek out stray draughts for and run messages for, it's rather nice to be indispensable to someone.' If Constance was a little in love with Wilfred, her feelings were not reciprocated. But she seems to have made the best of it. A week later, she was writing of how she liked to lie in bed late in the mornings and dream:

> The sky is blue and the sun shines into my little room and I feel so happy and at rest. I hear Eva's canary in the far distance, its voice quite modified and sweet. 'Distance lends enchantment' even to that discordant fowl. There is nothing like those late morning hours, one is so pleasant and contented with oneself. Mama is raging in the doorway so I cannot go on writing.

Constance did not go to Dublin for the Season that year. Within a week, she was in London, at the house of her cousin Josslyn, Lord Muncaster, in Carlton Gardens. Josslyn brought her shopping and gave her 'many pretty things'. On 19 February she went to see the Victorian Exhibition and was critical both of the exhibits and what the show represented: 'What vulgar people the Royalties must be. This is the conclusion I have come to after being to the Victorian Exhibition. No taste in anything and every family event, birth and marriage being celebrated by an awful daub by an incompetent painter.'

She went dancing at 'the Club' with Rhoda L'Estrange, later Lady Morpeth, a relation; she was very impressed by a 'first-rate sermon from Mr Eyton' at St Paul's and commented: 'Because scientific men could not find heaven among the stars with a telescope it did not exist. (This to me is Bathos) ...' There was a fancy-dress ball in Malmesbury where she 'met an old friend and danced a good deal with him'.

A book she read aroused rather anguished reflections on love and its elusiveness. This was *Ariadne by Ouida*, the pen-name of Marie Louise de la Ramée, the popular and rather risqué novelist. Maria Bashkirtseff had also read *Ariadne* and was no less unsettled by it: 'It is ... in the highest degree sensational the agitation it caused me three or four years ago. It treats of art and love and the scene is set in Rome.'[12] Constance who, like Bashkirtseff, had a sense of destiny and wanted to be an artist, was just as susceptible to the theme of Ariadne, which concerns the fate of a young sculptor, Gioja. Gioja has been brought up on Homer and Virgil and lives for art alone until she meets Hilarion, a capricious and sublime poet for whom she dies. Constance wrote:

> I have read *Ariadne* and loved it, unnatural and overstrained it may be, but there is a spark somewhere, the indescribable touch that carries one away and makes one believe in Love real true love – God is love and I do not know Him. How I hate the English language where I want to think in it, it seems poor and I feel a fool. Molly (Mabel) has her God whom she worships and why mayn't I have mine. To my eyes he is ... goodhearted, thoroughly English, and loves her as well as men do love and for that he is her God. She keeps nothing from him and every idea and word she speaks radiates to him, her very face in repose is nothing but a thought of him and for him. ... It's indecent to parade happiness, it makes one feel that there is something in it all – not something, this won't do – everything – and I don't want it to be so – what do I want? I don't know. Every thought has a contradiction tonight and I don't understand why. I wish Eva were here – she might. Anna Karenina loved and saw nothing wrong in her folly.

A few weeks later, an irritating, self-centred house guest and the role she and Duck (Eva) assumed, playing 'gooseberry for Molly and her lover', prompted her to return to the subject. She wished she too had someone to love:

> I feel the want. Women are made to adore and sacrifice themselves, and I as a woman demand as a right that Nature should provide me with something to live for, something to die for. Why should I alone never experience the best and at the same time the worst of Life's gifts? The happiest and the saddest.

Con's heightened mood suggests that she was feeling the pangs of unrequited love, perhaps for Wilfred Ashley.

By 2 April she was back in Ireland where she took part 'in fine style' in the final run of the Sligo Harriers, having arranged to be met with her hunter Max at the train station so she could go straight to the drag race. On 7 April 'Eva and I took our lunch to Knocklane – us two and the little tandem. We took no account of time having left our watches behind.' And next day, 'Planted the beautiful bed of White Arabis with coloured hyacinths. All day I worked barring lunch and tea. In the evening the canoe was launched and I paddled out and sailed back before the wind.' In this month she also mischievously stole and hid 'the Dillon's cow and calf', obliging the Dillon family to walk the Sligo road until midnight calling 'Sucky, Sucky'.

At the end of the month she was staying with her cousins, the Zetlands, at the Viceregal Lodge for the Punchestown Races; took in a visit to her aunt May Wynne whose son Captain Graham Wynne was an admirer of hers; and by 7 May was back at Lissadell when her father's yacht arrived and anchored in the bay for two weeks before it set out for Greenland. As it came in, Con went to meet it in the canoe. 'Crew met us in their whaling boat and were much astonished at our courage. Certainly we were nearly swamped. We came in from Rachley on the ship and stayed until nearly dinner-time.' The *Kara* was the centre of attention for some days:

> Spent the afternoon on Kara. All the countryside came on board. ... Mordaunt left. His Mama saw him off so I did not. We dined on the ship and had an excellent dinner. After dinner the crew entertained us with songs and dances and we were much amused notwithstanding

Mama and WG came on board to sit in judgement, which stiffened our marrow and wet our spirits.

When the *Kara* sailed in the early hours of the morning of 28 May, Con and some others got up to see it go and 'it was so dreary and sad watching the ship getting smaller and smaller, sitting on a bank and passing a telescope round'.

At this time Constance's problematic situation was apparent. She was restless and unhappy although her basic cheerfulness and capacity to absorb herself in her favourite activities made her unhappiness only fitful. Her mother and she were increasingly antagonistic towards each other. Lady Gore-Booth, as a Victorian mother, obviously felt her eldest daughter ought to be married and had perhaps come to realize that Con's singularity was too marked to ensure a conventionally successful match. Constance was chafing at her continuing dependence, a sense, perhaps, of failure, and at the prospect of a future that seemed to hold only an interminable and purposeless round of amusements.

But by the end of the London Season in July, Constance had clarified for herself and her family what it was she wanted. Throughout the Season Constance absented herself from many of the parties and receptions to take art lessons daily from a Miss Anna Nordgren, a Finnish artist then aged forty-six, who had studied in Paris, also alongside Maria Bashkirtseff, and had been exhibiting in London since 1885:

> Hilda married, Evey marrying, a whole London Season older and not engaged or even wishing to be. If I could only cut the family tie and have a life and interest of my own I should want no other heaven and I see an opening, daylight and freedom, if I can only persevere and drudge and get my parsimonious family to pay. All the season I have worked my four hours daily with Miss Nordgren and Miss Griffin and have got on beyond my wildest dreams and am encouraged to see success at the end of it if only ... Three years hard work and no money to do it on and no hopes of getting it. Success and Art walled round with family pride stinginess and conventionality. What is one to do? How am I to coerce them? How break away? If I was sure of myself and knew I could succeed for sure and make a name or more to the point money, I would bolt live on a crust and do. But to do all that with the chance of having to return and throw oneself on the charity

of one's family a miserable failure is more than I can screw up my courage to face. So many people begin with great promise and greater hope and end in nothing but failure and the poor house or improper.

She had clearly broached to her family the subject of her ambition to be a full-time art student but was given no cause to be hopeful. In late July, Lady Gore-Booth, Constance and Eva, and a friend, Rachel Mansfield, went to Bayreuth for the opera – then a thing for music-lovers to do, Wagner being a new and passionate enthusiasm – travelling across Germany through Aachen, Cologne, Nuremberg, etc. Perhaps because it was a rather stuffy thing to do, perhaps because she wanted to continue with her lessons in London, Constance seems to have gone unwillingly; and her remarks on the journey are girlish, whimsical and irreverent, peppered with barbed references to her mother. In Boulogne after the boat across the Channel she writes: 'Eva and Rachel went to read by a paddle-box while I took exercise ... We were all sick. Mama nearly died. She will never recover I'm afraid. We put her to rest and went out.' Lunch was 'in an awful place found by Mama'. In Cologne, they dined in 'a low pot-house, well and cheaply'. Constance went to High Mass and found the Cathedral 'sublime', although it was not liked by purists because of its mixture of architectural styles. The party visited St Ursula's shrine – 'quite comic, built up everywhere with skulls and bones. Mama kept saying in a loud voice "Professor Owen says all the bones are those of inferior animals"'. Constance was in a frame of mind that was supercilious and rather sceptical. 'I think Faith is a very pretty quality and am greatly interested to know if it can be combined with Knowledge and common sense.'

She and Rachel often got up very early or left the party in the afternoons to explore the towns through which they passed or to sketch scenes in market-places or meadows. 'We selected a meadow from which there was a lovely view ... I sketched Listz's grave for Squidge and made great friends with a small boy who sketched it too I supplying him with paper etc.' She used her sketching as an escape and equally as a proof of her seriousness. They also took photographs. Along the way they met acquaintances and the ubiquitous relations; in Nuremberg they met Rhoda L'Estrange who was with some friends, and again in Bayreuth when they at last arrived. Bayreuth then was uncomfortable and dirty and very hot. They were pleased to find their lodgings clean though they were cheated by the porters.

They saw *Parsifal* twice, *Tannhäuser* – 'one of the greatest sermons ever written' and *Die Meistersinger*. Constance was disparaging about her mother because she and Eva had to find seats in the gallery while Rachel and Lady Gore-Booth sat in the stalls – 'What comes of getting your tickets after you arrive.' She was as ready as any girl to be charmed by random acquaintances. At *Parsifal*, 'Our seats were very good and next me sat a man with a very interesting and nice face. I had a great many possessions – dropped them all … He retrieved them and offered to take care of them for me. That man must have a sense of humour.' They attended *Parsifal* again next day, but 'alas, alas, my charmer was replaced by a decrepit bore'.

Cursory accounts of tiffs, pot-houses etc. are interspersed with commonplace impressions of places and sketching expeditions. On the last day Constance met Mr Stuart-Wortley in the street who told her that a relation, Lady Sibell Grosvenor, had arrived in town and she rushed off to visit her. She was very sad that day, leaving Bayreuth; but generally, on this trip, Con's mood was juvenile and impatient, maybe because the difficulties between her mother and herself made her childish. Her flippancy may also have concealed a certain desperation about her future.

When they got back to London on 17 August she went straight to the studios to show her sketchbook. 'Miss Mackay gave me a kiss and tea, Miss Pfeiffer much good advice and I was happy. How nice these people are. So natural and simple, openly critical and straightforward … Mama awfully X and Squidge came to tea.' Back in Sligo Con 'revelled in a cool green country, a blue sky and a bluer sea. Tea on the shore and laziness and a sail in a boat. Oh the joy of seeing the people, trees and mountains of home again.' Next there was the Horse Show, where she 'missed W.'; a ball given by Lord and Lady Wolseley in the Royal Hospital, Kilmainham, where she 'danced most of the time with little Captain B. a silly little flirt quite in his element at a Ball'; a house party at Lord and Lady Erne's in Crom, Co. Fermanagh; and a respite at home of three weeks, sketching the country people.

In that time, she galloped across the sands to nearby Classiebawn where there were house guests. Her comments here suggest her critical faculties had an edge that young men might have found off-putting. 'Mr B.', she wrote, 'is a sleek and youthfully bald nonentity'; and Lord Shaftesbury 'has a nice face, beautiful eyes, a kind affectionate weak face and a good strong very young and plump figure'. Mary Leslie of Castle Leslie in Co. Monaghan was also there and she later described that first meeting with Con: 'I thought I had never seen anyone so lovely. In the evening she started off at a hard gallop over the shore as if she feared the tide would come up and stop her. Hatless, dressed in a brown corduroy frock, not a habit, she was startlingly beautiful as the sun caught her fair hair.'[13]

Mr Leslie took a great fancy to her when she went to stay at the Leslies' a couple of months later. He gave her grapes in the greenhouse, brought her out on the lake in a velocipede to look at the wild ducks and took his losing to her at picquet 'as lightly as most things'. In December she pasted in her journal a cutting from a society paper, which reported that an attaché in the suite of the German Emperor had said that the most beautiful women that he saw in England were the Irish 'Duchess of Leinster, Lady Carew, and Miss Gore-Booth'.

A round of house parties punctuated the hunting season. In January she and Eva went to the Dunravens at Adare in Co. Limerick where Randolph Churchill was among the guests. Much of the talk must have concerned politics and the imminent Home Rule Bill to which we can reliably assume the house party *en masse* was opposed; but Constance's passion was reserved for the servants whose own party downstairs was stopped early, despite Lady Dunraven's assurance that it could go on as late as they liked, and shows Con's characteristic impulse to support the underdog. 'That mean little rat Mr P. stopped them at 12.'

On her twenty-fifth birthday, 4 February 1893, there was no birthday cake and only one present. There is an implication that by now Con and her family were quite at loggerheads. In March there was a meeting in Sligo to oppose the Home Rule Bill, which Gladstone had introduced the month before in the House of Commons. Constance attended, but was bored and acted with defiance: 'Anti Home Rule meeting in Sligo Town Hall. Declined to be among the aristocracy and sat in the hall and drew caricatures of the speakers. Went to Hazelwood to see Mabel.'

Con's rebellions were still very minor. Usually they were on the level of horseplay and pique. But the direction in which her ambitions were leading her and an obscure lack of enthusiasm for her own circle show she was forming the identity of a *déclassé*, which no house party or suitable man could curb. She was taking a long time to grow up. At the age of twenty-five, she aimlessly scratched her name on the windowpane of the 'gloryhole', the small drawing room she and Eva had taken as their own when they were younger. In April, when she was staying at Aske, the Zetlands' house in Yorkshire, there was another anti-Home Rule meeting, on which Constance commented with approval. Lord Zetland made a voluble and rhetorical speech against the Bill and was followed by Lord Ashbourne who regarded the Bill as 'calamitous'. She wrote, 'Lord Ashbourn [*sic*] a real angel, speaks splendidly.' She could still be as unionist as anyone, according to her humour. Of course, she rarely, if ever met any 'Home Rulers', nobody to allow her any scope or test her incisive intelligence. How the great rooms at Lissadell, even the landscape around it, must have seemed to yawn sometimes, offering only diversions, however delightful. She needed to be challenged.

NOTES

1. *The Sligo Independent*, 12 February 1890.
2. *The Rebel Countess*, Anne Marreco (Weidenfeld & Nicolson, London, 1967) p. 31.
3. *W.B. Yeats and Georgian Ireland*, Donald T. Torchiana (Northwestern University Press, Evanston, 1966) pp. 185–6.
4. 'On a Political Prisoner' in *Collected Poems of W.B. Yeats* (Macmillan, London, 1982) p. 206.
5. The diary is in the National Museum, Dublin.
6. *The Rebel Countess*, Marreco, p. 32.
7. *Prison Letters of Countess Markievicz*, Esther Roper (Longmans Green and Co., London, 1934) p. 252.
8. *The Rebel Countess*, Marreco, p. 35.
9. *Seventy Years Young*, Elizabeth, Countess of Fingall (London, 1937) p. 121.

10. *Ibid.*, p. 191.
11. *Ibid.*, p. 129.
12. *Journals of Maria Bashkirtseff*, p. 266.
13. *The Rebel Countess*, Marreco, p. 53.

THREE

THE SLADE AND SUFFRAGE

IN THAT YEAR, 1893, when she was twenty-five, Constance's persistence at last wore her parents down. She entered the Slade. It was the 1890s, the 'gay nineties', happy, buoyant, full of illusion, decadent. Women of course were not encouraged to be decadent – the male artist Alfred Thornton wrote complacently, 'Confidence and complete assurance was abroad, and woman was the guardian angel of our virtues'[1] – and their study of art was limited by prudish attempts to protect their innocence.

Constance arrived at the Slade, however, at a fortuitous time. In 1893 Alphonse Legros retired from the Slade and was replaced as Principal by Frederick Brown, who was a member of the New English Art Club (NEAC), the avant-garde group, which had set itself up in 1885 in opposition to the Royal Academy (RA). The NEAC was deeply influenced by the French Impressionists, exemplified for a contemporary reviewer by Degas's *L'Absinthe*, which allowed him to claim that the NEAC only wanted to paint 'sodden people in a cafe'.[2]

Until 1893 women were confined to the Antique Rooms at the Slade where they had to make do with the casts of half-draped figures for models. In that year, after presenting a petition to be allowed to draw, like the men, from the live nude, they were given a male model wearing bathing drawers who was then swathed in a loin cloth nine foot long, which was kept in place with a belt as prescribed by the regulations. Constance continued to work with Anna Nordgren in less frustrating conditions at her studio in the Bolton Studios off the Fulham Road. Both women exhibited at the Society of Women Artists.

It must have been a great relief for Con to replace a life of covert husband-hunting in grand houses with the Alexandra House Hostel for Girl Art Students and Bohemian parties at the 91 Club in the Boltons where, according to a contemporary, 'the studios were full of artists in more or less shabby blouses, gay, hopeful, and chattering'.[3] Before very long she had managed to be set up in a studio of her own in Stanley Chambers. The strict rules in force at the hostel became intolerable when Con found herself locked out one night on her return from an outing to Twickenham with a cousin, probably Graham Wynne. Then, a woman seeking a room for the night at a hotel in London without luggage was considered very improper. Constance, irate at having been put in this position, asked her father to make representations to the hostel authorities. As a result they apologized and extended the curfew from 10 to 10.30 pm – and Con was able to move out to her own place.

At the Slade she developed an infatuation – along with a good number of the women students – for one of her teachers, Henry Tonks. Tonks was then thirty-two, a tall, gaunt fellow, severe both in appearance and manner. He was one of the eleven children of a Warwickshire brass-founder and had trained as a surgeon before becoming an artist. He was at that time one of the young and progressive set represented by the NEAC, although ascetic rather than Bohemian in his habits – certainly not an absinthe drinker. He was uncompromising in his dedication to art, and scathing in his criticism of the students' work. Students, however, sought his approval and one of his rare smiles, which were said to transform his grim face. He was proud and nervous, and a misogynist. He spoke with a laconic contempt for his women students: 'Speaking generally, they do what they are told. If they don't, you will generally find they are a bit cracked. If they become offensive it may be a sign of love. They improve rapidly from about sixteen to twenty-one, then the genius you have discovered goes off, they begin to take marriage seriously.'[4]

Tonks pitied women for what he saw as 'the sad destiny of their sex' and appreciated them best in the role of the intelligent and understanding mother who found her satisfaction in influencing the life of a great man. Constance distressed him because she communicated her love through provocative boyish gestures: sitting astride her donkey (drawing-stool), winking at him defiantly across the room, taking a bun from a paper bag and stuffing it into her mouth. He knew she was a 'lady' because he used to visit the house of Lady Wyndham Quinn who was a relation of hers and was shocked that Constance, as he told his friends, had 'the manners of a kitchen maid'.[5]

It was she who told friends of the grand plan she devised and carried out to get his attention. There were national schools at the top of Cheyne Row where the yards in front were asphalted and Con used to go there to practise 'rinking' – roller-skating. Tonks lived in Chelsea and walked down Cheyne Row every day on his way home. One evening Con waylaid him by running into him deliberately at full speed and knocking him down. But this did not improve their relations as she had hoped. Henry Tonks never married – he thought married life 'a mistake'. He became Professor of the Slade in 1917 and upheld the traditional ethos of the School in the face of the futurism and modernism of the 1920s.

Constance still spent much of her time at Lissadell, which, now that she was working and leading an independent life, she found less dull. Anna Nordgren came to stay and they painted together out of doors; and Constance was there in the winter of 1894–5 when the young poet William Butler Yeats became a regular visitor. Con already knew Yeats in London – in the summer of 1893 she had invited him round to Bryanston Square where she was staying with friends. And they had lunch together at least once, an occasion when a newspaper editor at a neighbouring table was so impressed by her beauty that he wrote a sonnet on the tablecloth, cut it out and passed it to her. He then left, and it was Yeats who had to face the irate restaurant proprietor and promise him a new cloth.

In the summer of 1894 Yeats inscribed a copy of his play *The Land of Heart's Desire* to Constance. Yeats was keenly aware of the protocols of Irish provincial society, which prevented the well-to-do Protestant mercantile class, to which the Pollexfens, his maternal relations, belonged, from seeking to mix with the aristocracy of the county:

> We would meet on grand juries, those people in the great houses – Lissadell among its woods, Hazelwood House by the lake's edge and Markree Castle encircled by wood after wood and we would speak in malicious gossip and know ourselves suspected in turn, but the long-settled habit of Irish life had set up a wall. One man, a merchant at the other end of the town did indeed sometimes drift a little into such society but we despised him for it.[6]

But at this point, now that he had published several books, he felt entitled to depart from these conventions: 'My going to the Gore-Booths was different, I had written books and it was my business to write books and it was natural to wish to talk to those whose books you liked and besides I was no longer of my grandfather's house, I could no longer say 'we do so and so or we think so and so.'

In the winter of 1894–5 Yeats stayed for six months with his uncle George Pollexfen in the town of Sligo, paid visits to Lissadell and was a house guest at least once for a few days. He described his doings and the Gore-Booths fulsomely in letters to his sister Lily who was very curious about what lay behind the walls of the demesne. He found Lissadell very impressive with its 'great sitting-room as high as a church and all good things in good taste'.[7] He took the credit for introducing the family to folklore. The Gore-Booths, he wrote, 'had not thought it existed' – that is, they were unaware of the significance Irish folklore was attaining in certain Dublin circles who felt in it the pulse of a vital Gaelic culture that was, until now, unrecognized. He thought them 'delightful people' and was kept busy telling stories – 'Old Irish stories – first to one then another and then telling them over again to the sick Miss Gore upstairs.' He doubtless also enlightened them on the occult and the cabalistic. Yeats was a member of the esoteric Order of the Golden Dawn; during the summer, Constance had asked him to arrange a meeting for herself and Althea Gyles (who was Irish and a student at the Slade in defiance of her father's wishes) with Mrs Mathers of the Order for the purpose of having their fortunes told. Yeats replied that Moina Mathers was 'always busy and very little of the world' and had consented only to read the fortune of the one whose affairs were 'at a great crisis'.[8]

The Gore-Booths had another friend at Lissadell in the vicar of the little Anglican Church on their estate, the Reverend Fletcher Sheridan Le Fanu, nephew of the novelist J.S. Le Fanu. Yeats returned to Lissadell to give a lecture on Irish folklore to Reverend Le Fanu's parishioners in the schoolhouse:

> I lectured [he wrote to Lily] in the schoolhouse on Fairy lore chiefly to an audience of Orangemen ... I found that the comic tales delighted them but the poetry of fairy lore was quite lost on them. They held it Catholic superstition I suppose. However I had fortunately chosen nothing but humorous tales. The children were I believe greatly excited.

It seems to have been the Gore-Booth women who were enthusiastic about Willie Yeats. He was not quite thirty, olive-skinned, and ardent behind his self-conscious pose as a poet, which demanded that he wear velveteen, loosely knotted silk ties, a pre-Raphaelite cloak and soft sombrero. 'These people,' he wrote to fellow poet Katharine Tynan, 'are much better-educated than our own people (meaning the middle-class) and have a better instinct for excellence.' Yet Yeats' provincial class diffidence made him rather defensive in his attitudes towards the family. He was disparaging about the men. Sir Henry 'thinks of nothing but the North Pole, where his first officer to his great satisfaction has recently lost himself and thereby made an expedition to rescue him desirable'. It was Sir Henry who said 'Go back to bed, Sir' when he met Yeats on the stairs in flight from his gloomy north-facing room where he saw a ghost he had not seen for twenty years. Josslyn was 'much troubled by the responsibilities of his wealth and almost painfully conscientious. He and the clergyman Le Fanu are full of schemes. He is not however particularly clever and has not, I imagine, much will.' Josslyn, for his part, hated Yeats.

That he was obsessively in love with the young woman called Maud Gonne made him more indifferent to the Gore-Booth girls than he might otherwise have been. Tall, beautiful, imperious Maud Gonne was involved in the occult activities, which appealed to Yeats; and though the daughter of an army officer, she was an Irish patriot. The Gore-Booths may have been already aware of her as a rather scandalous figure among their set. Willie Yeats found Con rather similar to Maud Gonne in appearance and voice, but shorter and of course a paler shadow of his beloved. He told Lily then that Eva 'has some literary talent and much literary ambition and has met no literary people' but he later wrote that he was drawn to her 'delicate gazelle-like beauty' that reflected 'a mind far more subtle and distinguished'.

Probably because she was quite different to Maud Gonne, Eva was, for a couple of weeks, his 'close friend':

> I told her all of my unhappiness in love. Indeed so close was it that I nearly said to her as William Blake said to Catherine Blake, 'You pity me, then I love you.' But now I thought this house would not accept so penniless a suitor and besides I was still decidedly in love with that other. ... I threw the Tarot, and when the Fool came up, which means nothing at all would happen, I turned my mind away.[9]

He felt that he was a nationalist influence on the Gore-Booths. He gave them the Irish revivalist Standish O'Grady to read and hoped he was diverting Eva into writing about Irish things. It was probably from Yeats that Constance first got a broader view of Maud Gonne whose extreme nationalism she would outdo in years to come. For now, nationalism was diffused among the variety of ideas that interested her. These included, in 1895, the collecting of autographs. Yeats sent her a selection that included the Fenian John O'Leary's, the poet Katharine Tynan's and Standish O'Grady's, torn from correspondence, and hoped that the rumour of her having been bruised at the hunt some days before was untrue. 'Sligo is always full of rumours and the slightest one about its wild huntswoman naturally and properly echoes from mountain to mountain.'[10]

There is the impression that the Gore-Booth acquaintance was exciting but somewhat demanding for Willie Yeats. In March the river was frozen and there was skating. 'The Miss Gore-Booths were there and made coffey on the shore.'[11] It took the weight of years and events for him to regard them with an unobscured and sentimental eye, 'that table and the talk of youth' in 'that old Georgian mansion':

> The light of evening, Lissadell,
> Great windows open to the south,
> Two girls in silk kimonos, both
> Beautiful, one a gazelle.[12]

By the mid 1890s Constance and Eva had established themselves as enlightened modern young women on the fringes of the theosophical and artistic *milieux* and somewhat marginalized from the country lifestyle of Sligo. Eva must have soon remedied her lack in literary acquaintance because in 1896 she was staying at the house of the writer George MacDonald in Bordighera on the Italian Riviera where she met Esther Roper with whom she was to spend her life. It was Esther Roper who brought inspiration and a framework to Eva's seriousness of purpose. For the previous two years, Esther had been working for the economic and political enfranchisement of women. In Bordighera she and Eva discussed at length these increasingly controversial questions, as well as the conditions of the cotton workers and sweated labour in Manchester, where Esther lived. 'For months,' wrote Esther Roper, 'illness kept us in the south and we spent days walking and talking on the hillside by the sea.' When Eva returned to Lissadell she must have made a radical decision about her future. In the following year, 1897, she left to settle in Manchester and to live and work with Esther.

In the autumn of 1896 Eva, Constance and Mabel were preoccupied with the question of women's suffrage, to such a degree, said Edward Rowlette, Master of the Sligo Hunt Club, that they discussed little else even in the field between runs in the course of a day's hunt. It was decided to form a committee. Their first idea of a committee to represent the county of Sligo was reluctantly discarded in favour of a more humble parish committee, which would seek to gain 'the active support of Nationalist MPs',[13] who were considered to be less conservative in their social views than unionists. An inaugural meeting was called in Ballinful schoolhouse in December at which Con was elected president, Eva secretary and Mabel treasurer of the new association, only the third of its kind in Ireland, although the Dublin Women's Suffrage Society had been in existence since 1874.

A couple of weeks later there was a public meeting at the schoolhouse in Drumcliff, which drew a large crowd, two-thirds of it men. The schoolroom was hung with pretty seasonal evergreens framing austere mottoes: 'Who would be free themselves must strike the blow' – 'Liberty, justice and equality' – 'No taxation without representation'. It was all quite jolly since it was Christmastime and many of the men went along to have some fun at the expense of the women. Clearly most of them had given the subject little serious thought. This first public address Constance gave to an ebullient audience showed how capable an agitator she might be: how sure was her grasp of tactics, how dashing and engaging her manner and her quickness in responding extempore to heckling. Eva's approach was more sober, more measured and she displayed a broader comprehension of the issues. Mabel's angle was rather mundane.

The thrust of Constance's speech was a call to action:

> Now in order to attain to any political reform, you all know that the first step is to form societies to agitate and force the government to realize that a very large class have a grievance and will never stop making themselves disagreeable till it is righted. John Stuart Mill said thirty years ago that the only forcible argument against giving women the suffrage was 'that they did not demand it with sufficient force and noise'. Now, one of the many sneers I have been accustomed to hear against women is that they make too much noise; and yet we are told the principal argument against our having votes is that we don't make noise enough.

At this point there was laughter and cheers and the speaker continued: 'Of course it is an excellent thing to be able to make a good deal of noise, but not having done so, seems hardly a good enough reason for refusing us the franchise.' There were again loud cheers and laughter. 'But,' she concluded, 'the sooner we begin to make a row, the better.' There were cries of 'Oh!' when she quoted figures to the effect that the number of women who signed a petition to Parliament increased from 11,000 in 1873 to 257,000 in 1893. A cycling tourist present was supportive. So was trusty Mr Rowlette, if also sexist in his well-meaning way, when he said that women, because of their special talents, should be entrusted with the administration of justice and negotiations between nations. A Mr Clarke, in opposition, said it would be 'home rule' with a vengeance.

Eva, in her address, said she had taken part in many arguments on women's suffrage and agreed that, 'home is a women's sphere. Of course I am not talking of the great number of women all over the world who have not got homes and therefore can hardly be shamed for neglecting them [but of those women] who pay their rates and taxes, I think you will find they look upon politics as very much their business.' This aroused a cry of 'Three cheers for Lissadell!' There were more cheers for the president's exchange with a voice in the crowd who called out 'If my wife went to vote she might never come back' – 'She must think very little of you then.' When the resolution calling for the franchise for women was carried, there were loud cheers and applause.

Meetings continued, but the Suffrage Society failed to maintain its impetus. The Gore-Booths were going their separate ways; and the rather whimsical support the Society received came from the Tory 'country' element whose power was rapidly declining. In the political climate of polarization between unionist and nationalists, or Home Rulers, the latter would never lend their support to an issue taken up by unionists. When, some months later, there was a meeting of the Irish Agricultural Organisation Society, set up by the unionist Horace Plunkett to develop the dairy industry and thereby improve the living standards of the country people – and of which the conscientious Josslyn was on the Sligo branch committee – the *Sligo Champion*, being a nationalist newspaper, commented: 'No doubt they mean well. … But Creamery Conferences are simply a weak attempt to tinker up the social drawbacks, which are naturally attached to this country because of the want of self-government. Home Rule and Home Rule alone will touch the spot, in fact the many spots, which are diseasing the body politic.'[14]

Constance seems to have spent much of 1897 in Ireland. She hunted often with the Harriers. In February, she attended a fancy dress ball given by Colonel Campbell, Master of the Sligo Hounds, in Sligo Courthouse, its interior transformed with tapestries, incandescent lamps and a profusion of hothouse plants. In this exotic setting, the Gore-Booth sisters kept the faith with Josslyn's earnestness about the dairy industry and went dressed as Drumcliff dairymaids. At the Horse Show in August, Con's mare Cherry Ripe was commended and lacework from her mother's school was admired at the Textile Exhibition. It was a bad summer. There were rumours of impending famine from the *Sligo Champion*.

In September there was the annual fête for the children of the national schools on the lawns of Lissadell. Josslyn and Mordaunt assisted the Misses Gore-Booth with the races and the picnic tea of cakes and fruit, and the Reverend Le Fanu was there, as well as the church organist and some neighbours. Eva was absent. She was preparing her first book of poems for publication and was establishing her new life as an agitator for women's suffrage and improved conditions for workers in Manchester. Her elder sister was pressing ahead with her latest plan; to go to live and work in Paris where everything new in art was happening. Artists' circles in London were buzzing with talk of the vigorous and exciting Parisian avant-garde. Art in London was in the doldrums, staid and dull again after the small convulsion it experienced in the early 1890s. Early in 1898 the Exhibition of the International Society of Sculptors, Painters and Engravers came to Prince's Skating Rink in Knightsbridge, showing works by Whistler, Puvis de Chavannes, Renoir, Rodin et al., and was found astounding. Artists and aspirants were rushing post-haste to Paris. Con, who was always attracted to the new and the iconoclastic, was among the exodus.

NOTES

1. *Diary of an Art Student in the Nineties*, Alfred Thornton (Sir Isaac Pitman and Sons, London, 1938) p. 52.
2. *Ibid.*, p. 67.
3. *Constance Markievicz*, Sean O'Faolain (London and Toronto, 1934) p. 46.
4. *Life of Henry Tonks*, Joseph Hone (Heinemann, London, 1939) p. 45.
5. *Ibid.*, p. 46.
6. *W.B. Yeats and Georgian Ireland*, Torchiana, pp. 185–6.
7. *The Collected Letters of W.B. Yeats*, eds Kelly and Domville (Clarendon Press, Oxford 1986) p. 418.

8. *Ibid.*, p. 393.
9. *W.B. Yeats and Georgian Ireland*, Torchiana, p. 186.
10. *The Collected Letters of W.B. Yeats*, ed. Kelly and Domville, p. 461.
11. *Ibid.*, p. 447.
12. From 'In Memory of Eva Gore-Booth and Con Markievicz', *Collected Poems of W.B. Yeats*, p. 263.
13. A full report of the meeting appeared in *The Sligo Champion*, 26 December 1896, under the heading 'Amusing Proceedings'.
14. *The Sligo Champion*, 16 April 1897.

FOUR

PARIS AND POLAND

IN GOING to Paris in 1898 to study art, Constance removed herself finally from the orbit of the average eligible lord and from all ordinary expectations. She was going to be a great artist. She wore a ring on her marriage finger as a declaration that she was married to art. She got a place in a studio of Julian's, who ran the only good studios for women, according to Maria Bashkirtseff who had studied there in the 1880s, where 'all distinctions disappear; you have neither name nor family; you are no longer the daughter of your mother; you are yourself. You are an individual with art before you – art and nothing else.' Julian's, run by the large, formidable Rodolphe Julian from the Vaucluse in Provence, was acceptable to Lady Gore-Booth because Sarah Purser, now a family friend, had been there, and was acceptable to Con because so too had Anna Nordgren.

In the 1880s Julian's claimed, with 400 students, to be the largest art school in Paris. Although, unlike the École des Beaux Arts, it had no entrance exam, Julian's insisted on high standards and serious ambitions. It was influential in Parisian art circles and its professors such as Lefebvre, Bonnat and Laurens sat on the jury of the Salon. Students worked hard, usually eight hours a day, starting at 8 am. Of the private ateliers that flourished in Paris at the time, Julian's was considered the most rigorous in its standards, the most hard-working and the most international. In its early years, Julian's had mixed classes but by the late 1870s the sexes were segregated. Constance attended the women's studio, then in the rue du Cherche-Midi in the sixth arrondissement. The principal men's studio was in the rue du Dragon nearby.

Julian's attitude to women was relatively enlightened. Maria Bashkirtseff was pleased to find a man posing nude when she went first to the studio and with Monsieur Julian's comment that 'sometimes the female students are as clever as the young men'. Julian's was the first to enable the women to compete with men on an equal basis in the monthly competitions for prizes, so the atmosphere in the studio was demanding and competitive as the students vied with each other for the distinction of being chosen to compete and for a good position in Salon exhibitions. Yet, it seems that in 1887 at least, fees for women were nearly double those for the men and there were complaints that they had only one professor to criticize their work while the men's atelier had several. Julian's did admit gifted students for a minimal fee or for free.

With her characteristic unconventionality, Constance in Paris frequented the places where Parisians went and avoided the expatriates. The writer Violet Hunt, daughter of the painter Alfred Hunt and novelist Margaret Hunt, became friendly with her when a mutual acquaintance, Camomile, ('a hard worker') asked Con to take Violet around. Constance, wrote Violet Hunt, 'had a supreme contempt for the pretty-prettiness of the Crèmerie Leopold Robert',[1] decorated in a very English way by some student in lieu of paying his bill. She took Violet not to the 'English-infested' Crèmerie nor to the Moulin Rouge nor to the Heaven and Hell – 'all got up on purpose for such as you' – but to relatively notorious haunts like La Cigale and Le Soleil d'Or on the Boulevard Saint-Michel.

Both Violet and Camomile declined to go to the Bal des Quatres Arts at Montmartre one evening. This was quite a risqué place to go since the artists brought their models there. But Constance went. She arrived at Violet's and Camomile's English *pension* in the rue de Rivoli at 2 am and slept on their floor rather than walk halfway across Paris to her room on the Left Bank, putting herself to sleep by reciting Swinburne's *Triumph of Time*. In the evenings, they would sit on the *terrasses* of cafés on the Boul' Mich' until 11 or so when Constance would set off alone to her room. Violet thought her 'hopelessly generous', even though she was very poor. According to Violet, 'her father and mother were niggardly with supplies in the hope of starving her back home to Lissadell'. She used to boast 'bitterly' that she could 'live on 2f a day and take her bath in a pannikin in the middle of the bare studio floor'. When her parents came to Paris, they 'went to one of the fashionable hotels and she had to see them, properly dressed with gloves and a hat'. Once they told her to order a new dress for the occasion and she made the assistants at Worths roar with laughter when, trying on a green one and gazing at herself in the mirror, she exclaimed that it made her look like a rabbit sitting in a head of cabbage. She was so poor that Violet Hunt was sure 'she had not ever quite enough to eat'. 'I am sure her very brain was starved,' wrote Violet in 1916, as if seeking to explain what most English people regarded as Con's outrageous actions in that year. 'She did not think, she had no emotions which she could not work off with a dance at the Moulin de la Galette.'

In 1899, the year in which Constance met one aspect of her destiny in the form of Casimir Dunin Markievicz, Maud Gonne, who would be almost equally instrumental in shaping it, was also in Paris. In those months, Maud Gonne was living on the Avenue de la Grande Armée and being cold to Yeats who was staying in the Boulevard Raspail: she had finally confided to him her long-standing relationship with the French journalist Millevoye and the existence of her daughter Iseult. He was depressed and she was preparing to return to Ireland and to the support and succour of evicted tenants in Co. Donegal. It is unlikely that Yeats met Constance at that time, but her meeting with the Polish Count Markievicz has been well, if rather snidely, documented by a fellow Pole, the writer Stefan Krzywoszewski, in his autobiography *A Long Life*.

In January, Constance was at a students' ball accompanied by Daisy Forbes-Robertson's brother, Eric. Before making their appearance at the ball, Casimir Markievicz brought his friend Krzywoszewski to dine at a small restaurant where they had a two-franc menu of *steak-frites*.[2] When the meat came to the table, Casimir, for the benefit of the other customers, indulged in the kind of obvious humour that Constance might have appreciated, issuing a series of neighs to convey that it had come from the *boucherie chevaline*. According to Krzywoszewski:

> At about ten p.m. we found ourselves at the ball. It was a bizarre gathering, every class and nationality was represented and the clothes echoed the diversity. ... Near me stopped two Englishwomen. The older was of the type that you could meet ten or twenty times and yet not be able to recognize her five minutes later. The other one, who appeared to be about twenty years of age, was conspicuous for her proud bearing. She was a living Rossetti or Burne-Jones. Her profile was delicately-drawn, her eyes grey-blue. Her ball dress, an over-stylish one and not too fresh, barely covered the skinny shoulder-blades and the smooth planes where men gladly look for convexities. Since she was looking at me in a friendly manner I asked her in French; 'Madame, don't you dance?' 'I have no-one to dance with, I do not like to dance alone.' I bowed, she stooped down a little towards my arm. We squeezed into the dense crowd of waltzers. A brief conversation enabled me to orientate myself to this new acquaintance. In spite of her easy, woman-of-the-world manners, typical of the Parisian art student world, this was an intelligent miss with a background of good society. No sooner had the music started again than the Englishwoman wanted to dance once more. Markievicz was passing at this moment. I stopped him: 'Do dance with this lady. You will be well matched in height and bearing.' Markievicz immediately seized her and started to talk animatedly in his broken English. They looked well together – outstanding in the lively, dancing crowd.

A week or two later, when Krzywoszewski was sitting on the terrace of the Café Flore, Casimir and Constance came up on bicycles, completely absorbed in each other, and talking and *tu-toi*-ing like old friends. They left together.

Count Casimir Dunin Markievicz was charming, handsome and exotic. He was hugely tall and broad-shouldered with black hair and blue eyes and, six years younger than Con, was a match for her high spirits. It is no surprise that when she was at last susceptible to a man, it should have been Casimir. He was remote from the conventional world she had rejected. He too was a painter, and a good one – the piece he was then working on, *Amour*, later won a *Médaille d'Honneur* at the Salon – and he was amusing and energetic. His foreignness, his European manners and attitudes appealed to her. He was perhaps the first man she knew or was attracted to who was not 'thoroughly English' as she had rather contemptuously categorized her sister Mabel's Perceval. She may have taken his Bohemian irreverence for a serious iconoclasm. He also had an interesting, and tragic, marital past – indeed, when they first met, Casimir was still married – against which Constance, though older, was an *ingénue* in experience.

Their country, privileged backgrounds were quite similar. Count Casimir Dunin Markievicz came from a landowning, horse-breeding family in the Ukraine, which was bequeathed a swan for its coat of arms by one Peter Dunin (the Dane) who arrived in Poland in the twelfth century. The question of whether the Markieviczes were entitled to call themselves counts is often raised. When Casimir used the title, as he did in Paris, the likelihood is that he assumed it as a mark of distinction as members of the Polish nobility were in the habit of doing when they were abroad, a habit that seems to have been regarded, among themselves at least, as normal and acceptable. Born in 1874 he grew up on Zywotowka, the country estate bought by his grandfather, attended the State Gymnasium in Kherson and studied law for two years at the University in Kiev.

Like Constance, he was determined to be an artist. In 1895 he was helped by his family, no less reluctantly than the Gore-Booths, to go to Paris; and was secretly accompanied by his lover, Jadwiga Splawa Neyman, who had persuaded her parents to allow her to go there to study music. Jadwiga and Casimir lived on the fourth floor of a house in the rue Bonaparte in the Latin Quarter, married, and had two children, Stanislas in 1896 and Ryszard in 1897. But the relationship seems to have floundered. Sometimes they lived apart and both of them may have loved others. The marriage was also interrupted when Casimir was called up to do his military service in Russia. After a year in St Petersburg he came back to Paris as a commissioned officer in a regiment of the Hussars. When Jadwiga fell ill, probably with consumption, as did the younger child, she returned to the Ukraine with both children. She died in 1899 and was quickly followed by the younger son. Stanislas, the firstborn, remained with her family. Casimir heard of the death of his wife and son during the first weeks of his friendship with Constance. Her ready sympathy was immediately available to him and drew them together. Their high-spirited companionable friendship in the Paris spring allowed him to forget the sad past.

Casimir's love for Con seems to have been something of an aberration for him. From what we know of other women he loved before and later,[3] he was attracted to more typically romantic women – the pale consumptive kind – while Con was boyish, angular and outspoken. He may have fallen for Constance because at this time he sought friendship in a woman rather than the romantic love that had just ended so badly. One senses that she had always wanted friendship and sought inspiration rather than romantic love. Comradeship was the emotional climate in which she felt most comfortable. Casimir, as a painter, consorted perfectly with her view of a satisfying future. They would be united in their mutual ambition; they would inspire each other to be great painters. Within these boundaries, they were extremely romantic about each other. Their courtship was conducted through the medium of French.

Bicycling was the new craze, and they made long cycling expeditions into the French countryside, wearing kerchiefs and the new, daring cycling knickerbockers. They sat around in cafés like the Flore and the Procope smoking cigarettes. When they ran out of allowance money, Casi washed trams in the depot at night for a few francs. He painted Con's portrait, *Constance in White*, and showed it in the Grand Palais at the Great Exhibition of 1900. He fought a duel on her behalf with a Frenchman who behaved insolently at a costume ball, wounding the fellow in the thigh with his fencing sword. He also developed an infatuation, that may have been quite serious, for a friend of Constance's called Alys, but his fondness for Con overcame it. By September, they were engaged.

Con's wish to marry was, understandably, strong. She was brought up in a society where taboos against unregulated sexuality, especially for women, were deeply entrenched. Society was changing but the sexual revolution was still in the distant future.

Con, though rebellious, had a streak, which compelled her to conform to the outward conventions of respectability. She liked to wear the right clothes to the right occasions, to be industrious, to excel. She would have hated to be thought 'improper'. There was also the consideration that marriage, like nothing else she might do, bestowed personhood on a woman. It gave independent status, the right to take one's own decisions about what one wanted to do or where one wanted to go. Constance, at thirty-one, found the status of girlhood and dependency an embarrassment when she gave it any thought.

Also, it was a status, since she was the eldest girl that weighed heavily on her younger sister Mabel. Mabel was betrothed now to Perceval Foster for several years; that they weren't yet married suggests that her family was adhering to the Victorian convention where a younger sister could not marry first. (Mabel's marriage took place within three months of Con's.)

Con's forthcoming marriage, all things considered, must have been quite a relief to Sir Henry and Lady Gore-Booth. Initially they were wary enough of Casimir's provenance and suitability to make alarmed enquiries about him involving international diplomatic circles and the Russian secret service. But in the end they accepted with a degree of equanimity the more undesirable factors in the situation of their future son-in-law. These were several: he was younger than she was by six years, a widower, an impecunious painter and younger son, a Catholic and a foreigner of dubious title. That Constance's idealism was still firm and unstifled by the prospect of love and domesticity is evident from the letter she wrote to Eva telling her about Casimir: 'He fills me with the desire to do things. I feel with the combination I may get something done, too.'⁴ The ambition of being great artists together was spurred by Casimir's success with *Amour* exhibited alongside *Constance in White*. Based on the Slav legend of St John's Eve, *Amour* was exhibited in Warsaw and St Petersburg, and elicited a visit to Casimir's studio from the President of the Imperial Academy in St Petersburg who wanted to know why the painter was not working in his native Russia. Casimir answered with the irony of a Pole who regarded Russia as having unlawfully annexed his native land: 'The climate there does not suit my health, your Highness.'⁵

In the early winter of that year Sir Henry and Lady Gore-Booth went to Switzerland in search of a cure for Sir Henry who was unwell. In January 1900 he died in St Moritz. Constance had always admired and been influenced by her father, and his loss affected her deeply. She returned to Lissadell with her mother for the funeral. In May Casimir came to join her and to make the customary acquaintance of her family and the neighbourhood. Having charmed everyone, he left in July for the Ukraine to see his family and small son, and in September rejoined Constance and her entourage in London. Constance later told her stepson, Stanislas, amusing stories of how she used to coach his father, whose English was still rudimentary, in his responses for the marriage service, generally while travelling around London on the tops of buses.

They were married on 29 May, three times: in civil services at a registry office and the Russian legation, and in a religious service at the Protestant church of St Mary's in Marylebone. The wedding was traditionally splendid: Constance in white satin, a pearl necklace and some diamond pieces given her by her mother, Casimir in Russian court uniform that included a rapier and a three-cornered hat. There were four bridesmaids, Eva and Mabel in violet satin, and Rachel Mansfield and Mildred Grenfell in green. The Reverend Le Fanu was there to officiate. The reception was held in the house of her friend Rhoda, now Lady Morpeth.

But the conventions were not quite unbreached. The promise to obey her husband was omitted from Con's marriage vows according to the Russian practice. And after the couple had been seen safely off to France on the boat train from Victoria, they got off at a station down the line and returned to London to throw a party for their wilder friends who weren't invited to the wedding. A honeymoon travelling around Normandy by bicycle took three weeks; then they settled down in Paris to live and work, in a rented apartment containing a studio and four relatively grand furnished rooms in the rue Campagne Première in Montparnasse. They were living in the heart of the Bohemian quarter of artists and their studios but were not poor enough to be typically Bohemian. Neither were they rich.

When Constance's father had made his will, he followed to what now seems a ruthless degree the convention of primogeniture.

His purpose was to keep intact the property he had inherited. Josslyn, as the eldest son, therefore got everything, down to the family heirlooms of diamonds and pearls. In comparison, the younger children, including the son, Mordaunt, got a pittance. On Sir Henry's death, Constance, Eva and Mordaunt each received the sum of £2500, which they were expected to invest wisely, as well as an equal share in a sum held in trust which amounted to only £33 each per annum, at most £2000 in today's values.

Girls were expected to provide for their futures by marrying well, and Sir Henry rewarded his daughter Mabel for her success in finding a suitable husband by substantially increasing her share of the inheritance. Not only did her yearly income from monies held in trust amount to over £300 – or more than ten times that of her sisters – but this sum was in fact provided for out of an amount that had, prior to the addition of a codicil in October 1899 before he left for Switzerland, been intended to be shared equally between all of the children.

Aggrandizement, or improvement of one's position, was rewarded. And Constance was not compensated for having married an impecunious man. Casimir did have a small income of his own. Constance also seems to have received a legacy from an aunt before she went to Paris. Other legacies may have followed since there was no shortage of wealthy relations. But Constance and Eva, who had overstepped so many boundaries, were not everyone's idea of favourite nieces. When Aunt Augusta, Wee Ga, died in 1906 she left her fortune to the Wynnes of Hazelwood, while Eva got some silver and books, excluding the 'set of the Temple Bar Magazine' – and Constance got Wee Ga's household linen.

Constance and Casimir intended to earn money. That year, Casimir was given some important portrait commissions. But neither he nor Constance were ever to make their reputations as painters. If they had had to, both of them were talented and competent enough to make a living as portraitists. But their joint income meant that was never necessary; it also allowed them to indulge their other interests and any tendencies to dilettantism. The principal reason why neither of them figures in the lists of remembered painters is that they did not have the commitment to originality which would allow them to compete in the great artistic event of the new century, the modernist movement. In 1901 when Casimir was painting Constance in the manner of Sargent, Picasso was already at work.

They spent the first Christmas of their marriage at Nice and the following summer at Lissadell because Constance was expecting a child. She wanted to give birth there, where her mother was and in the house where her sisters and brothers were born. The baby was born on 13 November 1901 with great pain and difficulty, the birth probably attended by one of those gynaecologists who travelled to great country houses from Dublin for these events. It was a girl and was christened Maeve Alyss, reflecting the Irish and French influence in her heritage; Maeve for the great legendary queen who was buried under the cairn on Knocknarea, the flat-topped mountain framed in many of the house's windows and familiar to the mother since her childhood; and Alyss, it is said, for the friend who had since married and died in childbirth, leaving Casimir a ring.

When the Markieviczes went back to Paris some months later, Maeve remained with her grandmother at Lissadell, setting a pattern that was to continue throughout her childhood and youth. That Constance cared for her daughter only fitfully is often cited as an indication of a flaw in her nature. There is a suggestion that the value of her love for people is diminished if her own child felt her mother did not love her. It is true that Maeve does seem to have felt unloved. As she grew older, she would complain that she had been farmed out to her grandmother and resented her mother for paying only occasional visits. She remembered with some bitterness how once, when she ran forward to meet her, she was greeted with the reprimand 'Watch out. Don't step on the dog.'[6] Later events meant that they were necessarily separated for years at a time.

But although their relationship was often distant and desultory, they were never estranged. It was a relationship more typical of friends than of mother and daughter; it conformed to Con's habit of camaraderie and talk of mutual interests in place of intimacy or emotional involvement. That she may have wounded Maeve through an apparent coldness was to distress Constance later and she often sought to justify the child's country upbringing to women friends. It seemed the best thing from every point of view for the baby to stay at Lissadell for the time being. It was winter. Con and Casi intended to make a journey to Poland in the near future. Meanwhile, they wanted to continue their artistic life in Paris, which, relatively bourgeois though it was, would provide an unnecessarily hazardous and insecure start for a baby. In those days, when babies died willy-nilly of all sorts of infections, a country upbringing where there were bracing ocean airs and experienced nursemaids was considered to be of much greater advantage to a child than the mere presence of its mother.

As the years passed, her grandmother became so attached to Maeve that she was loath to give her up – as early as 1906 Lady Gore-Booth made a will naming Maeve as her sole beneficiary – and her mother became so preoccupied and busy, and her life held such potential dangers, that she was glad to let the arrangement stand.

In May 1902 the Markieviczes left Paris to spend the summer at Zywotowka, Casimir's family's estate in the Ukraine. Zywotowka, a white-painted house, reminiscent of the American colonial style, was not as grand and imposing as Lissadell Court – Maria Bashkirtseff, who was also Ukrainian, complained that houses in her native land were not lofty as in Europe but low-level – yet the inhabitants of both lived very similar lives. Casimir's family, like Constance's, was large. There was his mother, a strong woman whose Eton crop anticipated the style of the 1920s; and four sisters and three brothers, the eldest of whom, Jan, was married. Jan's wife, Lena, gardened, and he bred English thoroughbreds. They were all very pleased with Con because she was so companionable and a fine horsewoman. But the most adoring friend she made in the Ukraine was Stanislas, Casimir's six-year-old son who lived with his mother's people twenty-five miles away. Stanislas always remembered the special smell she had then, of perfume, paint and tobacco, and how beautiful she seemed to him in her artist's overalls, how tall, and how soft her brown hair seemed.[7]

Like Lissadell, Zywotowka had its peasants who lived in wretched cabins and bared their heads as carriages approached. Sometimes, when you were out riding or driving on the dusty roads among the *versts* and *versts* of green cornfields, you might come upon one of them huddled in a ditch. In a letter home, Constance expressed her endemic if fitful unease about the plight of common people. She liked the Ukraine immensely but

> there are tiresome things about it as well. The peasants are miserable. Yesterday we went for a long drive and passed a man lying drunk in a ditch by the roadside. I wanted to get out and help him, but the horse galloped past and Casimir said he would be all right. So there was nothing to be done.

It is hard to see what could have been done by someone on holidays in a new country among a new family whose approval she wanted to keep. For her, it was enough for the moment to observe and remember.

People like the Markieviczes could anyway afford to be complacent about their hereditary privileged position in a way that the Gore-Booths could not. Since the eighteenth century, when the Ukraine was taken by the Russians, they shared with the people their Polish nationalist aspirations and with them they held on to their Polish language and culture, forming a united front against Russian imperialism. When Polish servants slept on the floor outside their masters' doors they expressed in most cases a genuine sense of fealty though foreigners usually thought the practice awful.

The Markieviczes found it charming rather than uncomfortably egalitarian when Con got herself a colourfully embroidered peasant dress. They had a pair of high red boots made for her to go with it. Maria Bashkirtseff, whose feelings were not at all democratic, had also got herself a peasant costume. It was summer so she and Casimir painted scenes of rural life out of doors and made a studio out of a little structure in the park where storks strutted about. Con made a pet of a crippled stork and fed it frogs at night-time. As autumn drew on, there was talk of hunting. Here in the Ukraine, they hunted wolves and hares and took a feast with them of brandy, mutton and roast pies to lunch on in the woods. Bashkirtseff was surprised that it was the custom to distribute the same repast among the peasants.

By the end of September it was cold. By November everything would be white under a grey sky. In October, when the stubbled cornfields reached to the horizon, Con and Casi returned to Paris and gave a fancy-dress ball for 150 people. They spent Christmas in Ireland. And the following May they were back in the Ukraine for a second summer. This time however, when they left in the autumn, they returned not to Paris, but to Dublin.

They saw Paris as a place to be students in – now they were going to be professional painters. They probably wanted to be with their baby daughter. Perhaps Constance liked her native country too much to stay away for very long and Casimir had no objection to taking on a new city. On one of their last visits to Lissadell, a man called George Russell was staying there who knew Con's brother, Sir Josslyn, through their common involvement in the cooperative dairy movement. Russell, who was a close associate of W.B. Yeats and all the artistic people in Dublin, had told them about the thriving cultural life of the city.

By late summer 1903 Con's mother had bought and furnished a house in the genteel south-city suburb of Rathgar for them to live in. The decision had also been made to take the boy Stanislas to live with them. He proved to be as enthusiastic about the prospect as they were about having him. His Polish grandmother was dismayed, however, and had to be promised that his Polish language and identity and Catholic religion would be kept up while he was abroad. Stanislas always remembered Constance's delight when she was told that his grandmother had finally agreed to his going.

On an October day in 1903 the newly formed family boarded the great wood-burning train at the country station of Oratowo, bound for Warsaw, Berlin and Paris. They arrived in Dublin some days later with sixty-four cases of property and zestful schemes for taking its artistic coteries by storm. More than a year before, after they had fired one another's ambitions at Lissadell, George Russell wrote in a letter to Sarah Purser that 'the Gore-Booth girl who married the Polish Count with the unspellable name is going to settle near Dublin about summertime [and] as they are both clever it will help create an art atmosphere. We might get the materials for a revolt, a new Irish art club.'[8]

Dreamy, theosophical George Russell was being more prescient than he knew.

NOTES

1. Violet Hunt wrote a piece about her now infamous friend in the *Daily Mail* of 3 May 1916.
2. Stanislas Dunin Markievicz's translation of Krzywoszewski's account of the meeting is cited in Anne Marreco's *The Rebel Countess*, p. 68.
3. Apart from Alys, Casimir's relationship with a young woman in Poland in the 1920s and early thirties is described in Sean O'Faolain's *Constance Markievicz*.
4. *The Rebel Countess*, Marreco, p. 70.
5. *Ibid.*, p. 72.
6. Told to the author by Seamus Scully who was acquainted with Maeve de Markievicz.
7. Stanislas wrote an autobiographical piece for *The Irish Worker*, 17 October 1931.
8. *Letters from Æ*, ed. Alan Denson (Abelard-Schumann, London-New York-Toronto, 1961) p. 39.

FIVE

MARRIED LIFE:
NATIONALIST AWAKENING

DUBLIN IN 1903 was, in the eyes of many of its citizens, a very pleasant city. It was happily located, the sea at its feet and the Dublin and Wicklow mountains at its back providing places of resort and recreation, especially since the advent of efficient transport: the train, the tram and the bicycle. Architecturally elegant, with Georgian squares and tree-lined streets still largely intact, at least on the south side of the city, its bars and cafes were numerous and quite European in style, saved from the dangers of provincialism and homogeneity by the presence of the British administration and the Viceregal Court. The Dublin of 1904 in James Joyce's *Ulysses* is depicted as a mellow, shabby-genteel place, alive with talk and bravura and the complex psychologies of its citizens. Its tone was unusually literary and intellectual. It seems significant that Dublin then had almost as many bookbinders as shoemakers. Servants were plentiful.

But for almost one third of its quarter million inhabitants, life was wretched. That one third, the unemployed and labouring classes, lived in its slums of fine Georgian mansions gone to seed.

These great houses were built in the eighteenth century when Dublin was prosperous and had its own parliament. Since the parliament had been lost in 1801 with the Act of Union, Dublin had fallen into decline. And houses, whose owners left Ireland, were abandoned and became tenements, the homes of landless people who migrated year after year from the countryside.

The Dublin poor were poor indeed. The city had few industries and the labour force was, for the most part, unskilled. Most of the employment available was in the unskilled commercial and distributive areas, in the casual occupations of carrying and labouring. It was a boss's market and wages were ruthlessly low. There was a shortage of accommodation, and rents, even for floor space in a tenement room, were high. The mansions in which poor people lived had once been beautiful. Many of them still possessed their original 15ft-high mahogany doors and, as plasterwork liked the damp cool climate, the neo-classical cupids and moulded decorations still nestled on their cornices next to the high ceilings. But the elegance was soured when a family lived in each of the four corners of what was once a drawing room. A family, even where there were several children, was thought fortunate to have an entire room to itself.

Baths were unknown. Privies, one to a building, were in back yards or unventilated basements, by the single tap. Some streets were still open sewers as in the Middle Ages. Cooking facilities were also primitive. People lived on bread and tea and whatever could be boiled or fried on an open fire – herrings, cabbage, potatoes. Many of the houses had fallen into decay and were structurally unsound. The degradation that resulted was horrible: the filth, the smell – the smell was said to be the worst of all – the overcrowding, the lack of such essentials as clothing and furniture. Children were often wrapped in rags and slept on straw. The number of prostitutes, even for a late nineteenth-century city, was inordinately high.

George Russell later wrote with an incandescent anger of how the poor were herded together 'so that one thinks of certain places in Dublin as a pestilence. There are 20,000 rooms in each of which live entire families and sometimes more, where no functions of the body can be concealed, and delicacy and modesty are creatures that are stifled ere they are born.'[1] The infant death rate in Dublin was the highest of any city in the British Isles – save, in some years, that of another Irish city, Cork – and rivalled that of Calcutta.

The Markieviczes' new house at Frankfort Avenue, Rathgar, was an elegant redbrick early Victorian villa with the traditional Dublin feature of a neo-classical doorway. It had ample gardens with a greenhouse and stabling, though Constance and Casimir did not keep any horses. They employed a cook-housekeeper and two maids, and even, for a time, a footman called Janko, to run it on smooth bourgeois lines. Janko was a kind of refugee, the son of a Jewish tenant at Zywotowka who, to avoid conscription into the Russian military service, had been smuggled across the border to Berlin where he joined the Markieviczes en route to Ireland. But he soon left up his livery and departed to the city with ten pounds Constance gave him to make his own way. Maeve was brought up to Dublin and for long periods during the next few years, she and her half-brother Stasko lived with their parents.

Casimir took to Irish life with gusto. Through his wife, he had an entrée to Castle society and, though not at all snobbish his favourite drinking companions were Martin Murphy, stage-manager and carpenter at the Gaiety Theatre, and a Polish tailor called Dubronsky – he thoroughly enjoyed the social round it offered. The Count and Countess Markievicz were mentioned frequently in the society columns alongside the titled notables of the day. The fashionable frothy confections Con wore were faithfully recorded: she was seen in black with a large leghorn hat at the Horse Show, in orange and gold satin at an 'empire ball', and 'picturesque' in purple chiffon at Lady MacConnell's, the wife of the Under-Secretary of State. They were regulars at balls and house parties where the Count sang Polish songs accompanied on the piano by the Countess.

They patronized the traditional charitable events that their friends organized, such as the La Floralia fête associated with the Spring Show of the Irish Horticultural Society, where the Countess had a stall that displayed her talent as a gardener. At an afternoon party on 15 March 1907 she 'looked very pretty in stone grey with a bright cerise toque',[2] and that evening wore her purple chiffon again at the St Patrick's Ball, which was attended by 1000 guests.

The social columnists regarded the events they described as the apex of Irish society but, within a few years, they would appear anachronistic, eclipsed by literary tea parties in draughty drawing rooms and meetings of obscure-sounding societies in ill-lit halls. In so far as history had ever inhabited the Castle and the Viceregal Court, it now forsook them finally for their grubby environs, the streets of Dublin. Constance had come back to the city to find a cultural revolution in progress.

After the fall and what was felt to be the betrayal of Parnell, there was general disillusionment with politics and many among the young generation turned from political to cultural nationalism. The Irish language, vitiated by emigration and urbanization almost to the point of extinction, had been taken up by intellectuals who saw it as the repository of all that was unique and distinctive in the Irish nation. A society called the Gaelic League had been formed in 1893, which sought to restore Irish as the everyday language of the people.

The learning of Irish quickly became a national occupation. In small country towns, large numbers of people enrolled in Irish classes. The more enthusiastic spent their holidays in the Irish-speaking districts in the West, the 'Gaeltachts', cycling around the remoter districts and engaging the native speakers in conversation so as to acquire the authentic accent, or *bias*. Rejuvenation was not confined to the language. Irish forms of dancing and music and games, especially hurling, an ancient game played with stick and ball that owed nothing in its conception to English ball games, came into vogue.

Much of this rediscovered culture was ersatz. Men were wearing kilts, appropriated from Scottish clansmen, which were closest to their idea of their Irish forebears. The vigour and vitality of native dances were subdued to fit Victorian drawing rooms and Victorian deportment.

What interested others like W.B. Yeats, his patron Lady Gregory and George Russell (increasingly known by his pen-name Æ) was not the language itself but the ancient Celtic myths and sagas it embodied. They regarded the Celtic past as a fund of inspiration. They liked to imagine Ireland as a place where gods and heroes walked among the people as they did in ancient Greece, and they popularized them in their stories and plays and poems so that the tales of Faery and Cúchulainn, Maeve, Queen of Connacht, Finn MacCool and the Fianna, which for centuries had been the mythology of the rural peasantry, became familiar to urban sophisticates.

This Gaelic revival or resurgence was not overtly political but was, all the same, profoundly nationalistic. Inherent in it was the belief that this threatened culture was innately superior to, and needed to be protected from, the contamination of the dominant English civilization. The attitude of the English towards the Irish was always one of complacent superiority; as a reaction to this, the Gaelic revivalists romanticized and idealized their own race. The idealism was not at all practical. Ireland would be made a perfect place; therefore she would not be modern with all the vices of modernity, but pastoral and Arcadian. Yeats said in 1903 that she would not have 'great wheels turning and great chimneys vomiting smoke' but would be a country where 'men plow and sow and reap'. 'We wish,' he declared, 'to preserve an ancient ideal of life.'[3]

For Douglas Hyde, the talented poet and painter who founded the Gaelic League, the reasons for bilingualism included 'the fear of becoming materialistic and losing our highest characteristics'.[4] All over Dublin people were translating their names and titles into Irish, using the Irish version of their name over their shop or pub and thereby loftily declaring their kinship with an old vanished nobility, which was greatly superior to the gentry of the present day. A new pejorative word was coined, *seoinin*, used to describe someone who rejected things Irish and cultivated English ways instead, who 'imitated' the English 'interlopers'. A *seoinin* was an English-Irelander, while an Irish-Irelander was approved of – except by the most discriminating, who thought extreme Irish-Irelanders pompous and chauvinist.

The Gaelic revival was supported by the Catholic Church, which, since the mid-nineteenth century, had exercised a tremendous hold on the people. The Archbishop of Cashel, Dr Croke, sponsor of the Gaelic Athletic Association (GAA), formed in 1884 to promote Irish sports, expressed the new disdain for Englishness:

> If we continue travelling for the next score years in the same direction that we have been going in for some time past ... effacing our national features as though we were ashamed of them, and putting

on, with English stuffs and broadcloths, her masher habits and other such effeminate follies as she may recommend, we had better at once, and publicly, adjure our nationality.[5]

This self-assertion was later to develop a raucous and reactionary character but in 1903, when Constance arrived in Dublin, it seemed like a springtime of hope and liberation.

These were heady and controversial times. Artists and writers were inspired with a new pride, a sense that what they said and did could influence their country's destiny. Everyone was ready to be influenced. Now that constitutional politics was in the doldrums, a more vital, anarchic and diffuse politics seemed to be taking its place. And it was a movement in which women, who anyway had little time for parliamentary politics since they had no vote, were active and important. But one political idea was dominant, and that was the separation of Ireland from the United Kingdom. That the overwhelming majority of the Irish MPs at Westminster were in the Irish Party, which was committed to achieving Home Rule, reflected the fact that the majority of Irish people were separatists of one kind or another.

The Markieviczes may have chosen to live in Rathgar because their close acquaintance Æ (George Russell) and his unconventional wife, Violet, lived on nearby Coulson Avenue. Next door to the Russells lived the redoubtable Maud Gonne who had moved out to Rathgar in 1902 from a flat in the centre of the city. Con had made Maud's acquaintance before during one of the London Seasons but it was on a different basis that she met her now at one of the Russell's Sunday 'at-homes', frequented by people from the art world and the theatre, theosophists, and the occasional political theorist. At that time in Dublin, these roles were often interchangeable. Æ for instance, was all of them.

Maud, two years older than Constance, already had a long involvement in politics. In the 1890s she made the cause of evicted tenants her personal campaign and now was notorious both for her political extremism and, with rather less justification, for her romantic liaisons. In 1898 she made a countrywide lecture tour to celebrate the centenary of the 1798 rebellion, and the following year, was a founder of the Transvaal Committee formed to support the Boers in the South African War.

She was famous for her leonine beauty and for being the unrequited love of W.B. Yeats and therefore the inspiration for his great poetry. She played the eponymous heroine in his play *Cathleen ni Houlihan*, personifying the risen Ireland with 'the walk of a queen'. This was the play, which was to spark revolutionary fires in many breasts with its challenging lines that included 'If any man would help me, he must give me himself, give me all.' She painted. And lived much of the time in Paris where she kept her daughter Iseult (by her French lover, the political journalist Millevoye), and where she produced a journal, *Irlande Libre*.

In 1900 (as a response to the exclusion of women from the nationalist Celtic Literary Society and indeed from other debating clubs such as the Contemporary Club), she founded a society for patriotic women called *Inighnidhe na hÉireann* (pronounced Inini, as it is in the simplified spelling of today's Irish),[6] meaning 'Daughters of Ireland'. The Inini engaged in activities ranging from the distribution of propagandist pamphlets to the production of nationalist plays and the organization of opposition to the customary visits royalty paid to Ireland.

In 1903 when King Edward came to Dublin, Maud's house in Rathgar had been the object of a siege by police when she hung out a black flag – actually a black petticoat – as a partisan gesture towards the recently deceased Pope, Leo XIII, who could not be officially mourned because of the proliferation of Union Jacks. In October, the month of the Markieviczes' arrival in Dublin, Maud had annoyed Yeats and Lady Gregory when she walked out of their production of John Millington Synge's *In the Shadow of the Glen*. Synge's new play was considered a radical departure in its realistic portrayal of the Irish country people, but Maud Gonne, who romanticized Ireland, aligned herself with what were regarded as the obscurantists who held that Synge's play degraded Irish womanhood. Maud's defence was: 'It is for the many, for the people that Irish writers must write and if the Irish people do not understand or care for an Irish play, I would feel very doubtful of its right to rank as national literature.'[7]

In the same year Maud had made what was an already disastrous marriage to the nationalist John MacBride, and after the row with Yeats, she rejoined MacBride in Paris. It was in 1904 when she was back in Ireland for the christening of her son Sean that she and Constance first met. Maud told of visiting the Markieviczes and of being taken to see Maeve in her bath; but there is nothing to suggest that they discussed politics then. Maud would have thought of Constance as at best apolitical if not actually unionist because of her background and her easy relationship with the Castle. After she separated from MacBride in 1905, she felt obliged to live in Paris to safeguard her custody of their son Sean, which left her effectively *hors de combat* in Ireland at its most crucial period.

For a long time, the Markieviczes were regarded by the nationalist middle-class intellectual establishment as parvenus. But gentle, vague Æ who managed to work with and be friends with everyone took them up. In March 1904 he wrote to Willie Yeats:

> I am painting as many pictures as I can for I am going to exhibit during Horse Show Week together with Markovitch the Polish painter all the best in the collection of pictures 'Ireland Visible and Invisible'. I hope it will irritate a good many people. I would never have thought seriously of it but Markovitch who is a medallist in the Salon and a really fine painter thinks my things are good and like nobody else's and he has persuaded me. ... Markovitch is devouring Lady Gregory's book and is going to do cartoons of old Irish subjects for the show.[8]

The Yeatses, at least among themselves, kept up the old Sligo middle-class disdain described by W.B. in his autobiographies. In 1907 John Butler Yeats, also a painter and father of W.B., wrote to his son: 'I saw Count Markovitch today. Nathaniel Hone had bought one of his pictures. Nathaniel Hone thinks very little of – He says he has faculty but no brains and that he is a stupid man.'[9] Casimir was not by any means stupid, but he was a bit of a dilettante who did not believe in seriousness. His method of dealing with the status quo, when left to his own devices, was to undermine it with a witty aside or a humorous parody. He learned his English in Dublin, which was perhaps what led the writer Padraic Colum to call him the only stage Irishman he had ever met. His Bohemianism was rather self-conscious in the manner of the time, exemplified by people like Isadora Duncan or Augustus John. He enjoyed and was accepted in the city's artistic drinking places but his mind may have been too European for him to be quite at home in this small intense world.

It is significant that both Casimir and Constance were each described, affectionately, as childlike by two different people who knew them around this time in their lives. Of Constance, Æ said she was 'straight as a lance, devoid of fear ... like a child who dibbles down flowers without a rod to make a ready-made flower-garden'.[10] (It was an inappropriate image to choose for such an expert gardener.) Æ also said she was gifted with energy and 'should have been born in America'. A friend of Casimir's, the Polish writer Makuszynski, wrote of how everyone loved him 'the way you love a nice, good child. And this child was a giant almost two metres high'.[11] Their aristocratic breezy insouciance tended to baffle the more cautious and complex middle-class people they moved among. Some of them looked askance at certain actions of the Countess; the occasion, for instance, during a heat wave when she was seen happily playing a water hose over Stasko and the Russell boys who were running around naked on the grass.

The projected exhibition that Æ spoke of duly took place in Horse Show Week. The three exhibitors, Constance Gore-Booth, Casimir Dunin Markievicz and George Russell (Æ) called their show 'Pictures of Two Countries'. Constance showed seventy-six pictures, Casimir eighty-five, and Æ sixty-three. The highest prices asked were £330 for Casimir's *Amour* and £150 for his portrait of Æ, now in the Hugh Lane Municipal Gallery. Constance asked £150 for *The Conscript*, a Polish interior in which a peasant family sadly regard the boy who has just been called up to serve in the Russian army. But these prices were not representative; most of the other pictures were priced at six guineas or three guineas, and the exhibition was well reviewed and well attended, even if not many of the paintings were sold.

In the opening week of the exhibition they went to the Antient Concert Rooms for a concert programme that included John McCormack and a young poet they had previously met at Æ's called James Joyce, who cherished ambitions for his fine tenor voice. In 1904 too, Æ published *New Songs*, an anthology of modern poetry in which Eva Gore-Booth had two poems. And in December when George Moore gave a lecture on Modern Painters of the Royal Hibernian Academy, Count Markievicz was chairman and introduced the lecturer in French.

In 1905 this loosely bound group of friends did what they had been talking about for a long time, and founded an Arts Club. It was located in one of the Georgian houses on St Stephen's Green. They called it the Dublin United Arts Club. Its members comprised the by now familiar nucleus of Dublin intellectual life: besides Æ and the Markieviczes there were Willie Yeats and his painter brother, Jack, J.M. Synge, the painter William Orpen and the comic songwriter Percy French, author of hundreds of popular music-hall songs.

It was largely a drinking club so women were not very much in evidence. But there was a monthly dinner, given on each occasion by a different member, and although the general tone was one of levity and amusement, the Arts Club played its part in developing an artistic life in the city. Members who were painters gave a life class two or three nights a week and one of them, Page Dickinson, has written that the Markieviczes were among the most helpful and 'could have been really first-rate if they had worked. They never did, however, their energies were too diffuse to concentrate on painting.'[12] It was the Arts Club which, in 1911, brought over to Dublin Roger Fry's Post-Impressionist Exhibition, showing Van Gogh, Picasso, Gaugin and Matisse, that had been so sensational in London where it was hated, a *succes d'execration.*

The intellectual atmosphere of the Arts Club and the circles in which Constance moved was nationalistic; but it was nationalism at a remove from the ardent separatism that was gaining ground elsewhere. The Viceregal couple, Lord and Lady Aberdeen, considered themselves enlightened and democratic and even welcomed moderate nationalists to the Lodge, among the 'doctors of medicine, divines of the various Protestant persuasions, skilful dentists and perfumers', Maurice Headlam, Chief Remembrancer in the Treasury, used to flit between the Castle and the Arts Club and described Countess Markievicz as 'a haggard and witch-like creature'. But Headlam was perhaps a misogynist: he was also scathing about Lady Aberdeen because she was the dominant partner in her marriage and was too democratic.

Nationalists, of the moderate kind, were not generally banned from mixing with the Castle people. A certain amount of encouragement was probably seen by the administration as a means of emasculating the movement, and added a fashionable spice to things. About the time Yeats was indoctrinating the Gore-Booths in the Irish heritage, he was also coaching Betty Balfour, wife of the Chief Secretary, in the subject, and tableaux from his play *The Countess Cathleen* (less inflammatory than the later *Cathleen ni Houlihan*) were being put on at the Lodge.

Yeats's nationalism was visionary and yet, ironic. Æ's version was mystical and evolutionary: he was employed by the unionist, Sir Horace Plunkett, to develop his cooperative creameries, an innovation in Irish agriculture that would endure. They were observers essentially, subtle, rather fastidious and exploitative. Then, some time in 1907, probably in the summer when Casimir was in the Ukraine, Constance came upon a direct, more extreme brand of nationalism.

She was renting a cottage in the country, a typical two-roomed whitewashed cottage in the Dublin Mountains near a village called Ballally. She used it as a retreat, a base from which to paint outside, to ramble in the hills and roam the countryside on her bicycle. The poet Padraic Colum used to live there for a time and browsing one wet day through some old newspapers he had left behind, Con found among them copies of *The Peasant* and *Sinn Féin* and the *United Irishman*. These were the propaganda sheets of the Irish-Ireland and national movement. They ran articles ranging from the inspired and quite sophisticated to the crudely sentimental and simplistic. Gallahers Irish Tobacco was eulogized, as was *Our Irish Games*, a novel by Mary Butler, for being 'An Irish national novel', and the newly established Woollen Mills as 'an outcome of Irish-Ireland ideas'. There were series on the Irish past, the Harpers and Pipers of the seventeenth century, life in early Ireland, and Irish heroes, couched in tones that were reverential.

By-lines were pen-names, usually in Irish: '*Lasairfhiona*', '*Marabhan*'. One 'Carrickburn' wrote: 'Emerging from the darkness of Anglicization into the health and warmth of an Irish atmosphere, I learned that Ireland had a language of her own full of the treasures of the golden past.'[13] The Irish culture was presented as high-minded, healthy and Spartan while the English culture against which it was fighting for survival was somehow, by implication, unwholesome.

Today, these publications seem quaint and rather tedious, comparable in many ways to the house magazines of a religious movement or some cranky minority cause. But to Constance, they showed the light. For the first time, she understood what Robert Emmet – whose face was familiar to her from childhood, affixed to cottage walls next to images of the saints – had died for. She understood the wonderful pathos and defiance of his speech from the dock that ended with: 'When my country takes her place among the nations of the earth, then, and not till then, let my epitaph be written.' She recognized his greatness and the greatness of those other patriots who were the heroes of the people: Owen Roe O'Neill who led the insurgency of 1641 and was popularly believed to have been poisoned by an English agent; Wolfe Tone, sent to the gallows for his part in the rebellion of 1798; Thomas Davis, the sweet-natured guiding spirit of the rebels of 1848.

She saw the significance in the bronze plaque of the man called Arthur Griffith that was hanging on the wall of this cottage in Ballally: 'I awoke,' she would later write, 'to the fact that Ireland had not surrendered and that there were men and women who had not acquiesced in the conquest.'[14] It was analogous to a religious illumination. A prospect opened before her of purpose, action, adventure, comradeship with a noble people united in a noble aim.

It has been said that Constance turned to the nationalist cause because she saw finally that she was never going to achieve fame as a painter. The truth is, that despite her undoubted talent as a painter, art had not succeeded in claiming her attention at a deep level. She did not quite possess an artist's nature: she lacked detachment; she had little natural faculty for reflection. At heart she was simple, fervent, spontaneous and responsive. But the complexities and subtleties of creative work bored her. Her instinct was to follow what was beautiful and simple and submit to it. And she was gregarious, verbal and active, talents that were thwarted by the solitary, quiescent life of a painter. She decided at once, she wrote, to get to know these people and to involve herself in their cause. And quite soon afterwards, one Sunday at the Russells', she met Arthur Griffith whom she recognized as one of the cause's leading lights and she gallantly offered her services.

Arthur Griffith was exerting a huge influence on his contemporaries through his gifted editorship of a weekly called the *United Irishman*. He wrote, as was customary, under a pen-name, *Cuaguan*, meaning Dove; and at this time, had moved from a vaguely militant stance to his pacifist 'Hungarian Policy'. He argued that since the Hungarians had won autonomy in the 1860s by withdrawing their allegiance from the Austrian parliament, the Irish should similarly withdraw from the English parliament at Westminster, setting up a parliament, law courts, and other institutions of their own in Ireland. He was also a strong advocate of economic nationalism, arguing that Ireland should develop her own manufacturing industries, which might be protected by tariff barriers enforced by a native government.

Griffith was a close associate of Maud Gonne and of Bulmer Hobson, a member, like himself, of the secret revolutionary organization, the Irish Republican Brotherhood (IRB). At the time Constance made his acquaintance, Griffith, like her, was in his late thirties. He had a forbidding personality. He was reserved, opinionated and caustic, and the enquiries this wealthy, brash, English-seeming woman made of him found him at his coldest. Constance wrote:

> I told Mr Griffith quite frankly that I only just realised that there were men in Ireland whose principles did not allow them to take an oath of allegiance to the foreign King, whose power they were pledged to break and overthrow. Mr Griffith was very discouraging to me and very cautious. I first thought that he merely considered me a sentimental fool; later on I realised that he had jumped to the conclusion that I was an agent of the enemy.[15]

Suspecting that she represented an attempt at infiltration from the Castle, he advised her to join the innocuous Gaelic League, advice that Con, whose ideals were already extreme, resented. She and Griffith never liked each other; and that she persisted after this unpromising introduction to nationalist councils is a proof of her seriousness from the start.

In December of that year Constance displayed publicly, if moderately, where her sympathies lay when she appeared in a production of Æ's play *Deirdre* with the Theatre of Ireland. The Theatre of Ireland was a new company, formed from some original members of the National Theatre Society of Ireland, which had been taken over by Yeats and Lady Gregory for their epoch-making productions in the Abbey Theatre. The new company was composed of an earnest and idealistic set of people who had broken away from the Abbey because of recent developments there. Under the patronage of Annie Horniman, it had ceased to be a cooperative and became a professional and hierarchical theatrical enterprise.

As a result, old hands like Æ and Padraic Colum, and the talented actress Maíre Nic Shiubhlaigh, left, partly because it was no longer democratic, partly because they felt it had shelved its commitment to serving the national movement. The members of the new Theatre of Ireland were, wrote Maíre Nic Shiubhlaigh, 'all amateurs, young men and women typical of the period, who strove first for a national ideal, secondly for a theatrical one'.[16] Yet they continued to put on some of their plays at the Abbey since the Yeats coterie rented out the theatre to other groups. In *Deirdre*, Maíre played the tragic Celtic heroine of the title and Con played the minor role of Lavarcham, the Druidess. On the committee were several names that became highly significant in the coming years: Eoin MacNeill, Patrick Pearse, Thomas Kettle, Arthur Griffith – and Constance Markievicz.

This colourful recruit used to arrive at the shabby rehearsal rooms in Harcourt Street, always, it seems, with a dog at her heels. The dog went everywhere with her. This particular dog, Jack, who first came to prominence alongside his mistress, was actually a Castle dog, a spaniel given to Casimir for Con by the wife of the Under-Secretary when he was doing her portrait. Maíre Nic Shiubhlaigh, who described Constance as 'the most remarkable woman I ever met',[17] remembered her, always with a dog, wearing brown tweeds and careless most of the time of how she looked 'but lovely all the same and full of vigour and enthusiasm'. Her usual attire, according to another contemporary, the writer Mary Colum, was 'a tweed suit and a mannish felt hat' but she would sometimes 'get herself up in a Paris frock and when few others in Dublin used cosmetics, put powder and rouge on her face'.[18]

Meanwhile, Casimir also got involved with theatre. In 1907 the amateur Irish Theatrical Club put on *The Pirates of Penzance* in aid of the Industrious Blind under the patronage of the Viceroy and his Vicereine. The part of Sergeant of Police was played by the Chamberlain and Casimir shared the coveted role of the Pirate King with Lord Farnham. Suddenly, the two Markieviczes were keeping very different company. A means of reconciling their apparent differences in attitude was found when Casimir set up the Independent Dramatic Company, which in the following years would present several plays that he wrote and produced.

The Independent Dramatic Company's first production in March 1908, *Seymour's Redemption*, at the Abbey, demonstrated his tendencies rather than Con's. It concerned the emotional turmoil and moral questionings of a politician who chooses the fulfilment of an illicit love instead of public success. It seemed to suggest the hollowness of political endeavour, and was too continental for Dublin's tastes. The reviewer in *Sinn Féin* wondered: 'Is it an impertinence to ask him (the author) to cast his eye about him in Dublin for some more familiar folly to satirize?' In fact, Casimir was not at all averse to nationalism. That year, he wrote, with Seamus O'Kelly a one-act play, *Lustre*, that consorted better with the kind of peasant plays the Abbey was known for.

With good humour he supported Con in what he probably regarded as her new enthusiasm. But nationalism never came to be a matter of principle or commitment with him. If he did have strong feelings on a political question, they were for the claim of Poland, his own country, to nationhood, a claim in many ways parallel to Ireland's. Basically, he sought to have a good time and to devote himself to artistic things.

By now the Markieviczes' married relationship amounted to a mutual tolerance and affection. Constance is reported to have told a friend that she lost sexual interest in Casimir after Maeve's birth and it was said that he, as a result, turned to affairs with other women.[19] It's true that she does not seem to have been someone who was conscious of a need for deep intimacy. Her emotional nature was satisfied in camaraderie and the sense of common purpose that being part of a movement lends. She and Casi really liked each other, they were the best of friends; but he was not necessary to her. Like many people, perhaps, who find their real place in a public milieu, she neglected her affective and domestic life. This has always been seen as unavoidable, even appropriate, for men who engage in life's 'important' activities. For women, it is more problematic. And Casimir was evidently not prepared, or expected, to take over the parental role.

In 1908, the year Constance began to get involved in nationalist circles, seven-year-old Maeve was sent to live in Co. Sligo with her grandmother who, on Josslyn's marriage (he married a cousin of the Gore-Booths, Mary L'Estrange-Malone), moved out of Lissadell to a house not far away, Ardeevan. In August, a governess, Miss Clayton, who was English, was engaged for her. Miss Clayton remembered how on her arrival at Ardeevan in the middle of a luncheon party, Maeve, just as her mother used to with her governesses, subjected her to 'a battery of embarrassing questions, which the grown-ups tried in vain to stem'. And when the child's parents came to visit some weeks later, Constance greeted Miss Clayton with 'So, you are the hated Sassenach, are you? If you think you're going to have any influence over my daughter, you jolly well are not.'[20]

Since the previous year Stasko had been a boarder at Mount St Benedict in Wexford, the newly established Jesuit school, which had a nationalist character and was where several nationalist intellectuals were now sending their sons. He and Constance clung together when he was going there for the first time. Stasko wrote that he wept and shook his head when she inquired 'You won't be ashamed to kiss your mother when you come back from school, like some boys?',[21] but with his departure her domestic life receded steadily in importance.

NOTES

1. Æ's 'Open Letter to the Masters of Dublin', *The Irish Times*, 7 October 1913.
2. *The Rebel Countess*, Marreco, p. 94.
3. *W.B. Yeats and Georgian Ireland*, Torchiana, p. 5.
4. *Culture and Anarchy in Ireland*, F.S.L. Lyons (Clarendon Press, Oxford, 1979) pp. 36–7.
5. I have used the modern form of the word from here on.
6. I have used the modern form of the word from here on.
7. *Maud Gonne – Lucky Eyes and a High Heart*, Nancy Cardozo (Gollancz, London, 1979) p. 238.

8. *Letters from Æ*, ed. Denson, 15/3/1904.
9. *J.B. Yeats. Letters to His Son and Others*, ed. Joseph Hone (Faber & Faber, London, 1944) p. 101.
10. Letter in private archive.
11. *The Rebel Countess*, Marreco, p. 83.
12. *Constance de Markievicz in the Cause of Ireland*, Jacqueline Van Voris (The University of Massachusetts Press, Amherst, 1967) p. 56.
13. *The Peasant*, June 1906.
14. *Eire*, 18 August 1923.
15. *Ibid.*
16. *The Splendid Years*, Maíre Nic Shiubhlaigh (Duffy, Dublin, 1955) pp. 142–3.
17. *Ibid.*, p. 101.
18. *Life and the Dream*, Mary Colum (Doubleday, New York, 1947) p. 278.
19. Recounted by Sean O'Faolain in his biography.
20. *The Rebel Countess*, Marreco, p. 126.
21. Stanislas in *The Irish Worker*, 17 October 1931.

SIX

'LIVE REALLY IRISH LIVES ...'

IN 1908 Arthur Griffith united the various separatist clubs under one umbrella organization called Sinn Féin. The name, meaning 'Ourselves', had been around since 1905 when it was coined by the Gaelic Leaguer, Maire Butler, and it was now the title of Griffith's newspaper. Sinn Féin's policies were more extreme than Griffith had previously expressed – its principal aim was 'the re-establishment of the independence of Ireland' – but Griffith wanted to accommodate those who held republican views. Since the achievement of this aim seemed as yet remote, there was the short-term aim of working for 'the creation of a prosperous, virile and independent nation'.

This was, as the name 'Ourselves' implied, Griffith's 'Hungarian Policy' of self-reliance. Ireland should set up its own national banking system, civil service, stock exchange and so on, should assume control of its seas, fisheries, transport, etc., and should eventually cease to recognize the authority of the British parliament. It was all more evolutionary than revolutionary and would soon have to compete with the growing republican activism of the IRB, the Irish Republican Brotherhood.

In spite of Griffith's rebuff, Constance began to attend Sinn Féin meetings and to be noticed in newspaper accounts of attendances. At one of these meetings she was noticed particularly by a young woman called Helena Molony. Helena, 'a very clever and attractive girl with a tremendous power of making friends',[1] was secretary of Inini na h-Éireann. Effectively running the organization during Maud Gonne MacBride's lengthy absences, she was looking for recruits. A mutual acquaintance introduced her to Constance and Helena suggested to her that she come along to an Inini meeting where the production of a new Inini newspaper would be discussed. Constance, who at this time would have accepted any invitation that emanated from any nationalist of any coloration, was delighted to accept.

Philosophically, the Inini – though they were often referred to affectionately or derisively as the Ninnies, suggesting feminine silliness – had militant republican ambitions. The first of its founding articles was unequivocally 'the re-establishment of the complete independence of Ireland'. Its subordinate aims included the encouragement of the study of Gaelic 'especially among the young', and of Irish manufacture, the discouragement of low English literature' and 'vulgar English entertainments', in fact, to 'combat in every way English influence'. Helena Molony brought a new thrust to the Inini. She was contemptuous of Sinn Féin's moderate tone and wanted to produce a paper that would counteract it. She wanted it to be a women's paper, 'advocating militancy, separatism and feminism'.

Sinn Féin was not actively anti-feminist; in fact it was a fond tenet recently among nationalist women that in the nationalist movement women were treated with an equal seriousness and 'a greater courtesy' than the men. The Gaelic League was the first nationalist society to accept women as members on the same terms as men; and in Sinn Féin women were elected frequently to the executive. Nonetheless, support for women's rights, which at this time centred on getting the vote, was never one of Sinn Féin's priorities.

On her introduction to the Inini, Constance created an unfavourable impression. The meeting to which Helena Molony invited her took place on a cold wet evening, everyone was in low spirits, and the talk was functional. Constance came late because she had been attending some entertainment, perhaps at the Castle, and dismayed Helena by appearing in the doorway of the dingy room wearing opulent evening clothes that included a blue velvet cloak with a train and diamonds in her hair. This did not endear her to the assembled company who were almost all women who had to earn their living. And they were not impressed, even when she kicked off her wet shoes, placed them on the hearth to dry, and joined them at the deal table. They snubbed her for most of the meeting, but this pleased Con who found their brusque manners a novelty. It was the first time, she told Helena, that she had not been 'kowtowed to as a Countess'.[2] And by the end of the meeting, Con had been elected to the committee, which would plan and produce the new paper, to be called *Bean na h-Éireann*, meaning Woman of Ireland, and she was a member of Inine.

She walked to the tram with Sidney Gifford, whose first meeting it also was, an aspiring journalist who felt obliged to write under the name 'John Brennan' because the name suggested, she thought, a strong Wexford farmer who should be taken seriously. On the way to the tram, Sidney was impressed when her companion said that it didn't matter about her train dragging in the puddles, as she soon wouldn't have any time for wearing elegant clothes. And Sidney was amused when Constance thoughtlessly handed the conductor some half-crowns instead of pennies for the fare.

That was in the autumn. The previous spring, Constance had been introduced through her sister Eva to an internationalist and increasingly important factor in politics, the labour movement. Eva had now been living in Manchester for eleven years (where ironically the Gore-Booths had property interests), and was entrenched in women's trade unionism and the suffrage movement, combining these robust political activities with the writing of ethereal poems and heroic plays. She was working for better conditions, for a better quality of life, for the right to work and the right to unionize, for diverse isolated groups: factory workers, barmaids. She held a variety of posts on trade union committees, spoke regularly at gatherings throughout England, edited the *Women's Labour News* ... In 1908 Eva, newly aware of Con's vigorous politicization, summoned her to Manchester to help campaign in a contentious by-election.

The major issue in the by-election was a Licensing Bill, which would make it illegal for women to work as barmaids. Winston Churchill, the Liberal candidate, could give no assurance that he would oppose this clause in the Bill, so the women trade unionists canvassed for his opponent, Joynson-Hicks, who did give such an assurance. In Manchester, Constance got her first taste of political success and gained a small reputation as a political activist.

The day before the election was frenzied, the streets crowded with speech-makers, marchers with banners and vehicles, including motor-cars advertising their slogans and exhortations. Through the *mêlée* Con drove a 'four-in-hand', and conveyed Eva from platform to platform. It was an impressive performance, handling four horses in such conditions and a man shouted defensively, 'Can you cook a dinner?' Yes,' she shouted back, 'I can. Can you drive a coach and four?'[3] She got a cheer from the crowd. And Joynson-Hicks won the election.

Bean na h-Éireann first appeared on the streets in the November of that year. It sold for one penny, and was supported by contributions of one shilling a month from the friends of those involved, who wrote for it without payment. Con's design for the cover and masthead incorporated an Irish, vaguely Celtic woman, an Irish round tower, and the rising sun. But she did not begin to write for the newspaper until the following March. In the meantime, through her assiduous attendance at Sinn Féin meetings (on 20 August she left the opening of the by now annual exhibition of her work with that of Æ, Casimir and others, to attend one) she was taken up by an opponent of Griffith's, Bulmer Hobson.

This bright, handsome young man in his mid twenties had been an active member of the reinvigorated Irish Republican Brotherhood since 1904 and was a close friend of that other bright young IRB man in Belfast, Denis McCullough. Hobson had engineered the infiltration of Sinn Féin by the IRB and he and Griffith were opposed temperamentally and ideologically. Constance was far more attracted to Hobson, with his decisiveness and aura of conspiracies, than to the acerbic Griffith, and she was of course flattered by his interest in her and his ready acceptance of her enthusiasm. She would in time be disillusioned enough to write that 'Griffith was infinitely more gifted than Hobson',[4] but for now Bulmer Hobson was her mentor and her purposes did gain enormously from his encouragement.

He gave her books on Ireland to read – he and his friends Dr Patrick McCarten and Sean McGarry 'educated me', she ironically wrote, 'and took me under their wing, explaining to me all the intricacies of such simple things as organizations and committees'.[5] He brought her up to North Great Britain Street (now Parnell Street) to see Tom Clarke in his newspaper and tobacco shop, and she became attached to that triumvirate of Hobson and his friends who were always in Tom Clarke's little shop talking about politics. Meeting the venerable Tom Clarke, and in this company, was for Con one of the first rays cast on 'the dark and obliterated path where I was wandering', she wrote. Compared to these young people who had never seen action for the cause they, to varying degrees, lived for, Thomas Clarke was a veteran.

He was now about fifty, but looked much older, a result of serving fifteen years in prison, nine of them years of horrific harshness in Portland, for his part in the dynamiting campaign in the 1880s when he had attempted to blow up London Bridge. He emerged as a ticket-of-leave man, as steely and as fanatic as ever, and after a time in America returned to Ireland in 1907 to be an anonymous tobacconist and to become a major figure in the Dublin IRB. To people like Hobson, and now Constance, he was one of those Fenian insurrectionists from the last century who, in this one, were venerated as heroes and martyrs. He was a small frail stooped man with a walrus moustache and brown eyes behind large tin-rimmed spectacles that were, Con wrote, 'like a searchlight turned on you and only afterwards you noticed the colour and how kindly they were and how they softened the fierce bushy eyebrows. ... What you got from him was interest in your schemes, encouragement for your hopes, support in your hours of despair.[6]

Con's friendships with Hobson, Clarke et al. show that she had made a real commitment to whatever nationalism might ask and that they took her commitment seriously. She continued to absorb rapidly the revitalized revolutionary principles they presented to her. If she had been invited to join the IRB, the usual method of introduction, we can assume she would not have hesitated. But the organization excluded women. The deep secrecy the Brotherhood practised and the wildly optimistic oath it administered to new members gave it an exciting, if sinister, aura to those who knew about it: 'I … in the presence of Almighty God, do solemnly swear allegiance to the Irish Republic now virtually established; and I will do my very utmost, at every risk, while life lasts, to defend its independence and integrity…'[7] But although Constance had, to an extent, the confidence of these men, the organization was so secret and had such a conspiratorial character that she was possibly not even aware of its existence at this point. Some of her other activities in this year do not, therefore, seem so incongruous as they might.

In December she appeared with Casimir's Independent Theatre Company in *The Dilettante*, the second of Casimir's plays, at the Abbey. This play was, again, rather European and again Constance played the principal role, Lady Althea. Its whimsical plot centering on a love triangle did not please the critics, but in having Lady Althea and Ella, the Steward's daughter, go off together leaving the poet Archie to his own devices, the plot pre-dated such *dénouements* in many continental movies of the 1970s. Casimir's urbane mind fed on the complexities of morals and manners while, for Constance and her new friends, full of antithetical certainties and intensities, examinations of personal relationships had little interest.

As an actress Constance was not wanting in enthusiasm. But this was one area in which she had little talent. Her accolades were suspiciously muted; words like 'striking', 'clever', 'unpredictable' were used to describe her acting. She tended to overact in a histrionic way. Acting was not her vocation; it was one means of serving the national cause. Of her role as Lavarcam, the amateur critic Joseph Holloway had remarked:'A n artist can be too intense and in earnest sometimes and appear ridiculous to those in front.' She used to act in Casimir's rather irrelevant plays, but as time went by she got him to write on themes closer to her heart.

At Christmas the Independent Theatre Company brought *The Dilettante* to Sligo to feature in a series of benefits organized to pay off the debt on the Temperance Hall. The play fitted happily in with the other entertainments on the programme, which were all English and middlebrow: *The Pirates of Penzance* was one and there was not a breath of Irish or Gaelic Leaguery anywhere. There was however, a meeting of the Gaelic League in the town at which Casimir discoursed convincingly on the importance of the use of the Irish language in the new National University, the alternative to Trinity College, an institution that saw itself, and was seen in these years, as a bastion of Englishness. In the days after Christmas, Casimir painted in the dining room at Lissadell those modernistic full-length figures with vaguely Russian faces that still stand on five of its columns. He painted himself and Mordaunt (Con's brother) very tall, Mr Kilgallon, the butler, with his tray, and the gamekeeper and the forester all very short, depicting humorously not only his great size but also the difference in social stature between master and servants.

Lissadell still had its complement of faithful retainers but it had changed in many respects. In 1903 the historic Wyndham land measures were enacted, brought into being by a relation-by-marriage of Constance's, George Wyndham, a romantic among chief secretaries. Under this Act, landlords were compensated, in fact paid, to sell their land to the tenantry, a facility that would lead to the rapid exodus of this class from the countryside and the creation of a new class of small proprietors. True to the Gore-Booth inheritance of not being hidebound by the practice of his peers in social matters, Sir Josslyn was one of the first landlords to sell off the greater part of his land, and was now concentrating his energies and resources on a kind of farming that was novel in Ireland.

Since the 1890s Josslyn had been associated with Sir Horace Plunkett who, in those years, was effecting a revolution in the dairy industry. The structures he created to modernize the backward, virtually non-existent industry have remained up to the present day. Plunkett pioneered a cooperative movement with his organization, the IAOS, which set up creameries (or dairies) throughout the country and brought a measure of prosperity and new patterns of social relations to farming communities. As well as being an agricultural reformer, Plunkett was unionist in his politics, autocratic and outspoken in his views and somewhat eccentric – he was, despite his interest in the dairy industry, macrobiotic in his diet. He met, therefore, with much opposition and hostility and his creameries did not thrive to the degree that they deserved. Sir Josslyn was now putting Plunkett's general ideas into practice and was an extensive grower of early potatoes, tomatoes, strawberries and peas, and was running a poultry farm and a dairy. Constance often cited with approval the work of the IAOS in her prescriptive speeches on Ireland's future.

In March 1909 *Bean na h-Éireann* carried Con's first gardening column. Political writings in those days were, from all quarters, far more visceral in their partisanship than they are today: witness, for instance, Gladstone's diatribes on the Irish Ascendancy during the long years of debate on the land question. The overtly subversive character of *Bean na h-Éireann* was not found remarkable or worthy of censure by the authorities. It was the first women's newspaper in Ireland and has remained unique because it combined a traditional *femInini* commentary with revolutionary exhortations: 'How perfectly lovely are the hats this season' with 'Arms, discipline and tactics should be the one thought, the one work, the one play of Irishmen and Irishwomen…'[8] 'I believe that the first thing to cultivate is your ideals for ideals are the soul of life,' wrote Con.

Her regular feature, titled 'The Woman with the Garden', was typically outrageous in its humorous parodying of gardening notes and easy appropriation of the nationalist propagandist style: 'It is very hard killing slugs and snails but let us not be daunted. A good nationalist should look upon slugs in the garden in much the same way as she looks on the English in Ireland…' She often wrote in the rhapsodic vein that the thought of Ireland's struggle aroused in her; of the crimson rose that brought one 'straight back to the reality of July '98 … the petals of Róisín Dubh lay as red and strange then on the green hillsides of Wexford, scattered a crimson shedding over the land from the sea-bounds of the Atlantic to the dusty streets of Dublin … reminding us that we must live so that our martyrs blood shall not have been shed in vain'. 'Lavender', the flower loved by Robert Emmet, called him to mind. And 'The Garden in Winter' recalled Ireland 'like a poor wee bulb buried in the dust and dirt of English rule and English influence and struggling to gain the light and air …'

The tone was assertively 'Irish-Ireland'. Recipes were given in Irish and there were advertisements for Gaeltacht holidays and for facsimiles of Celtic jewellery. The gardening notes followed this line in a more militant fashion: 'Ireland – like the garden – lies sleeping and resting, recouping her vital powers for the struggle that will come and now it is our duty to till and to dig and do all that which lies in our power to aid the tender plant of nationality in its struggle for existence.'

With such flamboyant leaders as Maud Gonne, Countess Markievicz and the charming Helena Molony, Inini na h-Éireann was seen as a vivacious and modern group and their paper was reputed to be read 'by all the young men'. Soon, the recipes and 'Hints on Furnishings' etc. were jettisoned due to pressure of space. This was confirmed as a suitable policy by an editorial: 'We confirm that month by month we were glad enough to cut out cookery recipes, millinery notes etc. in order to arrive at some clear thinking on more important national issues.'

They were not above vanity. John Brennan (Sidney Gifford) contributed a frivolous 'Lenten Pastoral to Irish Ireland' on the stodgy, earnest image of the species:

> The two great cults of the Irish Ireland movement are 'sturdy Gael' and 'shy cailin' ... The average Irish Irelander girl goes through the streets dressed very nearly as badly as an English suffragette, looking appallingly earnest and unflinchingly Gaelic. The very appearance of her is enough to send shivers down the Seoinini spine and to make the same Gael synonymous with dowdiness throughout the country.

The poets Æ and Katherine Tynan contributed, as did Arthur Griffith and James Connolly and Roger Casement, men who would be famous in the future. Helena Molony's own growing involvement with the labour movement and her position as editor meant it had a socialist tendency, best exemplified by her labour notes.

The columns of *Bean na h-Éireann* soon became the medium for a heated debate between the emergent women's groupings in the country, the nationalists and the suffragettes. Hanna Sheehy-Skeffington, one of the redoubtable Sheehy sisters and a co-founder of the Irishwomen's Franchise League (IWFL) in 1908, argued cogently that the first priority of Irishwomen must be to get the vote. She claimed that the nationalist societies might welcome women, but they only recognized them in, and confined them to, the 'purely incidental avocation' of mother, as nurturers of Gaelic young, and as housewife, in the role of consumer of Gaelic goods. Without political representation, she wrote, women were 'mere camp-followers and parasites of public life'. Each side perceived the other as participating in a dangerous diversion in which they would be used to further the concerns of men.

Nationalists considered that the suffragettes were seeking only a voice in the election of a parliament that had no right, as far as they could see, to legislate for Ireland. To recognize that parliament was to recognize the dominion of Britain over Ireland. They were indeed for women's suffrage, but they wanted to exercise the vote in an Irish parliament brought into existence through their efforts. All political questions were secondary to achieving an Irish parliament and, until its day came, the only form of citizenship that mattered was membership of nationalist organizations like the Gaelic League and Sinn Féin. 'Hitch your wagon to a star,' went one article. 'Do not work for the right to share in the government of that nation that holds Ireland enslaved, but work to procure for our sex the rights of free citizenship in an independent Ireland.'

The suffragettes on the other hand believed that the nationalists were foolishly naive and blinkered for presuming that nationalist men would be magnanimous when the time came for them to bestow rights or favours; no, they said, women should make sure of rights of suffrage before the new nation came into being so they would have a say in its nature. But neither nationalists nor suffragettes had any illusions about the commitment to either of their causes by the Irish Party at Westminster. The nationalists saw parliamentarianism under the present system as a stultifying force in Irish politics, which had betrayed them in the past, and might in the future achieve only what Britain was willing to give. And the scepticism of the suffragettes proved well founded in 1912, when the Irish Party, which held the balance of power, killed the Conciliation Bill that would have given limited suffrage rights to propertied women.

It was of course, far more heady and exciting to talk of fighting and revolutions, and more independent and courageous to consider seizing power than to lobby complacent and patronizing male politicians, and to have to plead, as the suffragettes seemed to, for what they wanted. Constance fell solidly in behind the nationalists.

It was the practice of Inini members to write under pseudonyms. Helena Molony's 'Emer' and Constance's 'Macha' were both taken from the names of women in Celtic mythology. Macha was the Celtic equivalent of Epona, the horse-goddess of Greek myth. But Macha was human and was reputed to run faster than any chariot. She was the consort of a king, and in one of those battles that were regularly fought between provinces, she was obliged – against her wishes because she was pregnant – to run a race against enemy chariots, which would decide loss or victory. Macha won the race, and the battle, and immediately gave birth to twins in full view of the vanquished. She was so enraged, however, at the plight in which she had been placed that she laid a curse on the losing side of Ulster.

In March 1909 'Macha' gave a lecture entitled 'Women, Ideals and the Nation' to the Students National Literary Society. It was a fluent and impressive speech, was published at once as a booklet by the Inini, and reprinted in 1919 when Con was celebrated as a heroine. This address of about an hour in length is a rational justification of the sacred idea of the Irish nation, based in part on practical material considerations that were, as yet, finding little voice in nationalist rhetoric. 'Macha' quickly disposed of the franchise question. In her rough outline for her address, she had alluded with heavy irony to the suffragette's motto 'Government without the consent of the governed is tyranny' and to their 'excellent' demand for the vote 'on the same terms as it is and may be extended to men'. 'Why stop there?' she asked, 'Why not demand the rights of citizenship *tout compris?*'[9]

She had alluded sarcastically to 'Mrs Wyse Power chained to Mr Redmond's or Mr T.P. O'Connor's doorsteps' and 'Miss Shannon ringing a dinner-bell in Mr Healy's ear'. But in her address[10] she discarded this undiplomatic tone:

> We are in a very difficult position here, as so many unionist women would fain to have us work together with them for the emancipation of their sex and votes – obviously to send a member to Westminster. But I would ask every nationalist woman to pause before she joined a Suffrage Society or Franchise League that did not include in their programme the freedom of their nation. 'A Free Ireland with no sex disabilities in her constitution' should be the motto of all nationalist women ... some day – as a woman and as an Irelander – you will have to face the question of how your life has been spent and how you have served your sex and your nation.

For her, for now at least, one's identity as an Irelander must come first:

> The greatest gifts that the young women of Ireland can bring into public life with them, are ideals and principles. … Let them remind their men that their first duty is to examine any legislation proposed, not from a party point of view, not from the point of view of a sex, a trade or a class, but simply and only from the standpoint of their nation.

She displayed her identification with Gaelic Ireland, but also made clear that she made no concessions to the elements that wanted Gaelic Ireland to be also Catholic:

> Our national freedom cannot, and must not be left to evolution. If we look around us, we will find that evolution – as far as Ireland is concerned – is tending rather to annihilate us as a nation altogether. We seem … little by little to be losing all that distinctiveness, which pertains to a nation, and which may be called nationality.

Even the educational system, native as it might appear, was destructive. 'The schools … usually under the patronage of the priest or parson of the district … concentrated on developing strong sectarian feelings in the children, instead of the broader creed of nationalism.'

She analyzed England's deliberately divisive influence in Ireland. She skilfully infused facts with rhetoric and in her description of how the English connection was exploitative of Ireland showed she had a grasp of economic relationships. She spoke of the Liberals' projected Land Tax, which would suit England's land structure, but not that evolving apace in Ireland; of the Conservatives' Tariff Reform where she digressed to speak of Sligo – 'my own county' – after free trade, where 'every little stream has the same tale to tell', of 'pitiful ruins of mills, great and small … and where even the bleak walls have vanished, you often find a record of bygone prosperity in names such as Milltown or Millbrook'.

In a country where taking a daily bath was not the norm, she must have caused some eyebrows to raise when she said: 'You must make Irish goods as necessary to your daily life, as your bath or your breakfast.' For, if women would only 'make it the fashion to dress in Irish clothes, feed on Irish food … LIVE REALLY IRISH LIVES, they would be doing something great …'

And if it all sounded boring and dull to start with, better things would come from it:

> You must make the world look upon you as citizens first and women after. For each one of you there is a niche waiting – your place in the nation. Try and find it. It may be as a leader, it may be as a humble follower – perhaps in a political party, perhaps in a party of your own – but it is there.

They should discourage their boys from enlisting in the British army. This was couched in terms that now seem unnecessarily offensive, but were terms that the Inini used blithely in their anti-enlistment pamphlets. The army was a 'mercenary army', 'the most immoral army in the world'.

It was not however, that all these activities were so important in themselves, but that they be fired by the one, holy, ruling idea: the concept of the nation. The language she used was already familiar from its religious applications and implied that what was needed was a change of heart or spirit:

> In every action we do in life, the idea behind it is the thing that counts – if you go deep enough – the soul as it were. And so it is only by realizing that unless the ideal, the spirit of self-sacrifice and love of country, is at the back of our work for commercial prosperity, sex emancipation, and other practical reforms, that we can hope to help our land. Every little act for Ireland's sake will help to build up a great nation, noble and self-sacrificing, industrious and free.

She had clearly discussed the question with Casimir, because she opened her address with harrowing images of brave nationalist Polish women incarcerated in 'the damp and mouldy gloom' of dungeons, or dropping 'exhausted on the long weary march through the snow-covered steppes to the land of exile'. And she ended with a call to the same heroic self-sacrifice that these distant sisters embodied:

> Arm yourselves with weapons to fight your nation's cause. Arm your souls with noble and free ideas. Arm your minds with the histories and memories of your country and her martyrs, her language, and a knowledge of her arts, and her industries. And if in your day the call should come for your body to arm, do not shirk that either.

As a final inspiring call, she cited a noble, romantic and familiar figure: 'May this aspiration towards life and freedom among the women of Ireland bring forth a Joan of Arc to free our nation.'

Today, the kind of things Constance was saying then with a new and passionate conviction are usually dismissed as tedious Gaelic Leaguery. But to her, and to her audience, they were novel. Even the prosaic details were exciting if you could see in them the gestation of a brand-new nation. How the new nation would be organized, and what life in it would be like, was never described. This vagueness created a semi-mystical idea of freedom and independence that individuals endowed with their own dreams and hopes. It was to this mast that Constance Markievicz definitively nailed her colours in 1909.

Of course she never went to the Castle now. Lady Aberdeen, the Vicereine, was a liberal and earnest soul who invited mild-talking nationalists from the Gaelic League to her tea parties in the hope that they and her unionists could somehow be reconciled. But Con was now so implacably 'green' as to be quite unacceptable, even if she had wanted to go to the Lodge. Her situation at times was somewhat forlorn because the society she had chosen still regarded her with a certain suspicion. Arthur Griffith was not alone in distrusting her background. And her artistic friends saw it as slightly abhorrent that one should commit oneself so fervidly to a political purpose, Yeats, who had always been prepared to maintain a vaguely Irish-Ireland stance, now began to dissociate himself from the distasteful practicalities of subversion. At the Arts Club, he lectured on the regrettable 'life of a young man and his gradual absorption in some propaganda'. And, speaking of Constance as much as of Maud Gonne, for whom his love was now less intense, he observed: 'Women, because the main event of their lives has been giving themselves and giving birth, give all to an opinion as if it were some terrible stone doll.'[11]

Constance's next endeavour looked harmless and philanthropic at first, but it was to lead her into the inner councils of revolution. In the spring of 1909, she was enraged by a report in the *Irish Times* that the Viceroy, Lord Aberdeen, had become the patron of a number of troops of Baden-Powellite Boy Scouts, and had reviewed a body of 800 boys on parade. The idea of them 'haunted' her. She recognized at once the hidden vein of militarism in Boy Scout activities and that these boys were absorbing the ethos of imperialism. She wrote:

> Surely nothing could be sadder than to see the sons of men who had thrown in their lot with the Fenians ... saluting the flag that flew in triumph over every defeat their nation has known. ... I could see these children growing to manhood and gaily enlisting in the British Army or Police forces and being used to batter their own class into submission.[12]

She conceived the idea of offering boys an alternative Boy Scout movement: an organization to 'weld the youth of Ireland together to work and fight for Ireland'.

She was now, on Bulmer Hobson's advice, a member of the Drumcrondra and Glasnevin Branch of Sinn Féin, on the north side of the city, and in mid 1909 was elected as the branch's delegate to the Executive Council, which annoyed Arthur Griffith greatly. She mentioned her grand idea in *Bean na h-Éireann*, and brought it up at the executive and at the open-air meetings, which were held several times a week, but was met with a wall of disinterest. Helena Molony and a few others were enthusiastic, however, and together they dreamed and planned, and eventually, and ironically, with the help of a sympathetic teacher at the school in Pearse Street, got eight boys together. They called themselves the Red Branch Knights after the ancient warriors of Ulster and began to practise signalling, scouting and drill in Con's back yard. 'It was rather funny,' she wrote, 'because none of us leaders understood boys in the least and no one knew anything about the subjects we set out to teach.' It was all very depressing until someone had 'the brilliant idea of a camp'.

Con wrote with a fond nostalgia of the camping weekend that ensued. She bought a scout tent, someone lent another; they filled up a pony and car that the Fitzgerald boys provided with tents, rugs, cushions, food, saucepans, books etc., and six boys, Helena and herself set out for the Dublin Mountains:

> We knew a little valley away up on the side of the Three Rock Mountain, with a little stream bubbling through it, and a lovely carpet of soft, close-cropped grass. ... After long hours of pushing, pulling, lifting, resting and pushing again, we arrived at the last gate at the

end of the track. A few minutes more saw us in the valley, kneeling on the soft green sward and bathing our dusty faces in the stream. We dawdled over a most delicious tea and dragging out poetry books and sketching things we lazily drowsed away the evening.

Twilight woke us to the necessity of fixing up things for the night. We started to pitch the tents on a grassy slope where the hill slid down to the stream. It took a long, long time. ... Tents are very hard to pitch if you don't know how, especially at night. ... Next comes the task of trying to disentangle jam from blankets, frying-pans, cushions, poetry books and all the other indispensable articles we had brought. Candles were the only important thing we had forgotten. But at last everything had found a place, the boys were comfortably settled, and we turned in and drifted into dreamland to the tuneful accompaniment of the snores of the six boys in the other tent.

We woke very early to find a bright, pleasant morning with a cheerful sun shining in through the flaps of the tent. Early as we were, the boys were still earlier and one was already improving his mind with W.B. Yeats's poems. The others were mostly blacking their boots and quite ready for breakfast. I didn't wonder that they looked fresh when at last I found my soap and towel – A brown dripping rag wrapped round a sticky mess. It was the only towel in the camp. After long experience I have come to the conclusion that the only thing that you can be quite sure that every boy will bring to camp is boot polish ...

After breakfast, the boys went to Mass, we put things straight and settled ourselves snugly to read. Suddenly some heavy drops of rain sent us scurrying into the tent. ... Luckily the rain stopped as suddenly as it began. The sun came out and did its best to dry our things. When it had to set, we took up the job, and, lighting a primus stove, we held the damp blankets to it, and watched the steam gradually growing less. The boys anyhow slept in dry coverings that night, and no one took cold.

The next evening saw the end of our holiday. We had some trouble in capturing the pony. A kind neighbour had allowed us to turn it into his park and graze with his own cattle and young horses. The pony found camp life just as much to his taste as we did, and would not allow himself to be caught and harnessed into bondage again.[13]

The camp showed how much fun scouting could be and it bound the group together. It was with these boys that Constance first shed the title of Countess and came to be called the more

democratic 'Madame'. It was a trend among active nationalist women to call themselves 'Madame'. There was Madame
Mac-Bride and Madame Despard, Madame Sheehy-Skeffington
and Madame MacSwiney. In eschewing the 'Mrs' of English usage,
they showed their identification with the French republican tradition. It was used by some women who weren't married as a feminist gesture. And there were others like the celebrated Madame
Toto Cogley who used it to suggest an identity with the artistic
world and a Bohemian disposition.

Madame Markievicz, as she soon became best known, saw
that her scouts could work. But the organization 'would have to
be run more on the lines of a Boys Republic and an army. There
would have to be a hall taken and an organization formed more
on the lines that Irishmen were accustomed to work in.' Then she
found that Bulmer Hobson had run the same kind of boys' organization some years earlier in Belfast, which had not worked. But
she asked him to help, and hired a hall in Camden Street – the
same rickety hall where the nucleus of the Abbey Theatre used to
rehearse – for ten shillings a week. In August, an advertisement
in the nationalist newspapers asked boys 'willing to work for the
independence of Ireland' to come to a meeting.

Such boys turned up in great numbers. Bulmer Hobson took
the chair. Con and Helena were on the platform. The women's
enthusiasm was checked, however, when one of the bigger boys
got up to speak: 'This is a physical force organization,' he said,
'and there are two women in the room. This is no place for them.
They must be put out.'[14] Hobson parleyed for them and the two
women were allowed to remain, 'on sufferance of course'. This
was an isolated incident. The boys, and there were several generations of them, in general not only accepted but respected and loved
Madame Markievicz.

A girls' *slua* or branch (the scouts followed the nationalist
custom of using the Irish forms for titles) called the Betsy Gray
was founded in Belfast by Annie O'Boyle. A recruit there who
would become well known was a little girl called Nora Connolly.
But Con was never passionately interested in forming girls' *sluas*.
Just as she felt happier with Stasko than with Maeve, she now
preferred taking boys off to camp and teaching them to shoot than

she did girls. Traditionally, it was men who did the fighting and the women bound their wounds. She may also have feared that girls' *sluas* would divert her energies into a lonely and essentially irrelevant feminist battle while the nation was at stake. Perhaps, most of all, it was a matter of temperament.

The Red Branch Knights soon changed their name to '*Fianna Éireann*', the name Hobson used for his Belfast scouts and which he had taken from the Fianna of legend. The first Fianna were the *corps d'elite* of Finn MacCool, chief warrior of the High King of Ireland. They were young men of exceptional strength and valour, sworn to the chivalric virtues of truth, fortitude and generosity; in order to be admitted to the company, they had to perform difficult feats of endurance and skill. The present-day Fianna now undertook to learn drill, signalling and other military accomplishments. Before long, the hall in Camden Street was in use every night and came to be known as the Fianna Hall. Con Colbert, a future captain, translated command words into Irish and these commands were in use from then on. There was a night devoted to learning the Irish language, and a night for games.

After Constance had taught Helena Molony how to use a gun, they both brought members of the Fianna on camping weekends to the cottage in the hills and taught each of them how to shoot. There was a grassy field in front of the cottage where the Fianna camped and learned the art of musketry and how to take care of guns, all quite legally since it was within the law to shoot on one's land or property. (Constance may have taken away a gun or two from Lissadell to use.) They wore a uniform: a dark-green shirt, black pants and a green 'crusher' hat, which they bought themselves if they could afford to; otherwise money was provided from benefits such as *ceilis* (Irish dances). A newspaper report, that was really an advertisement, said 'the youths learn to respect discipline', and part of Con's appeal was that she was very strict when it mattered, such as in the safe handling of guns, and not strict at all about the ordinary bourgeois proprieties.

Readers were told: 'In the enjoyment provided they soon forget the imaginary pleasures of smoking and other pernicious habits totally forbidden them, whilst upon their marches.' A branch of the Fianna had been set up in Maryborough in the Queen's County (now Portlaoise in Co. Laois) and the boys had walked from the town to the Rock of Dunamase, a distance of about five miles, and had set up camp. The following eulogistic report is an example of the impassioned propagandist tone to be found in many provincial papers of the time:

> The principles learned whilst members of the Corps will make them good and patriotic men and will help to soon win the glorious future fate has in store for our land. What is that future, boys of Ireland? … Commerce will be rife in our multitude of harbours – industry alive at every mill-site on our abounding streams – labour, hopeful, cheerful, abundantly profitable – peace in every district – comfort and contentment on every peasant hearth. The religious, the generous, the high-spirited, the admirable Irish people, at length freed from foreign interference, will make their own wise laws, by their own freely chosen, responsible and real representatives. The friend of human freedom abroad, the example of it at home the benefactor of nations in having shown the way to arise from the lowest depths of thraldom and degradation, to the highest pinnacle of prosperity and liberty, without the shedding of one drop of blood – respected, feared, loved, admired all this our country will be; all this she shall have.[15]

The part about no drop of blood being shed was either an exercise in deception, or the writer was a Sinn Féiner who was unaware of the soldier's training with which the boys were being indoctrinated.

In April 1910 Casimir showed his versatility, if not his change of heart, when his play *The Memory of the Dead* was presented at the Abbey Theatre. It would seem that his wife had a hand in it. The play's setting is the Rising of 1798. The plot involves a journey of some length on which a boy-guide – really Nora, the wife of a nationalist leader in disguise – leads a French officer to Killalla Bay to head off Napper Tandy's landing. There an ambush awaits him. The nationalist hero dies on stage of wounds sustained from English bullets and Nora vows over his dead body to carry on the cause.

The Fianna were given a part to identify with in the boy borne to safety by the French officer, 'a boy of 15 whose breast has been gored by a redcoat's bayonet, whilst fighting nobly for the freedom of his native land'. In the part of the boy-guide, Constance was a triumph. She was, in the words of the reviews, 'a charming guide', 'a very winning Nora Doyle'.[16] She seems to have liked playing male parts. In *The Shuilers Child*, Seamus O'Kelly's 'peasant play' presented by the Theatre of Ireland a year before, she played the part of a government inspector.

Her position in Sinn Féin was not eased by the founding of the Fianna. A notice appeared in *Sinn Féin* (the journal) dissociating the movement from the Fianna. 'Their reverence for dead heroes,' wrote Constance, 'was only of an aloof and mystical quality.'[17] And early in 1910 there was a row among the members of the Sinn Féin executive that alienated her still further from Griffith and showed she was the first to be distrusted when there was internal dissension.

At a special council meeting it became clear that Arthur Griffith proposed to join Sinn Féin forces with the All for Ireland League, a new breakaway faction of the Irish Party at Westminster. The All for Ireland League was headed by William O'Brien and by Tim Healy, the infamous opponent of Parnell in his great crisis. The League was now in opposition to John Redmond, their erst-while leader in the Irish Party who had great popular support. Constance, Hobson and some others disagreed violently with what Griffith was apparently planning, not because of the policies of the All for Ireland League, but because the very thought of entangle-ment with any section of the parliamentary party was anathema to them. Griffith would not come clean about his plans but became 'more and more silent and angry' as the heated debate went on.

Finally, the proposal was defeated. Con went to Sligo for Christmas so she missed a meeting. And at the following one, she was baffled to be met with a hostile reception. At the end of the meeting, Jenny Wyse-Power did, in Con's words, 'an awfully straight and plucky thing.'[18] She got up and said: 'Before we break up I want to ask you something that none of the men have the courage to ask you. You are being blamed for giving an account of the secret meeting to the press.' A full account of that meeting had subsequently appeared in *The Peasant*. Con was able to convince the assembly of her innocence. But the issue became an open controversy in the movement and she was given credit in many quarters for not having signed the incomplete account that appeared in *Sinn Féin* that *was* signed by Hobson and Denis

McCullough. The affair was an early illustration of the conspiracies and secrecies in which the men tended to indulge, but the women rejected.

NOTES

1. *Constance de Markievicz*, Van Voris, p. 61.
2. *Ibid.*, p. 62.
3. *Eire*, 18 August 1923.
4. *Ibid.*
5. *Ibid.*
6. *Leaders and Men of the Easter Rising, Dublin 1916*, ed. F.X. Martin (Methuen, London, 1916) p. 97.
7. This and succeeding quotes are from *Bean na h-Éireann*, April 1909 – February 1911.
8. From rough jottings in a notebook in the National Museum, Dublin.
9. This was published as a booklet, sixteen pages in length, by Inini na h-Éireann in 1909. The aims of the Inini are listed on the inside cover.
10. *The Autobiography of William Butler Yeats* (Doubleday Anchor, New York, 1958) p. 341.
11. *Eire*, 9 June 1923.
12. *Fianna*, Christmas 1914.
13. *Eire*, 9 June 1923.
14. *Irish Freedom*, May 1912.
15. *The Rebel Countess*, Marreco, p. 130.
16. *Eire*, 18 August 1923.
17. *Ibid.*
18. *Ibid.*

SEVEN

SINN FÉIN AND SOCIALISM

CONSTANCE WAS now forty-two. And at last she was successful in integrating those different aspects of her character: the keen, adventurous side that gave her such dash on the hunting field; the conscientious side, troubled by the bad circumstances of those around her, which she shared with several of her Gore-Booth antecedents and relations; the darker spiritual side that had looked for meaning and expression in the artist's life and was deeply bored by the social life of her class, which by now offered little more than a humdrum round of luncheon parties and gossip as her contemporaries headed for middle age.

She had found an ideal, that 'something to live for' she had fretted about in her twenties, and she accepted with an insouciance that was not uncommon in people before the First World War that she might be asked to die for it. This seriousness was often obscured by the quality that was one of the original things about her, and gave her charisma: her childlike irrepressibility. In 1910 she threw over the conventions of adult life as it was lived in the south suburbs and moved out to Raheny in north Co. Dublin with Helena Molony and several young Fianna boys. They had decided to set up a commune. This move was inspired by the famous commune of Ralahine. Ralahine was much spoken of at the time: in cooperative circles, by Sir Josslyn and Æ; by Bulmer Hobson who lent Constance an account by one of the ex-communards; by James Connolly who would be a future mentor of Con's, but who was at this time in America and wrote about it in his socialist journal, *The Harp*. She must also have heard of Ralahine from the Gifford sisters who were granddaughters of its proprietor, Vandeleur.

Ralahine was a small estate in Co. Cork owned by Arthur Vandeleur who, in the 1830s, made it into a model agricultural cooperative organized for the mutual prosperity of tenants and landlords. It worked very well. The production of crops and rearing of dairy and other animals on the typically run-down estate increased enormously, and the renowned community collapsed not because of any failure in organization, but because Vandeleur lost so heavily in the gambling halls that the Ralahine estate was seized in bankruptcy proceedings.

Helena Molony and Bulmer Hobson were as enthusiastic as Constance was about starting such a venture. When Casimir was absent in the Ukraine on his annual visit, Con let the house in Rathgar (for £90 a year) and took Belcamp Park, a Georgian farmhouse in Raheny, for £100. Belcamp Park was taken on a three-year lease from the prosperous nationalist Plunkett family, and seemed to justify, superficially at least, the hopes invested in the experiment. It was a spacious house, set in elegant country-side well planted with trees. There were a dozen bedrooms and seven acres of land, as well as the garden where fruit trees were blossoming. It seemed a haven of rural peace and potential fecundity. A gardener was hired, a graduate of Glasnevin Agricultural College called Donald Hannigan, who would also instruct the residents in horticulture and farming.

It set out to rival Ralahine. But Belcamp Park seems to have gone the way of most communes in more recent times. There wasn't much furniture, so eating and sleeping arrangements were rudimentary, with mattresses on the floors and cans for drinking out of. Bulmer Hobson was rarely there. Stasko turned up, upset, naturally, at not having been told that the family had moved house. Both Constance and Helena were often absent, between them maintaining a rigorous schedule of Sinn Féin executive and branch meetings, Inini na h-Éireann meetings, producing *Bean na h-Éireann*, theatrical activities, painting (Con was to exhibit again in August) and Fianna work, and they had to commute the seven miles into Dublin by bicycle.

The Fianna boys seemed to come and go as they pleased, and however brave and noble, they were urban warriors who knew nothing of country ways, and they wandered among the fields and boreens of the locality leaving a trail of havoc in their wake. But it was summer. The days were warm and pleasing and long.

There was a successful Fianna camp in August where 'a thorough Irish national atmosphere throughout was maintained'.[1] And the Fianna achieved a most respectable and worthy status in the same month when they held their first annual conference in the Mansion House by the kind permission of the Lord Mayor. Constance was elected President and Bulmer Hobson Vice-President. There were now seven *sluas* of the Fianna.

But then the autumn came, and with it came not only the cold but also Casimir, who arrived unannounced from the Ukraine one dark evening. Although he would regale the Dublin wits with stories of the anarchic household he found in Raheny, he was not amused. For a long time afterwards, the wits recounted Casimir's account of his homecoming, complete with Polish accent. According to one well-known version, a series of dirty ragamuffins or 'sprouts' greeted him as if he were a stranger, and when his wife finally appeared in the dark hall she was absent-minded and vague about whether there was anything to eat, and all the time the sprouts were whispering furtively around him. The gardener had appropriated the only lamp in the house and he was reading by its light in the drawing room. He did not get up when Casimir came in but kept on 'smoking some filthy tobacco with his feet resting on the chimney piece'.

Casimir was appalled. He sought Æ's advice and for days he pestered the heedless adults of the household with questions about the commune's economic base and financial incomings and outgoings. Constance ignored them but they made such an impression on Bulmer Hobson that he left for Belfast; and they caused Donald Hannigan such desperation that he cut down a large holly tree, which fetched 30s. for the kitty but cost Constance £5 in compensation to the irate landlord. When Bulmer Hobson pulled out, Helena Molony found she was responsible for a half instead of a third of the expenses. But she and the Markieviczes continued to live on at Belcamp Park until the following year when Constance moved to a temporary flat in Mount Street in town.

Her elusive wayward quality was caught in a description of her at that time written by Desmond Ryan who, as a boy, attended meetings of the Drumcondra branch of Sinn Féin. He was then a pupil at Patrick Pearse's famous Irish school for boys, considered approvingly by Dublin poets to resemble the school run by the Indian nationalist poet, Rabindranath Tagore:

> Madame de Markievicz sat in the middle of the room, pensive and beautiful with a costly lace collar draping her shoulders, ready to explode into the most unconvincingly bloodthirsty sentiments as the lecture and debate developed, but speaking with a gentle charm to anyone who approached her in private. She was, although her fury expressed in such polite accents had a comic aspect, a very courageous woman.[2]

In socialism, Constance found a counterbalance to those bloodthirsty sentiments. Her politics already had a social orientation and through the Fianna boys she was newly aware of the problems of the poor people. But what was the best way to tackle the problems of huge unemployment, exhausted workers, wages at starvation level and wretched accommodation? Nationalism alone might not be the answer, since in England the same conditions existed although to a much lesser extent. What she lacked was a systematic approach to their resolution.

One warm October day in 1910 at Belcamp Park, Constance read a newspaper account of the man called James Larkin, which filled her with 'hope, admiration, sympathy and delight. ... Here was a man who had the brains and the courage to demonstrate by his actions that International Socialism does not stand for the merging of our identity with that of England... '[3] James Larkin was a trade union organizer who brought to Ireland the inspiring insurgent brand of trade unionism that was sweeping Europe. His methods were syndicalist in that he believed in the use of the workers' strike as a weapon, and in the organization of the masses as a militant, self-conscious class. In Dublin his kind of trade unionism became known simply as Larkinism. In 1910 his star and that of his union, the ITGWU (The Irish Transport and General Workers Union) seemed to be on the ascendant.

It was not only his ideas however, that gave Larkin his importance. He was a formidable force, and was quickly recognized to be such by Dublin employers. With some alarm they acknowledged his physical charisma, his gift of oratory, and the unprecedented capacity he had to engage and sway a crowd. His enemies called him a demagogue; his people called him Big Jim, Big Jim Larkin. He had vision. He wanted to bring to the working-class homes of Dublin, the ghastly poverty of which so dismayed him, beauty as well as security. 'Here was a man,' concluded Sean O'Casey, 'who would put a flower in a vase on a table as well as a loaf on a plate.'[4]

When Constance first knew him, Larkin was in his early thirties. When she saw in the newspaper that this man was to address a meeting in Beresford Place, she mounted her bicycle and cycled into Dublin:

> It was a scorching day when I arrived and Beresford Place was already packed, but luckily, a friend of mine, Mr McGowan, saw me hot and weary in the dense crowd and brought me up on to Larkin's platform, a lorry, where I could rest in peace. Sitting there, listening to Larkin, I realised that I was in the presence of something that I had never come across before, some great primeval force rather than a man. ... It seemed as if his personality caught up, assimilated, and threw back to the vast crowd that surrounded him every emotion that swayed them, every pain and joy that they had ever felt made articulate and sanctified. Only the great elemental force that is in all crowds had passed into his nature forever ...
>
> Man without the trickeries and finickiness of modern civilization, a Titan who might have been moulded by Michaelangelo or Rodin, such is Jim Larkin, and this force magically changed the whole life of the workers. ... He forced his own self-reliance and self-respect on them. ... From that day I looked upon Larkin as a friend and was out to do any little thing I could do to help him.[5]

She and Larkin had the rapport that comes of mutual understanding and they often met because the Fianna sometimes met in rooms in Liberty Hall, the ITGWU headquarters at Beresford Place. By the following September Con's socialist ideas were sufficiently formed for her to address the new Women Workers' Union founded by Larkin and his sister Delia. She argued that women were absolutely at the mercy, not only of their employers, but of the men's unions. So, as well as being unfranchised, their wages were lower, their conditions more wretched, and their employment more uncertain.

Another man who would influence Constance had just arrived back from America. James Connolly, who like Larkin was not Irish-born – Connolly was of a poor Edinburgh-Irish family and had emigrated to America in 1903 to earn a living. There he became an organizer for the famous Wobblies, the IWW, International Workers of the World, and won a formidable reputation as a political writer and pamphleteer. By 1910 he was publishing his *New Evangel,* which brought an added and stringent dimension to the rapture of nationalism:

> The man who is bubbling over with love and enthusiasm for Ireland and yet can pass unmoved through our streets and witness all the wrong and the suffering, the shame and the degradation wrought upon the people of Ireland, aye, wrought by the Irish men upon Irish men and women, without burning to end it, is, in my opinion, a fraud and a liar in his heart.

Connolly was no dry intellectual. The same age as Constance, he was a warm, affecting man of imagination and emotional breadth, and his physical presence was large and memorable. His shape was rotund and he had fine eyes and a thick dark moustache. He was now working for Larkin's union in Belfast, where his daughter Nora joined the Fianna. He and Con were to become extremely close, but she did not get to know him until late in 1911.

The public event of 1910 that most concerned Constance was the King's visit. By this point, her rejection of the Crown was absolute and she made public gestures to show it. She always, for instance, remained seated for 'God Save the King'. While staying at her sister Mabel's house in England, she caused consternation among Mabel's in-laws, the Fosters, by refusing to join in the toast to the King ,which they always drank after dinner. The practice had to be suspended for the duration of her stay. In the mourning period for Edward VII, she wore a sensational red dress to the theatre.

Now that the new King, George V, and Queen Mary were coming to Ireland on one of those recurring state visits, she was determined to be in the thick of any nationalist protest. There was the usual alignment of interests. Unionist women organized an address to the Queen from the 'women of Ireland', which, it was said, employers were pressing shopgirls and frightened employees to sign. Nationalist women countered that with some success. On coronation day, 10 June, there was a huge nationalist meeting on Beresford Place with Arthur Griffith, James Connolly and Constance Markievicz among the speakers.

Since Larkin's ITGWU had established itself there in Liberty Hall, Beresford Place had become the new venue for political meetings in Dublin. Such meetings were traditionally well attended in Ireland, a tradition established by Daniel O'Connell, the politician who agitated for and won Catholic Emancipation in the early 1800s. In his day, they were called monster meetings, and in the nineteenth century were used by the people as a social outlet as much as a means of demonstrating political allegiance.

Beresford Place was a suitably dramatic scene for mass meetings. It was central and accessible – Sackville Street (now O'Connell Street), the city's principal street, was only a hundred yards away up Abbey Street, and it was close to tram and train termini. It is bounded by the river, the Liffey, on which the city stands, with the elegant Georgian building, the Custom House, alongside. Behind it, at that time, the slums of Mountjoy Square and Gardiner Street crept down towards the river. Modernity also intruded with the iron railway bridge that still runs overhead, while the Place curves in an arc towards the wide bridge that spans the Liffey. That day, a young man who was standing in the crowd, Éamon de Valera, teacher of mathematics, heard the stirring calls for the establishment of an Irish Republic, a concept which was new and daring then, at least when called out in a public place. De Valera, hearing it for the first time, thought it a fine ideal, but an unattainable one. From then until the visit itself, Constance was involved in several fracas. She helped to put up a banner in Grafton Street, which was pulled down. Union Jacks were pulled down in their turn. In a demonstration that attracted a full complement of people and policemen, she was in the centre of a tug-of-war between the two sides when she attempted to burn a Union Jack.

Helena Molony too, was in an incitatory mood. Outside Yeats's opticians at the corner of Nassau Street and Grafton Street, there was a huge pair of spectacles as an advertisement for their services, and now each lens was displaying a picture of George and Mary. Helena, who had filled her pockets with stones from a building site, pelted some at the offending glasses, and missed. But the stones made an impressive din on some corrugated iron. Constance got her away from the scene by seizing the reins of the brake – what Yeats would derisively call a 'waggonette' – and driving the horses up Grafton Street. But at Stephen's Green, Helena was arrested. Constance managed to bail her out in the early hours of the morning and the two wandered through the city in the slow delectable mid-summer dawn. It is clear from the way in which Constance wrote about it later, that it was a cathartic day for her:

> Dublin was asleep. The old grey houses stood calm and cool in the tinted twilight. Flaring torches, charging police and hysterical crowds seemed like a dream of purgatory. Peace floated in the air. We passed on the Quays and looked down the shimmering river to where the Custom House raised its stately dome. During the summer weather the day never quite dies in Ireland. ... It is Ireland's hour of beauty, when all the sordidness and sadness slips from her, and when she lies around us simplified and beautified in the coloured dusk.[6]

They went towards Beresford Place where there was a coffee stall, because they were tired and hungry – incidentally, the very coffee stall belonging to the shadowy 'Skin-the-Goat', where Bloom and Stephen have their coffee and buns in James Joyce's *Ulysses*. Con and Helena were refused refreshments, however, because women weren't served, probably a discrimination directed against the numerous prostitutes who worked in nearby 'Nighttown'. But when the stallholder heard that his customers were the heroes of the day, he gave in and gave them his best buns and coffee.

At Helena's trial (four people in all were prosecuted for their activities on the day of the demonstration) she got a month's sentence or 40s. fine. 'You will get no money from me, Sir,' she declared, and thus became the first woman of her generation to go to jail for a political offence. 'She was treated,' wrote Constance, 'like a common malefactor' and put into the grey dress and 'queer white cap' that female malefactors were made to wear. Helena had been apprehensive that she might have disgraced the Inini but in nationalist circles she was a hero, and Maud Gonne MacBride sent her a telegraph of congratulations from Paris.

A man called James McArdle was charged with burning the flag, and although Constance testified that it was she who burned it, McArdle was found guilty and was sent down for one month's hard labour. The events of the day itself, 8 July, when the King and Queen paraded through the city, were tamer than Constance and the Inini would have liked. Arthur Griffith, she wrote, was as usual 'in great dread of a riot' and most of the nationalist men were of the same mind. Their protest therefore took the form of a rival celebration, at Bodenstown in Co. Kildare, in honour of Wolfe Tone.

The Inini were 'always in favour of the most extreme action possible'[7]; they saw in dramatic public escapades the possibility of making converts to the cause. Nationalist men, especially the IRB, believed by tradition in proceeding by stealth, in keeping their methods and even their existence out of the public eye, and in patient infiltration rather than conversion. Their celebration at Bodenstown, some thirty miles from Dublin, was blatantly designed to keep 'all the turbulent young men' out of trouble, and of course as a by-product, to give the royals a smooth passage. They may have decided the royals had little importance – but to the turbulent women it looked like cowardice and they had remained in the city to carry out their form of protest.

Bulmer Hobson's stature diminished in Constance's eyes when he sought refuge in Bodenstown instead of joining them on the streets as he had promised he would. He preferred to win his laurels, she contemptuously wrote, 'by a fierce speech at a rebel's graveside' than by 'getting a hammering from the police or being arrested'.[8] The king would pass by the railings of Trinity College, the unionist stronghold; and there Con and an intrepid few took their places and handed out handbills: 'When will Ireland regain the Legislature which is by everyone granted to be her mere right?

... Long live Ireland.' As the royal carriage made its way through the sea of waving Union Jacks, she vigorously waved a black flag. An old man standing near her was so furious at this that he began to beat her about the back with the stick of his Union Jack. But her back 'was pretty stiff and the stick broke almost at once'.

The crowd as a whole was amused rather than incited by the little demonstrations. But from her lonely vantage, Constance saw in the King's passage through the streets at least from the hindsight of 1923 a vivid evocation of the Parisian tumbrils of 1793:

> So the King passed, passed through Dublin, through the blood-red laneways that had been built in his honour. Red streamers floated from pole to pole, and red paper flowers danced in the wind, red flags, red draperies, red carpets everywhere. But he passed, too, through sad grey slums, where the sorrowful eyes of a dispossessed people huddled together in misery, looked out and wondered; looked at all the splendour and force, and saw nothing but red. Red through a grey mist. Saw Dublin grey with the tragedy of 800 years, red with the memories of the past. ... And the King, the poor human symbol. ... A kindly-faced man seated by a smiling lonely woman.[9]

But of course, the crowds were there to cheer the King, not to jeer him. It could not be denied that only a small minority of the Dublin populace no longer saw him as their monarch.

Constance was able to make a bigger row on the occasion of her arrest in August. When James McArdle, convicted of the flag-burning offence, was released from prison, there was a meeting attended by over a thousand people in Beresford Place to welcome him. When Helena Molony spoke, she went so far as to call King George 'one of the worst scoundrels in Europe' and the police moved to the platform and arrested both Helena and Constance. They were able to do so only after what newspapers call a scuffle. The malefactors were marched to the nearby police barracks, accompanied all the way by a small Fianna boy who kicked repeatedly at the legs of their bulky captors as he shouted 'Ah, you devils. Ah, you brutes.'

In the excitement of the moment, they hoped for charges of treason and long imprisonment, but they were charged with only the mundane offences of 'making derogatory remarks', throwing gravel at policemen and resisting arrest. A long, hot afternoon in the barracks awaiting bail was relieved by a pot of tea Nancy Wyse-Power sent in. Sean MacDermott, the sweet-voiced IRB man, sent in grapes and roses. Arthur Griffith wanted to make the trial a test case for free speech and engaged a counsel. They were released in the end, without sentence, on the decision, it was believed, of a high authority, who prudently saw they would serve the cause better inside than out. But the trial was widely reported in the newspapers. And when the *Sligo Champion* ran the story, the Gore-Booths were made rudely aware of Constance's growing militant activities. After that, however, she disappeared from its columns for several years. Whether this was due to the editor's own sense of delicacy or to representations from Lissadell is not known.

By 1912 Inini na h-Éireann was so loosely organized as to be almost defunct. Its most dynamic members were no less active than before but they were dispersed throughout other organizations. Jenny Wyse-Power was Vice-President of Sinn Féin; Constance was on the Sinn Féin executive; and she, the Gifford sisters, Sidney and Nellie, and Helena Molony were involved with the Socialist Party.

By the end of 1910 *Bean na h-Éireann* had a rival in a new revolutionary newspaper, *Irish Freedom,* owned and controlled by the IRB. Early in the following year, *Bean na h-Éireann* ceased publication and *Irish Freedom* recognized their symbiotic identity when it announced that since *Bean na h-Éireann* would no longer be appearing, its own day of publication would from now on be the first rather than the fifteenth of the month.

At around the same time Constance came to realize that her position as head of the Fiana was in many ways titular only. Through Bulmer Hobson and Sean McGarry, the IRB had quickly seized on the potential for their purposes in the Fianna. They formed a special circle in the IRB, called the John Mitchell Circle – John Mitchell was one of the revolutionaries of 1848 – just for Fianna boys. When important questions of policy and administration were to be decided, at the annual Convention for example, it was the voice of the previously concerted John Mitchell Circle that carried the arguments. It was to Madame though that the Fianna boy Liam Mellowes went first to discuss his idea for developing the Fianna. Being in possession of 'a bicycle and a good coat' he wanted to give up his job and travel throughout the country setting up *sluas*. He wanted her advice and to know whether the sum of ten shillings a week might be available to cover his expenses. She approved the plan and Roger Casement, through Hobson's agency, provided the sum requested. Liam Mellowes cycled the length and breadth of Ireland, often arriving into a town in the small hours and leaving *sluas* behind him as he went. Constance succumbed with good grace to losing control of the organization she had founded and supported, just as Inini na h-Éireann surrendered the stance it had created with *Bean na h-Éireann*. Cultural assertion was being replaced by headier rumbles of revolution that were more and more audible if you listened carefully.

It was not naivety so much as a sense of magnanimity towards this development that allowed women to bow out so readily. But it meant that what concerned women would from now on be treated only at the whims of these men, well disposed though they might be. Women would be used where men decided they might be necessary or helpful. But they would have little, if any, say in revolutionary councils. Women were not alone in this. Many of the best thinkers and the most fervent among nationalist men were equally excluded. But only women were automatically excluded as a group.

In the midst of all this Constance was not letting her theatrical activities slide:

> Madame Markievicz was brilliant but most erratic. I was not at all sure that I wanted her to take the leading part in my play. There was a scene in which the heroine, the part which Madame Markievicz played herself, had to emerge from her bedroom in the middle of the night. I was anxious that my name should not be associated with anything risqué and I feared that Madame Markievicz would be inclined to wear as little as possible when making her appearance. I wrote her several letters urging the wearing of a dressing-gown, bedroom slippers and other similar garments. She wanted to reduce her clothing to a minimum.[10]

This particular play was the light and frothy *Eleanor's Enterprise* by George A. Bermingham, the pen-name of Canon James Owen Hannay, who gave it for its first outing to Con and the Independent

Dramatic Company. It was more Somerville and Ross than Synge and had a successful run in London in the 1920s. The Markieviczes' company brought it to Belfast and it was then that Constance became properly acquainted with James Connolly and his family. She stayed overnight at their house and when she politely ventured to hope, on leaving, that she had not been too much trouble, Lillie Connolly said, 'Oh, no more than one of the children.'

In that year the company also put on Eva Gore-Booth's *The Buried Life of Deirdre*, her *Unseen Kings* and Edward Martyn's *Grangecolman*, for which Constance often acted as stage manager as well as playing roles. They also presented Casimir's *Rival Stars*, a play, which suggests that he was giving thought to, and feeling keenly, his wife's political engagement. The play concerns the affectionate relationship between an artist and his wife, a writer and socialist, who drift apart as she devotes her time and interest to improving the lot of common humanity. In *Rival Stars* the woman, Dagma, played by Constance, has an affair with a fellow intellectual, leaves her husband, but returns to him in due course.

There is no evidence that anything so torrid occurred in real life. By now, Ireland was entrenched in the rigid morality of the Catholic Church on sexual matters and even men such as Larkin and Connolly kept a simple Catholic faith to the end. But more than that, a sort of idealistic puritanism seems to have prevailed in nationalist circles. Nowadays we would probably call it subli-mation. Yeats held that nationalism was producing eunuchs 'from the sexual abstinence it causes.'[11] Although there were courtships and marriages – Helena Molony had a fiancé, at least by 1916, and Éamon de Valera married his teacher of Irish, Sinead Flanagan – the cry of Irish nationalist youth was 'All for Ireland', not 'All for love'.

By 1912 the Markieviczes had moved into Surrey House, a sizeable Edwardian terraced house on Leinster Road, Rathmines, a suburb that is somewhat more central than Rathgar. Life at Belcamp Park had liberated Constance from the superfluous and tedious aspects of a bourgeois lifestyle. At Surrey House, she rolled up the carpets and took down the ornaments that gathered dust, and made it open house for Fianna boys and political activists from the republican, labour and suffragette ranks. It housed a small, platen-type printing press for printing posters and handbills.

Surrey House in fact became a hotbed of subversion and before long was under constant surveillance by detectives.

Casimir was apparently happy to make his own amusements. He founded a fencing club and brought over a fencing master from France, Monsieur Dain, of very Gallic temperament. When the great Pavlova came to dance in the Gaiety Theatre, Casimir and his friend, Martin Murphy, went out to Kingstown Pier to greet her, and were first onto the gangplank to kiss her in turn on both cheeks, crying out '*Ztradswite*'. For that day Casimir embraced Russia as his own nation, and set out the traditional Russian welcome in her dressing room of a cloth of unbleached linen, a jug of water and a loaf of bread. Maybe he was finding the nationalist/unionist conflict in Dublin, and therefore the exclusively English/Irish culture, oppressive and inward-looking. In 1912 he disbanded the Independent Dramatic Company and founded a new company to present European plays of quality. Despite her politics Constance continued to play with this largely unaffiliated group.

The Dublin Repertory Theatre, his new company, opened with François Coppée's *For the Crown*, a weighty tragedy about Balkan politics in the Middle Ages. Eric Forbes-Robertson, Con's old friend from her time in Paris, had put it on in Dublin some fifteen years before, and for this production he sent over some impressive props from London. Their next play, George Bernard Shaw's *The Devil's Disciple*, asked for a large cast and fifty extras and Casimir contrived a remarkable verisimilitude by enlisting students from Trinity to play the British soldiers, and Fianna boys and nationalists to play the crowd. The reviewers commented, apparently without irony, on the impressive realism of the fight that ensues between the two sides.

In 1912 too, Constance and her women friends reverted, in public anyway, to the more traditional female activities of feminist agitation and feeding the hungry. Throughout the preceding years, parliamentary politics had been proceeding in a steady if rather undignified fashion, and in April of that year the Irish Party saw the fruits of its labours when Asquith's Home Rule Bill started its passage through the House of Commons. This Bill promised only an attenuated form of self-government to Ireland and extreme nationalists gave it scant attention. Their plans for self-government were still embryonic but vastly more ambitious.

In July Mr Asquith came to Dublin; and for a change Constance recognized constitutional politics by joining the Irishwomen's Franchise League, the IWFL, in their protest against the government's continued intransigence on women's suffrage. Although she thought the energies of the IWFL were misdirected, she often spoke at their meetings, even if it was only to tell them so.

Asquith had been followed to Ireland by some militant English suffragettes, a type of woman he deplored, who planned to join forces with the Irish suffragettes. Hanna Sheehy-Skeffington, Delia Larkin and Constance were among the demonstrators at a meeting addressed by John Redmond, the leader of the Irish Party, and were set upon by, it is said, the stewards, who were members of the reactionary Ancient Order of Hibernians. Supporters of Home Rule joined in the attack and several of the women were injured. Some of them fled across Butt Bridge to the refuge of Liberty Hall in Beresford Place. Others had to be protected by the police as they made their way to their trams. Two English suffragettes, Gladys Evans and Mary Leigh, set fire to the Theatre Royal where the Prime Minister was due to speak and were sentenced to five years penal servitude, to be served in Mountjoy Jail.

The events of the summer may have recharged Constance's feminist consciousness. In August, she successfully overrode IRB attempts at the annual convention, the Ard Fheis, to prevent girls from joining the Fianna. It was a pyrrhic victory because, without encouragement from the IRB, girls could not go far in the Fianna. But at least a principle had been established.

The labour movement was proving to be a meeting ground for women who, though generally amicable, were divided on the issue of whether national independence or the franchise should come first. The labour movement had, in Connolly and Larkin, two leaders who were almost alone in Irish politics in their whole-hearted support for the aims of militant women. Arthur Griffith, for instance, was virulent in his opposition to Larkin and labour generally, and was hardly more accommodating on women's issues.

James Connolly was a socialist who was in the same dilemma about the winning of an independent Ireland as nationalist women were about the franchise. Should it be international socialism or should it be a nation state – which would necessarily be bourgeois to begin with – that should be given priority? But being flexible and pragmatic, he did not dwell on these problems. After the confrontations at the Theatre Royal, he came down to Dublin to lend his support to the suffragettes. 'In Ireland,' he had written, 'the women's cause is felt by all Labour men and women as their cause.'[12] He described the status of working-class Irishwomen as 'slaves of slaves'. In Belfast, he organized the women workers in the linen industry. In *The Irish Citizen*, the newspaper edited by the feminist and pacifist Sheehy-Skeffingtons, Hanna and Francis, Connolly was said to be 'the soundest and most thoroughgoing feminist among all the Irish labour men'. And in the imaginative and sympathetic political thinking of James Connolly, Constance found a nexus for the different strands of her developing aspirations.

It was in 1912 that she and her women friends had a kind of practice run for their work in the terrible labour troubles that would come in the following year, when they began to provide daily lunches for hundreds of schoolchildren. The Act of 1906 that enabled local authorities to provide school lunches had never been extended to Ireland. As a means of drawing attention to this, and to the plight of the children who were, if anything, more deprived that their English counterparts – it was a fact that many, many children were obliged to attend school all day having left home without a breakfast – a campaign was started in the columns of *Bean na h-Éireann*.

The women of the IWFL offered their help in any campaign. Most of the priests who were managers of schools would hesitate about inviting such notorious women inside their gates, but the open-minded Canon Kavanagh of St Audeon's asked Maud Gonne MacBride to provide meals for the children of his parish. Maud, Hanna, Helena, the Giffords, Kathleen Clarke (wife of Tom Clarke), Constance and others set up a canteen and fed 250 children a wholesome meat stew every day; except on Fridays, the day of abstinence from meat, when they got rice pudding with jam. Next, a Father Kearns asked for a canteen for his school in Johns Lane. Meanwhile, Maud spearheaded the agitation to have the Provision of Meals Act extended, but for legal reasons it was not until September 1914 that this was achieved. Helena Molony, for one, had her doubts about using charitable endeavour in this way as a stopgap for social ills. But in 1913 such soul-searching would seem redundant.

By 1913 Larkin had 10,000 members in his union, the ITGWU. In that year, he won substantial pay rises for the dockers and enabled agricultural workers in Co. Dublin to earn the unprecedented amount of 17s. for a 64-hour week during the harvest. Employers were deeply worried, and in June, at the determined instigation of one William Martin Murphy, they formed the Dublin Employers' Federation Limited.

William Martin Murphy was one of Dublin's richest men. He owned the city's tramway company and had interests in several tramway companies abroad. He owned the Imperial Hotel in Sackville Street, a department store, and a chain of newspapers, including the daily *Irish Independent*, the bulk of whose readership was the Catholic middle class. Murphy's public image was that of a gentleman, but in his aggression towards his employees, he was to evince a great brutality.

In August Larkin turned his attention to the unionization of the Dublin United Tramways Company – in which, ironically, Constance had shares – and the *Independent* newspaper. Murphy met him head-on by locking out those employees who had joined the union. On the morning of 26 August 700 tram-workers walked away from their trams leaving them and their consternated passengers wherever they happened to be. Larkin had replied to the lockout by calling the tramway men out on strike in the middle of Horse Show Week. Next he used the weapon of sympathetic strike action by calling out on strike the workers at Eason's, a newspaper store, which was continuing to sell the *Independent*. The dockers entered the fray and refused to handle 'tainted' goods, by which they meant consignments destined for Eason's.

But the employers had laid their own plans. Using the same tactic of solidarity, 400 members of the Employers' Federation locked out workers of theirs who were union members. The coal merchants, the builders, even the farmers, sundry industries big and small alike, locked out their workers. By the end of September

25,000 people would be out of work. It was a blatant attempt to crush the nascent trade unionism of Irish workers. The employers, declared Murphy, intended to starve the workers into submission. Keir Hardie, the Scottish socialist, who came to Dublin in the ensuing crisis, commented at a meeting: 'Most of you have served too long an apprenticeship to starvation to be very much afraid of that.'[13]

On Friday 27 August Larkin and four union officials were arrested for 'seditious conspiracy'. While on bail, he addressed a huge meeting at Beresford Place and burned the King's Proclamation, a police document prohibiting a 'seditious' meeting arranged to take place on the Sunday in Sackville Street: 'People can make kings and people can unmake them. I am a rebel and the son of a rebel. ... I recognize no law but the people's law. ... I will be in Sackville Street on Sunday next dead or alive and if I am dead I hope you will carry me there.'[14]

Another warrant was immediately issued for his arrest. Larkin was taken into hiding and it seemed natural that his refuge should be Surrey House. Casimir fortuitously arrived from the Ukraine that evening and Larkin was able to slip past the watching eyes of detectives by mingling in the cheerful entourage that Casimir brought back for a homecoming party. Getting him into town next day for his promised appearance at the meeting posed a problem. But in that theatrical household it was quickly solved.

A telephone call was made to the Imperial Hotel in Sackville Street, a hotel chosen with deliberate irony because it belonged to Murphy. Rooms were reserved for a Reverend Donnelly and his niece who would be arriving from the country next morning. The ploy of the niece was considered necessary as Larkin had such a distinctive Liverpool accent that speaking one word could give him away. He would pretend to be so deaf that his companion had to communicate for him. Nellie Gifford was chosen for this role because, since she worked as a teacher in Co. Meath, her face was not a familiar one in Dublin.

In the morning Big Jim was attired in a frock coat and top hat of Casi's, his hair and false beard were powdered, and he was elaborately coached in the stooped, careful walk of an elderly man. He and Nellie travelled into Sackville Street by taxicab, and alighted at the Imperial where a porter came to greet them and carried in their portmanteaux. They were closely followed by Constance, Casimir, Helena Molony and Sidney Gifford, Nellie's sister, who all waited in high spirits opposite the Imperial (later to be replaced by Clery's department store) for the burlesque they'd devised.

Sackville Street had a heavy police presence, but little more than its usual complement of Sunday strollers. The ITGWU had decided to avoid any trouble with the police by arranging a meeting at Croydon Park, the house Larkin was renting in Fairview, about three miles from the city centre, on behalf of the labour movement. Presently, a window on the second floor of the Imperial was thrown open and an elderly gentleman, now tall and upright, appeared on the balcony and shouted out in Larkin's unmistakable voice that he had kept his promise. His speech was brief because he was quickly seized by police. But Larkin had made his presence felt. There was a small buzz of excitement on the street and people gathered in groups to watch. Shortly afterwards, he emerged from the entrance of the hotel with a police escort and, as he was led down the street, Constance jumped from the car, ran forward, shook his hand and said 'Goodbye. Good luck'.

Almost at once, an occasion of ebullience and playful triumph turned into one of terror. Constance was struck on the face by a policeman who was accompanying Larkin and was knocked about by another. As she reeled in the centre of the street, she was overtaken by a surging mass of police wielding batons. Nora Connolly described the baton charge of which Constance experienced the beginning, and which ended in the deaths of two men:

> A lad beside me yelled 'Hey. The peelers have drawn their batons'. The next thing I knew the peelers were upon us. All you could hear was the thud, thump, crack of the batons as they fell on the heads of the crowd. ... The peelers came steadily like mowing machines, and behind them the street was like a battlefield dotted with bodies. Some of them still lying twisting in pain.[15]

Casimir, whose support for the trade unionists was lukewarm, was nonetheless one of many who wrote of what they saw in the *Freeman's Journal* of the following week:

> There was no sign of excitement, no attempt at rescue, and no attempt at a breach of the peace, when a savage and cruel order for

a baton charge – unprecedented in such circumstances in any privileged country – was given to the police. It was equalled perhaps, by the Bloody Sunday events in St Petersburg. Scores of well-fed metropolitan policemen pursued a handful of men, women and children running for their lives before them ... I saw many batoned people lying on the ground, senseless and bleeding. When the police had finished their bloodthirsty pursuit, they returned down the street batoning the terror-stricken passers-by who had taken refuge in the doorways. It was, indeed, a bloody Sunday for Ireland. I at once sought out Sir James Dougherty (Under Secretary for Ireland) and told him what I had witnessed. I felt it my duty also to inform the foreign press. No human being could be silent after what I saw, and the public should insist on a sworn inquiry.[16]

Over 430 people were treated for their injuries in the city hospitals. Most of them were uninvolved with the labour movement, defenceless onlookers who had been chased up side streets by frenzied policemen. By evening, the scattered party that were the cause of the trouble had reassembled relatively unscathed in Surrey House. Early on Constance had been removed from the *mêlée* by some men who took her down Sackville Place and inside a house, 'to stop the blood flowing from my nose and mouth and to try and tidy my blouse'.[17]

'As the industrial atmosphere has approached fever heat,' wrote a society magazine, 'the social barometer has fallen to zero; Dublin is plumbing the lowest depths of the dead season.'[18] The city was polarized. The workers were angry and determined, the populace apprehensive. Connolly, summoned from Belfast, was in jail for having attended Saturday's seditious meeting. He promptly went on hunger strike and, after a week, was released under the terms of the new 'Cat and Mouse Act', which meant he would be arrested again once he had regained his health. On his release he went straight to Surrey House.

When Larkin was released on bail on 12 September he went to England to seek support for the strike from the unions there. In Dublin the labour leaders were buoyant and hopeful. The workers were firm. Plans were set in train for successful defiance. In fact the response of the British TUC was disappointing. It failed to order the sympathetic strike action in Britain that Connolly and Larkin hoped for, but it did raise almost £100,000 for the strikers' fund.

With 25,000 workers and their dependents without an income apart from strike pay, the major problem to be faced was the averting of mass starvation.

Liberty Hall had been a hotel in the previous century, so its basement housed ample kitchen and store-room space. Constance was appointed to administer a commissariat of enormous scale. Every day, a team of volunteer helpers peeled tons of vegetables and potatoes and prepared gallons of soup in huge coppers. And every day, thousands of people streamed into Liberty Hall to line up in the steamy, humbly aromatic atmosphere for their ration of nourishment. The suffrage women were prominent among the volunteers and insisted on wearing their IWFL badges to show their separate affiliation. Hanna Sheehy-Skeffington described the scene:

> The children, ever the hungriest and the most eager, used to file past with mugs, tin cans, porringers, old jam crocks which she filled and with a jolly word for all, for Madame had a personal contact and real sympathy with the poor that removed all taint of the Lady Bountiful and made her a comrade among comrades.[19]

It was Sean O'Casey, later a renowned writer and then a secretary of the relief fund with a deep temperamental antipathy to Constance, who painted her with his characteristic fanciful venom as a scatterbrained Lady Bountiful. Eager for attention, 'scintillating in the suit of a harlequin lozenged with purple, old gold and virgin green',[20] only rushing for a gigantic ladle and busy 'as a beebeesee' whenever a photographer showed in the doorway. It's an amusing image, the Countess awhirl amidst her pots, but it springs from a febrile imagination. No amount of mere vanity would drive anyone to seek notoriety on such an unpopular stage; those caverns beneath Liberty Hall, bleak, sweltering and odorous, the work menial, for company the rabble or 'Maud Gonne's unwashed' as the Inini had been called, and regarded with contempt by the Dublin middle classes.

Constance may have known, and comrades such as Connolly did know, that much of her appeal for ordinary people was her exoticism. Her background, which O'Casey so resented, embodied in her voice and foreign name, had a libertarian freshness for them in the dreary homogeneity of Irish life. They, like everyone else, liked colourful dresses, and the way she wore a sack for an apron over hers and always had a cigarette hanging from her lower lip were cheerful symbols of her defiance of convention.

The work was gruelling and endless, the scrubbing and peeling of mounds of potatoes, the scraping of bones, the stoking of fires, in the midst of a procession of countless gaunt and despondent faces – those faces to which the painter William Orpen, who had been at the Slade in Con's time there, responded by coming in to sketch. To work in that place could be nothing other than a labour of love or, at least, of selfless dedication. Constance brought to it her unstoppable energy and unwavering hope along with a welcome injection of gaiety and lightness and high spirits.

The strike began with great optimism. On 26 September the first consignment of foodstuffs from the English TUC arrived at the North Wall on the SS *Hare*. Tea, sugar, bread and other basics were distributed among the workers while foods that required longer cooking were taken to Liberty Hall. Clothes were donated for the coming winter and seamstresses on strike set up a sewing workshop in Liberty Hall to alter them to fit. On 6 October a government inquiry into the deadlock reported. It was critical of the employers but was irresolute in offering a solution. As the days passed, hostility and antagonism increased. The nationalists were silent, apart from the intellectuals such as Pearse, Plunkett and MacDonagh. The SS *Hare* was condemned by Sinn Féin because the goods it carried were not Irish. Arthur Griffith declared the strikers should be bayoneted. Constance was evermore contemptuous of Bulmer Hobson because of his lack of support. The newspapers, including the nationalist *Freeman's Journal*, weighed in behind the employers. Many of the clergy, who saw in socialism only irreligion, even atheism, denounced the strikers.

At the end of October some philanthropic women, including the feminist Dora Montefiore, proposed that children from the homes in direst straits might be sent to England to stay with sympathetic families for the duration of the strike. Some parents welcomed the proposal because it meant that their children at least would be well cared for until the worst was over. But the Church raised a clamour of 'proselytization' and 'deportation'. After a week of controversy, during which the Church was assured that the children would be taken into the care of Catholic homes and

Catholic priests, three respectable ladies were marshalling a group of 'deportees' at the train station when they were besieged by a hysterical crowd and the children were 'rescued'. However, the furore did result in more convents and more conscientious middle-class homes around the city opening their doors to the hungry.

Throughout an exceptionally cold winter, the strike went on and the people's morale grew lower. They were virtually isolated. Among Con's middle-class friends, Æ was practically alone in his agitation for their cause. In a Swiftian invective in *The Irish Worker,* he wrote 'of the admirable experiment in the evolution of the underman', which the employers were conducting and which Larkin had frustrated:

> It is quite possible that after exhaustive experiments had been carried out we could have produced the really economic worker who would be content with five shillings a week, which would suffice for his simple wants; we might have found out that human beings could be packed comfortably in rooms like bees in a hive, and could generate heat to warm themselves by their very number without the necessity for coal. Nothing is more annoying to scientific investigators than the unscientific humanitarian-like James Larkin, who comes along and upsets all calculations.

Æ also wrote a withering 'Open Letter' in the *Irish Times* to the Masters of Dublin, to that 'oligarchy of 400 masters deciding openly upon starving 100,000 people and refusing to consider any solution except that fixed by their price'. He wrote of their insolence and ignorance, of the 'preposterous and impossible demand' they had made of the labour unions, of how they had chosen as their spokesman the contemptible Tim Healy, 'the bitterest tongue that ever wagged in this island'.[21]

But the support of the English unions on whom the whole endeavour depended was gradually waning. They were scared by the revolutionary tactics of the Irish unions who were still pressing for sympathetic strike action, and by the stormy unpredictability of Larkin's speeches. On 9 December at an extraordinary meeting of the British TUC, Ben Tillett, considered the most militant of the trade unionists and a mainstay of English support, shocked everyone when he deplored the methods of the Irish leaders.

Constance, meanwhile, was being viewed with a more serious

kind of hostility than she was used to in certain circles. Hanna Sheehy-Skeffington considered Con's work during the strike her greatest achievement, and she earned the undying love of the Dublin poor for it. However, to other eyes she was estranged. Nationalism was all very well, it was respectable and Con cut a flamboyant figure as a nationalist. But to descend to the level of Jim Larkin who talked about class war and to spend one's days with Larkin's rabble was something else altogether. In the early days of the strike, she was frozen out of the Repertory Theatre Company that Casimir had founded because of her connection with Larkin. Casimir left with her in solidarity. But in December he also left Dublin. When she was engaged in making up Christmas stockings for thousands of children, Casimir set off for the Balkans to take up a position as a war correspondent.

His situation was clearly becoming more and more difficult. He was not against Constance, but neither could he be wholeheartedly with her. He was an artist, not an agitator or an activist; and his home, Surrey House, was both a hotbed of political activity and often little more than a *pied à terre* for its inhabitants. Since Larkin's re-arrest, James Connolly remained in Dublin as strike organizer, staying with the Markieviczes and contributing 10s. a week to the household.

It is also likely that Casimir left because he needed to make money. The Markieviczes seem to have been somewhat short of money at this time. The previous year for instance, Casimir had been about to take Stasko with him on a long-awaited trip to the Ukraine when he discovered he would have to pay £4 to the authorities for each year Stasko had been away. The boy was sent to stay in England with the Fosters (Constance's younger sister Mabel) instead. Constance was inclined to give money away freely to whomever or whatever she thought needed some: there are several stories of how she threw her diamonds and jewels on the table when the subject of funds came up at meetings. And the hunger and distress of the strikers in 1913 must have seemed to her a very glaring need.

Con and Casi said goodbye on the assumption that they would see each other again before very long. With him went the last vestiges of her old life, the rarefied life of art, of ease. Of Edwardian glamour, of first-night parties, last-night parties, homecoming parties. Having fun would never be so easy or simple again.

The winter, with its attendant hardships and indignities, was wearing the strikers down. Funds from England were reduced to a trickle. And the strikers returned, not in droves, but in twos and threes or singly, to their workplaces and signed the pledge the employers were demanding that they sign. On 1 February the Builders Labourers Union with its 3000 members went back to work on the employers' conditions that:

> None of its members remain or become in the future a member of the Irish Transport Workers Union. Its members will take no part in or support any form of sympathetic strike; they will handle all materials, and carry out all instructions given them in the course of their employment. Further, they will work amicably with all employees, whether they be unionists or non-unionists.[22]

Ten days later, the money in the Relief Fund had come to an end. Connolly wrote: 'So we Irish workers must go down into Hell ... eat the dust of defeat and betrayal.'[23]

NOTES

1. *Eire*, 9 June 1923.
2. *Remembering Sion*, Desmond Ryan (Arthur Barker, London, 1934) p. 82.
3. *Eire*, 16 June 1923.
4. *Ireland Since the Famine*, F.S L. Lyons (Fontana, London, 1978) p. 276.
5. *Eire*, 16 June 1923.
6. *Eire*, 28 July 1923.
7. *Eire*, 14 July 1923.
8. *Ibid.*
9. *Ibid.*
10. *Pleasant Places*, George A. Bermingham (London, 1934) p. 170.
11. *The Autobiography of W.B. Yeats*, p. 330.
12. *Constance Markievicz*, Van Voris, p. 101.
13. *A History of the Irish Working Class*, Peter Beresford Ellis (Pluto, London and Sydney, 1985) p. 194.
14. *Constance Markievicz*, Van Voris, p. 103.
15. *Portrait of a Rebel Father*, Nora Connolly O'Brien (Four Masters, Dublin, 1975) p. 179.

16. *Freeman's Journal*, 1 September 1913.
17. *Eire*, 28 July 1923.
18. *Constance Markievicz*, Van Voris, p. 109.
19. 'Constance de Markievicz', Hanna Sheehy-Skeffington in *An Phoblack*, 14 April 1928.
20. *Drums Under the Windows*, Sean O'Casey (Pan, London, 1972) pp. 212–13.
21. *The Irish Times*, 7 October 1913.
22. *A History of the Irish Working Class*, Beresford Ellis, p. 202.
23. *Ibid.*, p. 202.

1. *Lissadell* (The Sligo Champion)

2. *The Gallery at Lissadell* (photo by Peter Haugh 1987)

*3. Group at Lissadell about 1886; includes Mabel, Constance,
Sir Jocelyn Gore-Booth and Captain Grey Wynne*
(courtesy of Miss Aideen Gore-Booth)

4. Drawing (of Eva Gore-Booth?) by Constance
(photo by Peter Haugh, courtesy of Miss Aideen Gore-Booth)

5. Constance at Lissadell about 1905 (Lafayette)

6. Constance with the Fianna boys (National Museum)

7. *Thomas MacDonagh (in Irish-Ireland kilt) with his wife and baby*
(courtesy of Lucy Redmond)

8. *Members of the Irish Women Workers Union (IWWU) (National Museum)*

9. *Constance in the uniform of the Irish Citizen Army 1916* (National Museum)

10. *Constance in 'Irish-Ireland' dress* (National Museum)

11. *Constance in* banin *dress, n.d.* (National Museum)

[v]

12. *Maeve de Markievicz at Lissadell* (Lafayette)

13. *Casimir Dunin Markievicz before he left*

14. *O'Connell Bridge and Eden Quay 1915 – the building of the IWWU is visible on the right* (South Dublin County Library)

16. *James Connolly* (Lafayette)

15. *Éamon de Valera, with the* fáinne *worn by Irish speakers in his lapel* (Lafayette)

POBLACHT NA H EIREANN.

THE PROVISIONAL GOVERNMENT
OF THE
IRISH REPUBLIC
TO THE PEOPLE OF IRELAND.

IRISHMEN AND IRISHWOMEN : In the name of God and of the dead generations from which she receives her old tradition of nationhood, Ireland, through us, summons her children to her flag and strikes for her freedom.

Having organised and trained her manhood through her secret revolutionary organisation, the Irish Republican Brotherhood, and through her open military organisations, the Irish Volunteers and the Irish Citizen Army, having patiently perfected her discipline, having resolutely waited for the right moment to reveal itself, she now seizes that moment, and, supported by her exiled children in America and by gallant allies in Europe, but relying in the first on her own strength, she strikes in full confidence of victory.

We declare the right of the people of Ireland to the ownership of Ireland, and to the unfettered control of Irish destinies, to be sovereign and indefeasible. The long usurpation of that right by a foreign people and government has not extinguished the right, nor can it ever be extinguished except by the destruction of the Irish people. In every generation the Irish people have asserted their right to national freedom and sovereignty ; six times during the past three hundred years they have asserted it in arms. Standing on that fundamental right and again asserting it in arms in the face of the world, we hereby proclaim the Irish Republic as a Sovereign Independent State, and we pledge our lives and the lives of our comrades-in-arms to the cause of its freedom, of its welfare, and of its exaltation among the nations.

The Irish Republic is entitled to, and hereby claims, the allegiance of every Irishman and Irishwoman. The Republic guarantees religious and civil liberty, equal rights and equal opportunities to all its citizens, and declares its resolve to pursue the happiness and prosperity of the whole nation and of all its parts, cherishing all the children of the nation equally, and oblivious of the differences carefully fostered by an alien government, which have divided a minority from the majority in the past.

Until our arms have brought the opportune moment for the establishment of a permanent National Government, representative of the whole people of Ireland and elected by the suffrages of all her men and women, the Provisional Government, hereby constituted, will administer the civil and military affairs of the Republic in trust for the people.

We place the cause of the Irish Republic under the protection of the Most High God, Whose blessing we invoke upon our arms, and we pray that no one who serves that cause will dishonour it by cowardice, inhumanity, or rapine. In this supreme hour the Irish nation must, by its valour and discipline and by the readiness of its children to sacrifice themselves for the common good, prove itself worthy of the august destiny to which it is called.

Signed on Behalf of the Provisional Government,

THOMAS J. CLARKE,
SEAN Mac DIARMADA.   THOMAS MacDONAGH.
P. H. PEARSE,   EAMONN CEANNT,
JAMES CONNOLLY.   JOSEPH PLUNKETT.

17. Proclamation of the Irish Republic 1916

EIGHT

'I AM GOING TO TALK SEDITION':
THE IRISH CITIZEN ARMY

'POURS OUT water on the ground. ... Prefers applied science to truth. Will make gas bombs. Also will succeed through cleverness in politics. ...'[1] In 1893 Eva copied this into a notebook as Constance's horoscope for the sign of Aquarius. It was a crude reading from the hand of one of those casters of horoscopes of the nineteenth century who tended to be more morbid and melodramatic about their subjects' futures than astrologers nowadays. It suggested depredation and anarchy were Aquarian qualities. But, interpreted with more sympathy, it might describe Con's impulsive, iconoclastic and revolutionary nature.

In 1899 Standish O'Grady, one of the first of the Gaelic revivalists, declared with a prescience induced by whiskey: 'We now have a literary movement, it is not very important; it will be followed by a political movement, that will not be very important; then must come a military movement, that will be important indeed.'[2]

It is possible to see Con's later career as the embodiment of the third of those movements forecast by O'Grady; of the spirit of the age.

The passive resistance of the workers had failed. It may have been a drawn battle in that, while they sullenly signed the employer's pledge, they still retained a secret membership of their unions. But on the face of it, the bosses had triumphed. For many workers, hope and defiance were salvaged by a new idea: active resistance. At the height of the strike, on a pink autumn evening, a densely packed crowd in Beresford Place listened to James Larkin say, in one of those speeches that used to lead to his arrests, that it was now necessary for the workers to use their collective strength, that they must learn discipline and military training to defend themselves against the violence of the police to which they had been subjected on Bloody Sunday. To prevent their elemental rights from being taken from them, they must have a Citizen Army. And Larkin presented to the cheering crowd Captain Jack White who was a military man and would be in charge of the workers' Citizen Army. Constance stood on the platform with Larkin and Connolly and Captain White. 'Listen to me,' shouted Connolly, 'I am going to talk sedition. The next time we are out for a march, I want to be accompanied by four battalions of trained men. I want them to come with their corporals, sergeants and people to form fours. Why should we not drill and train our men as they are doing in Ulster?'[3]

On Sunday 23 November a number of men turned up in Croydon Park and gave their names to Captain White, who undertook to drill and train them in soldiering.

Jack White was another of those unlikely figures who wandered, apparently by chance, onto the Dublin stage at this time. He had an impeccably patriotic English background. His father was the near-legendary Field-Marshal George White of Ladysmith. He himself had fought in the Boer War and been decorated, unwillingly, for gallantry. 'I feel I am odd,' he wrote to his father, 'and I cannot be odd without making more or less of a scandal. Will you agree to my leaving and help me to do something else?'[4] His father replied that he was already quite odd enough and should get on with his work. But Jack resigned from the army, dallied a little in Ulster, came south to Dublin, and was moved by Æ's letter in the *Irish Times* to place his unorthodox form of valour and organizational flair at the service of the strikers. His Citizen Army drilled regularly during the winter with hurley sticks for rifles, and though it flagged in the aftermath of the strike, it was reconstituted in March 1914 on a sound footing.

It may now seem strange that people turned with such open enthusiasm to the prospect of armed conflict, and that their preparations should be tolerated, on the whole, by the authorities. But this was the pre-war, in retrospect a golden age of innocence. The Great War, the first modern industrial war, was still in the future. Decent men and women had an almost medieval attitude to armed combat. They saw war as chivalric, manly and glorious. When war came, they would go to it with a curious exhilaration and very little fear. Near at hand, the Citizen Army already had an example in the Ulster Volunteer Force. When Connolly cried out on that glowing autumn evening: 'Why should we not train and drill our men as they are doing in Ulster?' he was speaking of those thousands of fellow citizens in Ulster, the province in the north of the country, who, the January before, had formed themselves into a private army. Their purpose was to oppose by violence a Home Rule parliament in Ireland. By the end of 1913 the Ulster Volunteers numbered 50,000 and, although the government liked to believe it drilled with wooden mock-up rifles, it was rapidly arming itself with very real weapons.

A great section of the population of Ulster had been firmly opposed to Home Rule since Gladstone in the 1880s first committed the Liberal Party to achieving it. Since the 'conquest', the province was divided, largely for economic reasons, both within itself and from the rest of Ireland. It was industrialized, therefore richer. More than half of its population was of 'planter' descent and felt itself to have a coherent identity of its own lent it by its Scots-Presbyterian ancestors. Its politics, especially since the inception of the Home Rule movement, was an emotive mix of religion and economics in which fear of submergence in a Catholic state, the attempt to maintain a level of comparative prosperity and privilege, and deliberate manipulation by the employing class, all played their part.

Partly in a bid to unseat the Liberals, the Conservative Party had been playing the 'Orange card', i.e., supporting the Ulster Unionists; and the Unionists had recently found a formidable leader in Sir Edward Carson, a former Solicitor-General. The Ulster

Volunteers gave concrete form to the catch-cry of the 1890s: 'Ulster will fight and Ulster will be right.' The rise of a paramilitary force in Ulster was seen in certain quarters in the south, not so much as a threat to the long-awaited Home Rule Bill, but with admiration.

Eoin MacNeill, who was prominent in the Gaelic League and a Professor of History at University College Dublin (a constituent college of the National University), wrote an ingenious article in the Gaelic League newspaper to the effect that the UVF represented a 'decisive move towards Irish autonomy'. 'Really,' he wrote, 'what matters is, by whom is Ireland to be held?'[5] It was an opportunity that the IRB saw at once it could exploit. Bulmer Hobson and a sympathizer, The O'Rahilly, called on Eoin MacNeill and suggested that he form the Irish National Volunteers recommended in his article. On 25 November moderate nationalists from the Gaelic League and Sinn Féin flocked to the Rotunda Rink to join the National Volunteers. The object of this rival paramilitary force was to protect the Home Rule Bill from being hijacked or diminished in any way. As far as the IRB was concerned, Eoin MacNeill as leader made an ideal front man; and he seems to have implicitly understood that this would be his role.

The Irish National Volunteers was founded just two days after Captain White's little assembly in Croydon Park; and while the Citizen Army grew ragged and bowed and wavered in its resolve, the Volunteers swelled into a solid and countrywide body. By May 1914 the Volunteers numbered about 75,000. Sean O'Casey detected a snobbism in the popularity of the Volunteers. 'Many,' he wrote, 'no doubt preferred Caithlin-ni Houlihan in a respectable dress than a Caithlin in the garb of a working woman.'[6] But it's also likely that what the average nationalist preferred was the simple hallowed call to the cause of Ireland than the class warfare the Citizen Army seemed to intend.

In March the Citizen Army rallied again in response to the urgings of Sean O'Casey. While Constance joined the Volunteers and maintained strong connections with the different organizations to which she belonged – Sinn Féin, the Fianna et al – the Citizen Army got her first attention from now on. All her aspirations found a voice in this little army: the cause of Ireland, the cause of the people, the cause of women, and her wish for action.

The argument for such an army was strengthened in March when the people were involved in another conflict with the police. In that month, Con marched behind Captain White with a group of the unemployed who intended to march through the city as a protest against joblessness. They had barely emerged from Beresford Place when they were confronted by a band of the metropolitan police wielding batons. There was a riot and Captain White's head was beaten 'to a bloody pulp', he would say. Constance 'hung on the flanks of the enemy throughout'. And she was 'magnificent' at the police barracks:

> She forced her way in and demanded that a private doctor should be sent for at once. The first time they flung her out but she ducked between policemen's legs and got back again somehow. Madame insisted on getting a solution of Jeyes fluid and bathing my head at once for fear of it getting septic, and got her way in having' a private doctor summoned at once.[7]

He claimed that her ministrations saved his life. By 22 March he was well enough to chair the inaugural meeting of the newly revived Citizen Army.

The first principle of the constitution of the Citizen Army was: 'The ownership of Ireland, moral and material, is vested of right in the people of Ireland.' The second was that it 'shall stand for the absolute unity of Irish nationhood'. Another object was 'to sink all differences of birth, property and creed under the common name of the Irish people'. The Citizen Army (its proper title was the Irish Citizen Army, hence its abbreviation to the ICA) was open to all, with the proviso that 'every applicant must, if eligible, be a member of his Trades Union'. This excluded only those who elected not to join the union of their trade, so the unemployed, the non-unionized – and *rentiers* like Constance were eligible.

An Army Council was duly elected. Constance was one of two treasurers. Captain White was chairman. Jim Larkin and Francis Sheehy-Skeffington were among the vice-chairmen; and Sean O'Casey was secretary. The scattered army was reorganized into battalions and before very long had expanded to a body numbering some hundreds of men and women. The secretary, Sean O'Casey, had not yet embarked on his career as a playwright and he and Con were old combatants from the Drumcondra branch of Sinn

Féin when the brilliant O'Casey, contrary and argumentative, proved to be one of the few who did not take to her. 'A dull and fiery figure swathed in labourer's garb,' was how Desmond Ryan saw O'Casey then. 'He speaks ... very fluently and eloquently in Irish, then launches out into a violent Republican oration in English, stark and forceful, Biblical in diction with gorgeous tints of rhetoric.'[8]

One of the first arguments in the Citizen Army concerned uniforms. Captain White felt the men needed uniforms to give them a sense of unity and pride. O'Casey argued that they should operate in anonymity as urban guerilla fighters so that they could easily melt into the crowd and thus avoid capture. But almost everyone was in favour of uniforms. Indeed, fifty uniforms of dark green serge were already ordered from Arnotts. Those who could not yet afford a uniform wore, at Constance's suggestion, armbands, blue for the men, red for officers. They all wore a green slouch hat with the wide brim pinned up on one side with the ITGWU badge depicting a red hand. They marched to a song Constance adapted from the Polish.

O'Casey displayed his implacability too in his hostility to what he saw as the rival army of the Volunteers. He regarded the Volunteers as bourgeois and Girondist, therefore the enemy of the Citizen Army. 'Let others who may prate about rights and liberties common to all Irishmen. We are out for the right to work and eat and live,' was typical of what he wrote in *The Irish Worker*. 'Soon all workers shall realize that it is good to die for one's friend, but foolish to die for one's enemy.'[9] It was the same old fraught question that kept rearing its head: whether everyone join together as allies in the fight for Ireland's independence, leaving all sectional demands for the national agenda that would follow. Captain White was optimistic: 'I think [the Citizen Army] will result in compelling the National Volunteers to cease from the suspicious aloofness for anyone connected with labour and draw together the Labour and National movements ...'[10]

That spring, Constance and O'Casey were still amicable enough to go canvassing together in the County of Dublin for new recruits to the Citizen Army. One fine Sunday they with Captain White and P.T. Daly 'proceeded to Lucan in the Captain's motorcar'.[11] In both Lucan and Clondalkin they were received with 'an ominous quietude' and the residents 'stood afar off for quite a long time, gazing fixedly at the Captain's motor-car as if it were some dangerous machine calculated to upset forever the quiet rhythm of the pastoral life. ...' Only Constance's 'nervous and passionate eloquence' aroused any interest. But the party persisted on succeeding Sundays and soon there were companies in Lucan, Finglas, Kinsealy and other outlying areas.

Jim Larkin designed a travelling caravan in which he and a few followers could tour the country, forming companies in every village in the land. But nothing came of it and the Citizen Army remained confined to Dublin and its environs. The ICA had an enlightened attitude to women members. They drilled with the men and classes in first aid were coordinated, given by Dr Kathleen Lynn who taught classes throughout Dublin to the various mush-rooming paramilitary organizations. The Volunteers on the other hand had a macho ethos and nationalist women formed themselves into a separate women's branch, Cumann na mBan (meaning the Women's Society). The members of Cumann na mBan at this stage tended to be sisters, wives, sweethearts, etc. of the Volunteers and the Volunteers stated in no uncertain terms that their role was what they themselves saw it as, by and large: an auxiliary branch. They could be helpmeets, nurses, messengers, fundraisers for arms and equipment, but they could not expect to have a voice.

The Inini na h-Éireann women joined the ICA; and middle-class women like Nellie Gifford, Madeleine ffrench-Mullen, Kathleen Lynn and of course Constance marched beside ex-factory workers from Jacobs and women such as Rosie Hackett who ran a news-paper stall. Characteristically Constance maintained links with Cumann na mBan and the Volunteers, taking perhaps, a leaf out of Bulmer Hobson's book. It was this ubiquitousness that gave O'Casey a reason for seeking to oust her from the ICA, because of her bourgeois tendencies, he claimed, but really because he disliked her. He called a special meeting of the Army Council and proposed a motion that since the Volunteers were 'inimical to the first interests of labour', the Countess must now be asked to sever her connection with either the Volunteers or the Irish Citizen Army. The motion was resolutely opposed. Constance won a vote of confidence by one vote after she had prudently voted for herself. O'Casey was asked to apologize, and resigned from the ICA rather than do so.

Frictions were inevitably occurring as well in the ranks of the Volunteers. In June the Government bowed to the wishes of the unionists and amended the Home Rule Bill to exclude Ulster from the terms of the Bill. John Redmond, the moderate gentlemanly leader of the Irish Party determined to show his teeth as the unionist Carson had. He issued an ultimatum to the Irish Volunteers that they co-opt twenty-five representatives of the Irish Party onto the committee. The extreme members were horrified, seeing in this the threat of emasculation. The moderates wanted to avoid a split. But Bulmer Hobson agreed, lamely and treacherously in the eyes of his brothers in the IRB, to Redmond's demand and the Irish party had its way. Tom Clarke, watching from the sidelines, was outraged. From then on Hobson was ostracized from the inner circle of the IRB. Clarke, who, it was said, had regarded Hobson as a son now rounded on him bitterly with: 'How much did the English pay you?'[12]

Apart from Hobson's contretemps, events moved fast and as furiously that summer as a single-minded revolutionary like Clarke, or indeed Constance, could have wished. At the end of April, the Ulster Volunteers landed about 30,000 Mauser rifles and two million rounds of ammunition at Larne, which they had bought in Germany. The army and police looked the other way. In London the Government managed to raise no more than a whimper of protest. The *Manchester Guardian* would write that the Ulster gun-running won as many titles and honours for its patrons 'as if it had been an incident in the first battle of Ypres'.[13] Thus challenged, and encouraged, the Irish Volunteers set their own gun-running venture in train.

London too, had its coterie of enthusiastic nationalists – again, such unlikely figures as Erskine Childers, novelist and Committee Clerk to the House of Commons; Alice Stopford Green, daughter of the Archdeacon of Meath, historian, highly strung and friend of the Fabians; and the tanned and interesting Sir Roger Casement, a consular official who was knighted for his exposure of the iniquities of the Belgians in the Congo and the Brazilian rubber-planters in the Putamayo. Between them they raised the sum of £1500 from sympathizers, bought about 1500 rather antiquated rifles in Hamburg, and Childers' yacht, the *Asgard*, set out for Ireland. On board the *Asgard* with its cargo of guns and 2600 rounds of ammunition, were Erskine Childers and a crew that included his wife, Molly, and Mary Spring Rice, daughter of Lord Monteagle and a niece of the British Ambassador to Washington.

Erskine Childers was an expert sailor and, having safely made its way through heavy seas and the British fleet on review at Spithead, the white yacht with its sunburnt crew and illicit arms came into Howth Harbour in North County Dublin on the afternoon of 26 July, just three quarters of an hour behind the time agreed with Bulmer Hobson for their rendezvous. The pick-up of the arms was smooth and efficient. That morning, 700 Volunteers had walked out from the city to Howth on what most of them saw as a routine route march. At their head was a detachment of the Fianna with two handcarts into which many of the rifles were quickly landed from the *Asgard*, while each of the Volunteers got a gun to carry away with him. But as they marched proudly back into town, bearing their new weapons, things took an unfortunate turn. On Malahide Road, they were intercepted by police and a company of soldiers from the King's Own Scottish Borderers who had been alerted by the Police-Inspector at Howth.

At first, all was well. The leaders succeeded in engaging their opposite numbers in arguments while the men slipped away and stashed their rifles in hedges or wherever a hiding place offered in nearby parkland. While small clashes broke out in front, the Fianna boys trundled their handcarts up a lane and buried their rifles in a garden – the inhabitant of the house was under the impression that they were innocently striking camp. Meanwhile, the protagonists remaining on the Malahide Road dispersed and the soldiers were marched back to barracks. As they came into town, they were beset by jeers and stone-throwing from people in the streets. When they reached Bachelors Walk off Sackville Street, the soldiers turned about and fired into the crowd of bystanders. Three people died at once and thirty-eight were badly injured, of which one more would later die.

Dublin, indeed all of Ireland, was incensed. The incident produced another set of martyrs. And it was a glaring example of how the authorities repressed such actions as sedition in the south, while they seemed to allow them to go unchecked in the north. At Larne, £60,000-worth of guns had been landed without interference. At Howth, the landing of £1500-worth was met with hostilities and four people died. The immediate result was that the ranks of the Volunteers swelled with new recruits. And despite the tragedy of the deaths, the arms had been landed and taken into their proper keeping. Constance must have been grieved at her exclusion from this exploit. But again on this occasion, women were made to understand that they were *de trop* when it came to real action and real excitement.

That weekend of 26 July Constance and the two spirited Connolly girls, Nora and Ina, were camping with some Fianna boys at the cottage in the hills. On the Sunday morning, the boys went off, wrote Ina, 'saying they were invited out and no girls were welcome. We were to pass the day as best as we could and they would be out in the evening to see us. This was most unusual; even Madame had not been asked.'[14] Bulmer Hobson wanted to use the Fianna for the pick-up at Howth because they were the only really disciplined corps available. But he did not intend to use Constance or any of the Fianna girls, even though Ina was secretary to the Belfast branch, the Betsy Gray. They were deeply upset: 'When we heard that guns had been run in at Howth and us sitting pretty a few miles away, it nearly broke our hearts. How could we face up to Belfast and father and say we knew nothing and did less? It looked as if we were not to be trusted. ... Had I been a boy,' I said, 'I should not have been overlooked.'

Next day, when Constance had gone, possibly in some indignation, into Dublin, a taxi arrived at the cottage laden with the guns retrieved from the Malahide garden where the boys had hidden them. When they were taken away again because, as they were warned by a sympathetic neighbour, a police sergeant lived down the road, Nora and Ina sat on the guns on the journey back to Dublin so as to lend the appearance of an innocent outing. Girls were expected to hide guns and mind them and to be happy to risk the consequences; and yet to share in none of the glory.

Everybody wanted a rifle; and Nora and Ina did get one each as a reward for their work. Even Arthur Griffith, 'always in dread of a riot', marched out to Howth for his. They were, as it turned out, very ancient models. And the ammunition was quite useless. 'It consists,' wrote Patrick Pearse to his confidants in Clan na nGael, the counterpart of the IRB in America, 'of explosive bullets which are against the rule of civilized war and which, therefore, we are not serving out to the men.'[15] But the Howth guns were nonetheless an improvement on their wooden predecessors.

A month before the Howth gun-running, the Archduke Ferdinand and his wife were assassinated in Sarajevo. Two days after Howth, Austria declared war on Serbia. And for the British cabinet, arguing wearily about the amendment to the Home Rule Bill, and for much of Ireland, as much as for Winston Churchill: 'The parishes of Tyrone and Fermanagh faded back into the mists and squalls of Ireland and a strange light began immediately, but by perceptible gradations, to fall and grow upon the map of Europe.'[16] The problem of Home Rule with all the intractable difficulties it presented was summarily and with great relief shelved by the cabinet until the European war should be over and won. But for a handful of conspirators in obscure places, the light fell with an ever-more intense glow on Dublin City. For them, England's difficulty would be Ireland's opportunity.

The majority of the Irish people did not see the war in this way. The Volunteers, apart from the few pockets of IRB revolutionists, adopted Redmond's revised view of their role. England could remove her troops to Flanders with an easy mind. The Volunteers would take over their station in Ireland and would defend the country from German invasion. Posters advertising for soldiers in the patriotic war were pasted up on Irish walls as they were on English. In Ireland, they were shrewdly designed for Irish eyes and thousands of young men enlisted, many of them foot-loose, property-less labourers who were attracted by the prospect of regular pay as much as by the prospect of adventure or the saving of small nations.

In September, Redmond, fatally conciliatory and malleable as always, went farther. In his famous speech at Woodenbridge, Co. Wicklow, he called on the Irish Volunteers to enlist: 'Account yourselves as men, not only in Ireland itself ... but wherever the firing line extends, in defence of right, of freedom and of religion.'[17] The result of Woodenbridge was an immediate split in the Volunteers. The majority, about 150,000, remained solidly behind Redmond, calling themselves the National Volunteers. But they were as vacillatory as their leader. Most of them had no intention of enlisting and, though they continued to drill and parade, they ceased to have any real importance. The others, who kept the name (Irish) Volunteers, were undaunted by their relatively small numbers. They were 16,000 after all, temperamentally more zealous, more romantic, more open to republicanism. Their leader, or Chief of Staff, was the relatively moderate Eoin MacNeill. But, unknown to the rank and file, at least half of the staff at headquarters were IRB men.

In the eyes of the IRB, the split in the Volunteers satisfactorily clarified a confused situation. It had separated, as far as they were concerned, the sheep from the goats. They now had under their control a sizeable force of men, unified in its decisive approach to the national question and on which they might rely. Jim Larkin, somewhat broken by the outcome of the strike the year before, had departed in October for America. The IRB now seriously began to court the man who had succeeded him as head of the Citizen Army, James Connolly. From now on, the Irish Volunteers and the Irish Citizen Army sank their differences and made friendly bedfellows.

These quite momentous events and imminent conclusions were the foreground where only men had parts to play. Constance was unique among the women in that she had a position on the stage, which was colourful and quite in the forefront. Her position was tenuous but she was determined to keep it. The mutual understanding between her and James Connolly was valuable. He gave her a commission in the Citizen Army (the manner in which the revolutionaries maintained the structures of the established organizations is somehow poignant) and kept her informed. Cumann na mBan, too, aligned itself into two camps as the Volunteers had done. For the more extreme or impatient or romantic, the Irish Volunteers presented a glimmer of possibility. 'I would not like to think of women drilling and marching in the ordinary way,' said Patrick Pearse, 'but there is no reason why they should not learn to shoot.'[18] In general, however, the women were in the background, occupied with raising funds, printing and distributing anti-enlistment pamphlets, getting first-aid boxes together and attending the endless round of meetings these things demanded. Constance soon became President of Cumann na mBan, which added to her busy schedule.

Much of it of course was fun; like the *tableaux vivants*, a popular form of entertainment at the time, that the IWFL put on to raise funds. Their thirteen *tableaux* featured great women: Madame Toto Cogley was Sappho, Maire ni Shiubhlaigh, Saint Brigid. Sidney Gifford was Robert Emmet's protector, Anne Devlin. Constance was able to indulge her heroic self-image as Joan of Arc. There were actually two Joans of Arc, Kathleen Houston as Joan at the stake, and Con as Joan in full armour. Hanna Sheehy-Skeffington remembered how Con typically toiled over illustrations of the period to get it right. 'What fine fifteenth-century pieces she contrived out of cardboard silvered over, and what a characteristic Joan she was. She posed as Joan appearing to a suffragist prisoner in her cell. Her alert, gallant bearing was well set off by her silver armour, helmet and uplifted sword.'[19]

That summer the ICA set up a marquee in Croydon Park and people who knew only the greyness and squalor and crowded conditions of the city were able to spend nights under canvas, and days among the red poppies and chestnut trees in the company of songbirds. There were concerts where Jim Larkin sang 'The Red Flag' and 'The Rising O' the Moon' in his hoarse tremulous voice and James Connolly sang the new songs he had just written. 'Bands played, artistes sang and children danced desperately at the same moment,' wrote Sean O'Casey, ... and the gallant Countess Markievicz tried to be in ten places at once.'[20]

And there were always convivial times at Surrey House. Constance had a delightfully casual attitude towards guests, extending to her domestic life her liking for an ambience of people and activity. 'Until she came down in the morning she never knew what guests she had under her roof,' wrote Margaret Skinnider, a new friend of this period. 'In order not to disturb her, they often climbed in through the window late at night.'[21] Contrary to O'Casey's statement that she never read anything, Margaret Skinnider said that the place was full of books and 'you could not walk about without stumbling over them'.

Constance would invite talkative and amusing acquaintances to come round in the evening with 'The gas is cut off and the carpets up but you won't mind.' They would talk,' said Hanna Sheehy-Skeffington, 'round the big fire, sitting on her large divan in the big bow window, by the light of innumerable candles stuck around.'[22] Frank Kelly remembered how crowds used to gather there at night:

> We had tea in the kitchen; a long table with Madame cutting up slices of bread about an inch thick and handing them around. ... She had lovely furniture and splendid pictures. Then we used to go into the sitting room and someone would sit at the piano and there would be great singing and cheering and rough amusements. She had lifted her lovely drawing-room carpet but had left her pictures on the walls and on the bare boards there was stamping of feet.[23]

James Connolly was usually there, lost in thought and his manner distant. And Constance, who found it hard to sit still and just talk, might be working on one of the four large curtains of unbleached linen she was embroidering with a Jacobean design.

That year, the first Fianna handbook was produced and Con supplied the illustration for the cover, her favourite motif of a Celtic goddess posed before a sunburst. The handbook was both a training manual and a collection of inspiring sentiments. It was the best source of instruction in soldiering available and Eoin MacNeill recommended it, not only for the Volunteers but also for use in boys' schools throughout the country. At Christmas, Con helped produce a Fianna Christmas annual in which the tone is both *Boys Own* and seditious at the same time. It reflects the curious atmosphere and circumstances of the epoch. Next to Con's account of the Fianna's first camp and a piece by Patrick Pearse on 'The Fianna of Fionn' were advertisements for shops and businesses. McQuillans offered cutlery, scouts' equipment and revolvers; Whelan's advertised their official status as outfitters to the Fianna; tailors offered to make uniforms for the Volunteers, and readers were advised, when buying books for Christmas, to get *Sheaves of Revolt*, verses by Maeve Cavanagh dedicated to the Fianna. Only Stasko's contribution was free of national preoccupations. His was a horror tale of grave-robbing in the Arctic, probably told by Sir Henry to the Gore-Booth children and passed on to Stasko by Con.

Stasko was now almost a young man. His future demanded some consideration. In 1915 he was learning French and Russian at the Berlitz School in Grafton Street and considering going to Trinity. Con could not entirely approve of this plan as she was afraid he would join the Officers' Training Corps there and become identified with the enemy. In April a long-awaited letter from Casimir arrived. It revealed that her husband had stolen a march on Constance in being first to fight his patriotic war. When war broke out, the Grand Duke Nicholas had issued a proclamation appealing to the Pan-Slav feelings of the Poles and Casimir had responded. He threw up his position as a newspaper correspondent in the Balkans, took a horse and rode 700 miles to join in his old cavalry regiment of the Imperial Hussars. He was wounded in the Carpathians during the bitter winter fighting, contracted typhus and almost died in Lwow.

For months he was very ill. His brother Jan arrived in Lwow to find him and brought him home. He was now in Zwyotowka and wanted Stasko to come. To finance the journey, he enclosed 300 roubles. To raise more money, Stasko sold his two rifles and his two bicycles to his stepmother – though of course Stasko always regarded her as, and called her, mother – and on 15 June was seen off at the North Wall by Con, in tears, and by his friend Brian, Æ's son, on his long circuitous journey to the Ukraine via Scandinavia.

NOTES

1. Notebook in family papers.
2. *The Damnable Question*, George Dangerfield (Quartet, London-Melbourne-New York, 1979) p. 137.
3. *Ibid.*, p. 106.
4. *The Rebel Countess*, Marreco, p. 166.
5. 'The North Began', Eoin MacNeill in *An Claidheamh Soluis*, 1 November 1913.
6. *The Story of the Irish Citizen Army*, P. O Cathasaigh (Sean O'Casey) (Maunsel, Dublin and London, 1919) p. 9.
7. *Constance Markievicz*, Van Voris, p. 128.
8. *Remembering Sion*, Ryan, p. 2.
9. *The Irish Worker*, 18 March 1914.
10. *Constance Markievicz*, Van Voris, p. 129.

11. The account of the trip is from O'Casey's *The Irish Citizen Army*, pp. 20–3.

12. *Leaders and Men of the Easter Rising* (Martin, Dublin 1916,) p. 104.

13. *Constance Markievicz*, Van Voris, p. 133.

14. *Unmanageable Revolutionaries*, Margaret Ward (Pluto, London, and Brandon, Dingle, 1983) p. 105.

15. *The Damnable Question*, Dangerfield, p. 121.

16. *Ibid.*, p. 119.

17. *Ibid.*, p. 129.

18. *Ibid.*, p. 135.

19. *The Irish Press*, 4 February 1936.

20. *The Story of the Irish Citizen Army*, O'Casey, p. 37.

21. *Doing My Bit for Ireland*, Margaret Skinnider (Century, New York, 1917) pp. 10–11

22. *Prison Letters*, Roper, p. 12.

23. *Constance Markievicz*, O'Faolain, p. 209.

NINE

CLOAK AND PISTOL

WITH STASKO went the last representative of the ordinary and the familial from Con's life. By now all her friends and associates were in one way or another involved with the political movement. This movement had achieved a quickened impetus in the last year that gave everyone a sense of zest and expectation and lit with a roseate glow the dreary halls where they met. Talk gave way to drills and manoeuvres in the hills. The Citizen Army became a familiar sight, Connolly and Constance at its head, as it tramped about the city at night. Twice it carried out a training exercise in which the occupation of Dublin Castle was enacted. The Fianna boys were secretly drilling IRB members in a hall in Parnell Square.

Liberty Hall at night became Nora Connolly's favourite place,

> when the long, dimly-lit hall was filled with men. Stacked around the walls were the rifles, bandoliers and haversacks, and the men sat in groups busily cleaning and polishing parts of the guns, or sharpening the bayonets, while the ruddy light of the fire glinted around them.[1]

Sean O'Casey, sullen on the sidelines, thought it was vanity that sparked the Citizen Army. Vanity 'sparkled from Connolly's waddle, from the uniformed men stiff to attention and from the bunch of cock-feathers fluttering in the cap of the Countess'.[2]

And in a way it was vanity, because what they all knew was that a revolution was planned in which they would man the barricades. They did not know who precisely was planning it or when it would happen; but they knew and hoped that before very long they would be called on to rise as those heroes who were their forefathers had risen before them in every century. They were now familiar with an argument that was reiterated again and again in speeches at political meetings, in the columns of political newspapers, even in the poems of their poet leaders like Pearse, MacDonagh and Plunkett – that it was essential to rise before the war was over and England free from distraction, and that the Irish people were in need of a sacrifice of life to move their minds and imaginations. For too long now, the republican tradition had been to hand on the torch of liberty to the next generation. The intention of this republican generation was to seize the torch and happily sear their hands as they did.

In 1913 at the annual Wolfe Tone celebration at Bodenstown, Patrick Pearse spoke of Tone's object of breaking the connection with England; 'the never-failing source of all our political ills'. The attempt might end in failure as Tone's had, but such, he said, 'is the high and sorrowful destiny of our heroes ... to blind their eyes to the fair things of life ... and to follow only the faint far call that leads them into the battle or to the harder death at the foot of a gibbet'.[3] By 1914 Pearse had been sworn into the IRB by Bulmer Hobson who equalled Constance in his ubiquitousness. The following year at Bodenstown, the Volunteers, the Citizen Army, the Fianna with Con at their head, and Cumann na mBan paraded together for the first time under a unified command.

In 1915 the revered old Fenian, O'Donovan Rossa, died in exile in America and his body was brought to Ireland for burial. All the usual organizations turned out for his funeral procession plus the girl guides and hurling teams. There were thousands of people in the streets. In retrospect, the day can be seen as a kind of dress rehearsal for the organized anarchy that would soon follow. Soldiers and police were conspicuously absent. The various groups took over the stewardship and the control of traffic. And in the gloomy late afternoon, Pearse gave an oration by the graveside:

Life springs from death, and from the graves of patriot men and women spring living nations. ... They think they have pacified Ireland. ... They think they have foreseen everything, they think they have provided against everything; but the fools, the fools – they have left us our Fenian dead, and while Ireland holds these graves, Ireland unfree will never be at peace.[4]

As he finished, three volleys reverberated over the grave. While Pearse's lofty bellicosity was echoed increasingly in all nationalist oratory, his oratory was the most awesome and the most inspiring. 'Bloodshed,' he wrote *in The Coming Revolution* (1913), 'is a cleansing and a sanctifying thing. ... There are many things more horrible than bloodshed; and slavery is one of them.'

In 1915, he spoke of the war in Europe, how

the last six months have been the most glorious in the history of Europe. ... It is good for the world that such things should be done. The old heart of the earth needed to be warmed with the red wine of the battlefields. Such august homage was never before offered to God as this, the homage of millions of lives gladly given for love of country.[5]

These are nakedly bloodthirsty words. But we should not judge Pearse's mystical attitude to violence solely from the standpoint of the present. Long before the outbreak of war, fellow poets such as Stefan Georg, Gabriele d'Annunzio and Rudyard Kipling had, in a similar way, glorified bloodshed; and the first months of the European conflict itself were greeted on all sides by romanticizations of war as a purifying and redeeming and ennobling thing.

The poems of Rupert Brooke are the best-known English examples of this efflorescence. The culture of the day, particularly in the imperialist countries, was euphoric, almost feverish, about war. As late as the summer of 1916 the war correspondent Philip Gibbs could write about 20,000 deaths at the Battle of the Somme: 'It is a good day for England and France. It is a day of promise in this war, in which the blood of brave men is poured out upon the sodden fields of Europe.'[6]

War was not brutal. It was an adventure, for men, where rules were kept and deeds were noble and death was glorious. O'Casey described it as an illusion, 'all guns and dreams but no wounds'. For Irish nationalists, their war had the added element of a religious conflict. The ideas of the Republic were supposedly secular; but many undoubtedly saw themselves as going out to join those who in past generations had been martyred for religion as well as nationality. In Pearse's rhetoric, there was the identification of the soldier dying for Ireland with the crucified Christ dying for humanity. As in a holy war, your martyrdom won you eternal redemption. A young Cumann na mBan woman assured Constance that she was not at all afraid of dying since she knew she would go straight to Heaven.

Women of course, did not have an *entrée* as of right to the councils of war. Those who, like Constance – and she did not come from generations of soldiers for nothing – resisted their given role as cooks and nurses were often accused of being deficient in femininity. But Con's martial ardour was not in itself a problem for her contemporaries, except in so far as it might have been considered inappropriate for a woman. Our present-day attitudes to violence, their probings of our consciences as to whether or whenever it is justified, were not common then, except for a handful of vegetarian, anti-vivisectionist oddballs like the Sheehy-Skeffingtons. Nearly everyone saw violence in a good cause through a gracious haze. Constance's solution to her femininity for the moment was to disregard it, to adopt male attitudes and male practices. What she worried about was whether she should wear breeches as the men soldiers did, and whether her male colleagues were keeping vital information from her.

Her unique position in balancing male and female roles, and in being both part of and apart from things, was pointed up early in 1915 when the Citizen Army and ITGWU presented her with an address, its edges illuminated with Celtic knots, Lissadell in one corner and Liberty Hall in the other, and between them her picture at her most beautiful and Bohemian:[7]

> Madam, the members ... desire to present to you this address as a memorial of the high esteem and affection in which you are held as a result of your unselfish and earnest labours on their behalf during the Great Dublin Lockout 1913–14. At a time when all the forces of Capitalism had combined to crush the workers ... when the prisons were full of innocent men, women and girls, and all looked black before us, you came to our aid to organise relief; and for months worked amongst us and served the cause of labour by such untiring

toil, far-seeing vigilance and sympathetic insight as cheered and encouraged all who were privileged to witness it. ... Inspired and enthused by your example, we were proud to have you amongst us, and now that the fight is over, we desire that you remain one of us, and to that end we unanimously elect you, Countess, as an Honorary Member of our fighting Irish Union.'

It was signed by ten men, including James Connolly. Constance was immensely gratified.

The 'address' was a customary means of expressing loyalty in Irish life. Usually it was presented by a 'grateful tenantry' on the succession of a son and heir to the 'big house' or on marriage and, rather less often, for services he had rendered. Lissadell had its fair share, notably, one presented after the Famine in 1881 in recognition of the efforts the Gore-Booth family made to relieve distress. Constance was not at all put out by any connotations of *noblesse oblige* hers might have. Anyway, the gratitude of those who presented it was decorously combined with their new pride and independence.

An acute observer could have seen that things were hotting up. Each week, Connolly, in *The Irish Worker*, discussed insurrection. He discoursed on Moscow in 1905 and the Tyrol back in 1809. He described the Alamo as 'one of those defeats that are often more valuable to a cause than loudly trumpeted victories'. Elsewhere, the theme of insurrection appeared through the mists of symbolism, but with such opacity and in such obscure publications, that Birrell, the Chief Secretary, and Lord Wimbourne, Viceroy, might be excused for not heeding it: 'The little dark rose shall be red at last,' wrote Joseph Mary Plunkett, using, as Pearse and MacDonagh did, the traditional symbol of the dark rose for the Irish Nation. 'Praise God if this my blood fulfils the doom/ When you dark rose shall redden into bloom.'[8]

A wider readership absorbed the idea from the popular novelist Canon Sheehan's *The Graves at Kilmorna* (1913): 'The country is sinking unto the sleep of death and nothing can awake it but the crack of the rifle. ... As the blood of martyrs was the seed of saints, so the patriot will be the sacred seed from which alone can spring new forces and fresh life to a nation that is drifting into the putrescence of decay.'[9] That this idea of resurrection through blood sacrifice was in the air, part of that strange European zeitgeist, made it less conspicuous, the normal stuff of ranters and poets.

Augustine Birrell, Chief Secretary, was a literary man, a reader and essayist. His attitude to the Irish scene was liberal and benign; and necessarily distant because he spent much of his time in London or rambling in the rural havens of the West of Ireland. He had long decided on handling the Irish situation with tolerance: 'Be aisy, and if you can't be aisy, be as aisy as you can,' he said in a stage-Irish witticism to Sir Matthew Nathan when he sent him over as his Under-Secretary in 1914.[10] He never bothered to proscribe *The Irish Worker* when it began to publish again in 1915 after the general wartime proscription of radical newspapers in the year before. He saw in the signs of disaffection that came to his notice just talk and bluster; and, aware of the might of the British army, would have been of the same mind as Eva and Esther Roper when they saw a parade of the might of Irish nationalism on a visit to Dublin in 1915. They watched from a window as men and women in uniform marched by from the Citizen Army, the Volunteers et al., and Esther, while she thought with admiration of all the gifted people in those ranks remarked with relief to Eva, 'Well, thank goodness, they can't be planning a rising now, not with such a tiny force.'[11]

Birrell knew from police sources how badly armed the Volunteers were. And he knew nothing at all of the renascence of the IRB and its grandiose plans. In fact, by the end of 1915 the IRB Military Council had made a momentous decision. They would lead a revolution against the Crown in the following year. And they had set the date: it would be 23 April, Easter Sunday: Easter Sunday 1916. Joseph Mary Plunkett, the consumptive, flamboyant poet, had been sent to Germany to seek men and arms. Sir Roger Casement followed him there. Both men were met in turn with prevarications and lame compromises from the Germans. Only arms would be sent and, as it would turn out, the usual antiquated lot at that. The conspirators were undaunted. It is now clear that they were impelled by a sense of destiny and inevitability, which it is difficult to rationally comprehend.

The plans taking shape for the Rising were not the work of the Volunteers nor of the members of the IRB who had infiltrated the Volunteers, but of an inner circle, the IRB Military Council, answerable in theory but not in fact, to the Supreme Council of the IRB. Within the Military Council, Tom Clarke was the chief orchestrator. In the years since his return to Ireland in 1907, ironically the year too of Birrell's arrival as Chief Secretary to unwittingly smooth his passage, Tom Clarke watched the demeanour and commitment of promising nationalists, and from them handpicked his fellows on the Military Council.

He chose Patrick Pearse, founder and head of the Irish-speaking school, St Enda's, where inside the door there was a fresco of the boy-hero Cúchulainn with the motto, in Irish: 'I care not if my life has only the span of a night and a day if my deeds be spoken of by the men of Ireland.' Pearse was 'as utterly poetic in his nature as Shelley' wrote the *New York Tribune* later, 'and just as revolutionary and impractical'. He chose Eamonn Ceannt, a minor civil servant from Galway, and son of a policeman; the charming young barman and IRB stalwart, Sean MacDermott; and Joseph Mary Plunkett, the poet-son of Count Plunkett, Director of the National Museum. Plunkett was now in his late twenties, a theatrical fellow who wore rings and bracelets like a hippy of a later day, a taste probably acquired in Algeria and Malta where he spent much of his youth because of bad health. He was chosen largely for his expertise as a military tactician – although his greatest boast was that he could ride a camel with one hand while rolling a cigarette with the other. He was a drinking companion of, and co-edited a literary magazine, the *Irish Review*, with another of Clarke's chosen ones, Thomas MacDonagh.

Thomas MacDonagh was also a poet. He had taught at St Enda's but was now Assistant Professor of English at the National University. He was married to Muriel Gifford, Nellie's sister. He wore a kilt; and was said to be the first man to wheel out his baby's perambulator in the streets of Dublin, harried always by a gaggle of jeering children. These members of the Military Council represented the earnest, romantic, progressive element of their generation. And they were an odd, unlikely and motley set of revolutionary conspirators.

Early in 1916 the Military Council was completed with James Connolly. Connolly was not even a member of the IRB, but by the end of 1915 it was apparent that he had embarked independently on a road to insurrection that was parallel to the Military Council's, and that he might actually lead the Citizen Army in a revolution before they did. On 19 January 1916 Connolly disappeared and, as far as his friends were concerned, went missing for three days. Constance was distracted. She obviously believed he had been seized by the IRB – that much was known through contacts, that he was with the IRB – and, as well as the fear she felt for his safety, she saw the prospect of the revolution they had planned wither away. Michael Mallin found her in the street, quite frantic. She considered mobilizing the Citizen Army and leading a charge on Dublin Castle there and then. She was dissuaded from that course of action.

On 22 January she and some Fianna boys and Helena Molony were having tea in the kitchen at Surrey House when Connolly calmly walked in and stood warming himself by the fire, quite silent and composed. The boys were sent up to bed in double-quick time and Connolly was met with questions and expostulations. He would only say: 'I have been in hell; but I have conquered my conquerors.' During supper, someone else arrived and to her questions he only smiled and said cryptically, 'Oh, that would be telling.'[12] What had happened was that for three days, he was locked in tortuous discussions with Pearse and some other members of the Military Council. They had revealed their secrets to him; that they controlled the Volunteers through the 2000 IRB members in its ranks; that they themselves formed an inner group within the IRB, the existence of which was known to no one; and that they intended to stage-manage a rising on Easter Sunday.

Connolly would have appreciated the necessity for all this secrecy. After all, it was a truism of Irish history that insurrection and rebellions in the past were time and time again done down by informers. His hellish dilemma was that while he was all for a revolution, he was not in sympathy with the aims of the bourgeois nationalists who were about to revolt. He wanted to lead a revolution of the working class. But bargains were struck, adjustments were made in the manner of thinking of both parties, and Connolly emerged as a member of the Military Council.

By February, the rational and realist James Connolly was expressing himself in the rhetoric of Pearse:

No agency less powerful than the red tide of war on Irish soil will ever be able to enable the Irish race to recover its self-respect. ... Without the slightest trace of irreverence but in all due humility and awe, we recognize that of us, as of mankind before Calvary, it may be truly said 'without the shedding of blood there is no redemption'.

Equally, the mystical Patrick Pearse, in his last essay, 'The Sovereign People', appeared to be moving closer to the social ideas of Connolly. So that all of the men and women who make up a nation may benefit, he argued, sovereignty must extend to the material possessions of the nation and 'no private right to property is good as against the public right of the nation'.

Connolly's writings in *The Irish Worker* became ever more militant. The Volunteers and the Citizen Army stepped up their route marches and drilling and target practice in the pleasant open spaces surrounding the city. Various methods of action were pressed on Lord Wimbourne and Mr Birrell by the military, but in their steadfast pursuit of a policy of 'minimum action and maximum inaction' they refused all requests to arrest leaders or seize arms or proscribe organizations.

At Christmas, a young woman called Margaret Skinnider came over from Glasgow to stay at Surrey House. She was a teacher of mathematics, and a militant suffragette, and she brought some detonators hidden about her person. The next day, she and Constance spent the afternoon in the Wicklow Hills trying them out. They succeeded in blowing up a wall; and devised a plan for dynamiting the barracks at Beggar's Bush (near Ballsbridge).

It is rather intriguing that Constance told Margaret that a boat would land in Ireland around Easter Sunday carrying arms for a rising. It suggests that Con had a line of her own to IRB councils before Connolly was implicated. Perhaps she knew through her friendship with Tom Clarke – although it is extremely unlikely that he would have talked about such important matters to someone who was not even in the IRB, let alone on the Military Council. Perhaps she knew it from Sir Roger Casement himself, whom she knew – he had attended a performance of *Memory of the Dead* and went backstage afterwards. But Casement was languishing in Germany then, and so dispirited by his sojourn there that this too is unlikely. One day, a caller at Surrey House found Con at the drawing board at work on a map of Dublin, and was inquisitive about what she was doing. Constance pushed some papers around to hide the map and said she was preparing a housing plan, to replace the tenements, for James Connolly.

On St Patrick's Day, 17 March, 1600 soldiers of the Volunteers and 200 from the Citizen Army marched around Dublin and its environs with their new bayonets, on show for the first time, and glinting in the sunlight. Constance was armed, and to the teeth. 'So much so,' wrote *The Irish Worker*, 'that the casual onlooker might be readily pardoned for mistaking her for the representative of an enterprising firm of small arms manufacturers.'[13] They paraded through Dundrum and Booterstown, Con in her element, as she always was on these long marches. 'She was lovely in uniform,' a Citizen Army man recalled. 'I can remember seeing her marching at the head of the Citizen Army with Connolly and Mallin at a parade one Sunday afternoon. My God, she was *it*.'[14] A week later, there was a scare, which almost resulted in the rising in revolution by itself.

One afternoon when Con was shopping in Liffey Street, she heard that the police were raiding Liberty Hall. There was now a formidable arsenal there and she feared that the arms would be seized and Connolly arrested. She raced over there at once and found Connolly signing mobilization forms for the Citizen Army. 'It looks,' he explained, 'as if we are in for it and they are going to force our hands.'[15] But all the police wanted was the latest edition of *The Irish Worker,* which was in the Co-Operative Shop next to Liberty Hall and they left in fact with the wrong edition, and without entering Liberty Hall at all.

Meanwhile, mobilization was in full swing and unstoppable. Within an hour, 150 men were making for Liberty Hall, having downed tools, abandoned carts, and left customers unattended:

> Staid middle-class men in the streets, aristocratic old ladies shopping, well-fed Government officials returning from lunch, were transfixed with horror when they beheld the spectacle of working men with grimy faces and dirty working clothes rushing excitedly through the streets with rifles in hand and bandoliers across shoulders, on the way to Liberty Hall. Dublin Castle and the Viceregal Lodge were immediately besieged by batteries of telephone calls imploring the British authorities for news.[16]

From then until the fateful day approximately a month later, Liberty Hall was under continual guard and Constance took her turn at the sentry post. But that James Connolly was also playing a shrewd game with the authorities was told by Helena Molony. She would often arrive at Liberty Hall to find some outrageously provocative placard placed prominently outside. 'Citizen Army – Attack on Howth tomorrow. Such and such a company to assemble here. Arms to be carried. Or, Dublin Castle to be attacked at midnight.' Why, she asked Connolly, why 'bring the police on us?'[17]

'Don't you know the story of Wolf, Wolf?' he replied. It was a tactic to lull the authorities and indeed the city into the assumption that the would-be attackers were no more than deluded and harmless fantasists. And it worked. It became a commonplace to say that the Citizen Army was only showing off.

What to wear at the revolution was an absorbing question. It was, after all, an occasion for which there was no precedent. Constance put together an uncompromisingly soldierly rig-out: dark-green woollen blouse with brass buttons, green tweed knee-breeches that could be concealed under a long skirt, black stockings, and heavy boots. She wore a cartridge belt around her waist, with an automatic hanging from it on one side and a Mauser rifle on the other, a bandolier and haversack on her shoulder. 'What do you think of my rig-out?' Constance asked Nora Connolly who calls herself Nono in the following account:[18]

> 'You look a real soldier, Madame,' said Nono admiringly, and Madame beamed as if she had received a tremendous compliment.
>
> 'What's your rig like, Nono?'
>
> 'Something similar. Only I have puttees and my shoes have plenty of nails in the soles. I was thinking of wearing my Fianna hat, but maybe a tam would be better.'
>
> 'This will be my hat,' said Madame, putting on her best hat – a black velour with a heavy plume of coque feathers.

Madame also had had made, with her characteristic generosity, a lovelier uniform than her own for Margaret Skinnider whom she would soon summon as she had promised, in time for the revolution. It was a uniform of fine green moleskin, knee-breeches, a belted coat, and puttees.

Holy Week, the week leading up to the appointed day, began well with plans laid and a revolution on target. It would end in chaos. On Tuesday, the leaders of the Citizen Army were called and told that Sunday was the day. Constance, as a Staff Lieutenant, was there and was appointed as the second of Connolly's 'ghosts'. 'Ghosts,' she wrote, 'was the name we gave to those who stood secretly behind the leaders and were entrusted with enough of the plans of the Rising to enable them to carry on that Leader's work should anything happen to himself.'[19] Michael Mallin was appointed Commandant, second-in-command to James Connolly. Dr Kathleen Lynn held the rank of Captain as chief medical officer.

On Thursday, the idea came to Constance that a flag would be needed. She was at Surrey House with two members of Cumann na mBan, Maire O'Neill and Delia Brennan along with the MP Lawrence Ginnell and his wife who were staying there. Con seemed 'on edge', as she had been all week, and suddenly said she needed material to make a flag 'without giving any indication why the flag was needed' according to Maire O'Neill. She was reminded that the shops were closed, since it was Holy Week, but went upstairs and returned carrying the green bedspread from Larry Ginnell's bed. She cut it out on the drawing-room floor and then, said Maire, placed it on top of the grand piano and directed her and Delia to pull it from both ends:

> Poppet, Madame's pet dog, always had to play a part in whatever she was doing and kept jumping up and down, pulling at the material, until eventually he tore a piece out of the side. ... Wolfe Tone Fitzgerald entered the room as Madame was rescuing the material from Poppet, and she asked him to bring down a tin of gold paint from the attic. She had done no painting for some time and, as might be expected, it had dried up, so she went to the kitchen for a tin of mustard, which, after moistening, she mixed with the paint. ... She commenced to paint the words 'Irish Republic' on the material while we continued to hold it taut.[20]

During the weekend Constance moved into town, staying in the flat over Jenny Wyse-Power's vegetarian restaurant on Henry Street, a meeting place for nationalists. She had her photograph taken, wearing her Citizen Army uniform, in Keogh's Studios on Parnell Street.

There followed in the next few days a baffling series of orders, countermanding orders, and the arrest of the boat, the *Aud*, off Kerry, carrying the German arms.

On the Thursday Bulmer Hobson, although no longer in Clarke's confidence, got wind of the projected rebellion and called on MacNeill. Outraged when he heard of this independent conspiracy, MacNeill countermanded Pearse's significantly couched orders to the Brigade Commanders. Pearse, in turn, told MacNeil of the imminent arrival of the shipment of arms from Germany, and assured him there was a good prospect of success. MacNeill, mollified, rescinded his countermanding orders.

On Good Friday the *Aud*, posing as a Norwegian trawler, was nosing around the Kerry coast in search of the rebels assigned to meet it when it was taken into custody by HMS *Bluebell*. That morning Sir Roger Casement, travelling separately in a German submarine, was put ashore on the beautiful Banna Strand in the vicinity of the rendezvous that was never achieved. Half dead from the water and quite exhausted, he knew some hours of peace in a field amidst 'the primroses and wild violets and the singing of skylarks'[21] before he was found and arrested later in the day. He was sent to Dublin by train and at once on to London to face in due course a terrible and ignominious trial for treason, and for his homosexuality. Sir Roger Casement ended his life on the scaffold in Pentonville Prison the following August.

MacNeill, horrified anew by the loss of German arms, the 20,000 rifles, the ten machine guns, rescinded yet again the orders to move. He also became bitterly aware of the other deceptions practised by his comrades, Pearse, Clarke and others, and was sure he had been badly used. He issued a fresh countermanding order, to be carried by taxi to every corner of the country by The O'Rahilly and others: 'Volunteers have been completely deceived. All orders for action are hereby cancelled and on no account will action be taken.' But the message that most damagingly undermined the plans of the Military Council was an advertisement MacNeill placed in the *Sunday Independent*, which was read countrywide: 'Owing to the very critical position, all orders given to Irish Volunteers for tomorrow, Easter Sunday, are hereby rescinded and no parades, marches or other movement of Irish Volunteers will take place.'

Constance, dressed up for the revolution that would commence that evening at 6.30 pm, read with great shock, like thousands of other would-be rebels, the advertisement in the morning's newspaper. She rushed into Liberty Hall and found Connolly, MacDermott, and Clarke deliberating the new situation. Helena Molony said everyone was 'heartbroken ... When they were not crying they were cursing.'[22] Constance's grief was cut short by Connolly's words: 'MacNeill has cut the ground from under our feet. ... But it will be alright, we are going on. It will only mean a little delay.'[23] They would revolt on the next day instead.

All that evening the self-appointed Provisional Government of the Republic – Clarke, Pearse, MacDermott, and Connolly – directed revised operations. Messengers set out into the city and off on the train to the country districts with the latest set of orders. Copies of the *Proclamation of the Republic* rolled off the printing press. Con picked up a copy and read it out on the front steps, with the print still wet, to the small crowd assembling in Beresford Place with scant regard for the detectives inevitably mingling among them. All the signatories of the Proclamation were men; in fact, the members of the IRB Military Council. But Constance was the first to publicly proclaim the Republic.

Previous risings, such as the Fenian Rising of 1865, had been bedevilled by the arrest of the leaders before the event, on the word of spies. In 1916 the Provisional Government escaped this fate by the skin of its teeth. The authorities, like the rebels, had their own secrets. The Secret Service had succeeded in cracking German radio codes and knew for a long time about the *Aud* and Sir Roger Casement and the rising that was planned for Easter. It tried to pressurize Birrell into arresting the Sinn Féin leaders, as it called them, around Easter Sunday.

Since Birrell could not be told, for vital security reasons, how the Secret Service knew about the trouble it was predicting, he failed to be convinced of the urgency of departing from his long-standing policy of quietude. Anyway, he was in London that weekend, at a remove from Dublin 'where the air was thick with rumours', and his anxious under-secretary and army officers were more or less appeased when they saw MacNeill's advertisement and Easter Sunday passed without apparent incident. Under the circumstances, however, this latest bid for freedom could not but go off at the traditional inglorious half-cock.

The degree of diminution of the revolutionary forces is shown by the experience of Éamon de Valera, Commandant of the Third Battalion of the Irish Army of the Republic, as the combined forces of the Citizen Army and the Volunteers were now called. Only at five o'clock on Sunday evening did de Valera learn with relief that the rising would now take place on the next day, at noon. He tried to let as many of his men as he could know this; but when his battalion met at Great Brunswick Street (now Pearse Street) at 10 am to march to their post at Boland's Flour Mills, they numbered only 140 out of an expected 500. Boland's Mills was recognized as a key position. It overlooked the road by which it was thought reinforcements of troops arriving from England through Kingstown Harbour would try to enter the city. De Valera's well-laid plans for its defence demanded 500 men. In the same way, the commandants of each of the five commands found their muster sadly reduced and their plans in jeopardy.

NOTES

1. *Portrait of a Rebel Father*, Connolly O'Brien, pp. 266–7.
2. *Drums Under the Window*, O'Casey, p. 267.
3. *Ireland Since the Famine*, Lyons, p. 333.
4. *The Damnable Question*, Dangerfield, p. 147.
5. *Culture and Anarchy in Ireland*, Lyons, p. 90.
6. Now hangs in Liberty Hall, Dublin.
7. *Culture and Anarchy in Ireland*, Lyons, p. 89.
8. *Ibid.*, p. 91.
9. *Dublin Castle and the 1916 Rising*, Leon O'Broin (Helicon, Dublin, 1966) p. 27.
10. *Prison Letters*, Roper, p. 14.
11. *The Irish Press*, 11 February 1937.
12. *The Workers Republic*, 1 April 1916.
13. *Constance Markievicz*, Van Voris, p. 167.
14. *Portrait of a Rebel Father*, Connolly O'Brien, p. 263.
15. *The Workers Republic*, 1 April 1916.
16. *Portrait of a Rebel Father*, pp. 265–9.
17. *Prison Letters*, Roper, p. 38.

18. Report of a conversation with Maire O'Neill, *The Irish Times*, 28 February 1968.

19. *The Black Diaries of Roger Casement*, eds Peter Singleton-Gates and Maurice Girodias (Grove Press, New York, 1959), p. 414.

20. *Eire*, 26 May 1923.

21. *The Black Diaries of Roger Casement*, eds Peter Singleton-Gates and Maurice Girodias (Grove Press, New York, 1959), p. 414.

22. BMH (Bureau of Military History) Records, WS Helena Molony.

23. *Eire*, 26 May 1923.

TEN

THE EASTER REVOLUTION, 1916

IT WAS NOON. And it was comparatively hot for a Dublin spring day. Being Easter Monday, it was a holiday, and the citizenry strolled in the sun-lit streets, moving desultorily along Sackville Street, the widest street in Europe it was said, stopping on the bridge to gaze up the torpid Liffey at the graceful eighteenth-century building of the Four Courts, or downriver towards its sister, the Custom House, that faced Liberty Hall. If the activity there seemed more frenzied than usual, they took little notice. After all they were used to zealots in uniform milling about and parading in the streets.

Past Trinity College and up fashionable Grafton Street they sauntered, under the pleasant shade of summertime awnings, to take a turn in the public gardens of St Stephen's Green where Edwardiana, relatively unmolested by the war or rumours of war, still thrived. Couples promenaded, the ladies in new hats and dresses to the ground. Nannies flopped on park benches under the trees while their charges fed the ducks on the dappled pond. The promenaders were fewer than they might have been, and there were hardly any military men, because there was a race meeting at

Fairyhouse and many had gone there, or to the sea at Kingstown or Howth, or into the country for the day.

Down in Beresford Place, Constance watched with great happiness as the Army of the Irish Republic left Liberty Hall and proceeded up Abbey Street towards Sackville Street. A less fervent observer would have noted, perhaps with a degree of amusement, the pathos of this small marching army on its way to battle. The Headquarters Group at the front was smartly turned out. James Connolly was at its head in his Citizen Army uniform, his bayonet and hardware gleaming and his boots highly polished. On his right was Patrick Pearse with his pale, striking face. On his left was Joseph Plunkett, paler still with mortality, his smart grey-green Volunteers uniform consorting oddly with his throat bandaged from an operation he had undergone for glandular tuberculosis a few days before and the bangles and heavy rings he always wore.

Behind them, the column presented a motley appearance. Some were in full Volunteer uniform; others had concocted a military look for themselves from incongruous hats, leggings, tunics and bandoliers. Many had only an armband or brassard to show their allegiance and many of them did not yet know why, or to where, they were marching. Their fighting equipment revealed an equal dearth of resources. Two drays rumbled along in the rear, bearing Howth Mausers; shotguns, rifles, pikes; and ammunition and explosives from Belfast that had been ferried around in Dr Kathleen Lynn's car during Holy Week. The column turned into Sackville Street and drew up almost at once directly opposite the great Palladian structure of the General Post Office. 'Company halt,' shouted Connolly. 'Left turn – the GPO – charge.'

The charge was a short one; and then of course there was some jostling as they rushed the door. Bewildered customers queuing up for stamps were informed that they were impeding a revolution and were firmly hustled, protesting, outside. Within minutes, the GPO was a fortress in the possession of the Irish Republic and an unfamiliar tricoloured flag, green, white and orange, flapped above the classical pediment with, next to it, Constance's green flag with a gold harp and the words 'The Irish Republic', in case the tricolour defied interpretation. Half an hour later, Pearse emerged on the low step of the Post Office and read out to an unimpressed group of bystanders the Proclamation of the Irish Republic that he and Connolly had composed: 'Irishmen and Irishwomen: In the name of God and of the dead generations from which she receives her old tradition of nationhood, Ireland, through us, summons her children to her flag and strikes for her freedom ...'[1]

The Proclamation is an obvious compromise between Connolly's socialist aspirations and the mere democratic nationalism of the IRB. In declaring the right of the people of Ireland to the ownership of Ireland, it could be greeted with approval by both parties and its generalized statements left future arrangements open to discussion. It was the first Constitution to include the principle of equal suffrage: 'The Irish Republic is entitled to, and hereby claims, the allegiance of every Irishman and Irishwoman. The Republic guarantees religious and civil liberty, equal rights and equal opportunities to all its citizens ...' It has nobility of its own, and among the declarations of revolutionary intent that have appeared since the American Declaration of 1776, it is noteworthy both in its prose and in its aspirations.

The Proclamation was signed, with their habitual exclusiveness, by the seven members of the Military Council. Constance, doubtless, would have dearly liked to put her name to it, and she did deserve to, more than most. She, meanwhile, in her role as liaison officer between the various posts, had driven off with Dr Kathleen Lynn to deliver medical supplies. Dr Lynn's car was about the only four-wheeled transport this revolution could boast. The bicycle, on the other hand, was everywhere. Each battalion had a Cycle Corps. Revolutionaries turned up at their posts on bicycles. Michael Noyk, the IRB's solicitor, saw 'several Volunteers on bicycles with guns strapped across their shoulders cycling fast up Camden Street'. Bicycles carried messengers, food and ammunition from outpost to outpost. And Maire ni Shiubhlaigh made sure to leave hers safe at a friend's house on Camden Street before reporting to Jacob's, where she found Volunteers in their green uniforms climbing up the front walls of the factory and breaking windows to get inside. Even years later, she thought it the greatest moment of her life.

The rebel plan was to occupy public buildings strategically ringed around the city and adjacent to the different military barracks. By now this was accomplished, although plans of campaign had to be altered and improvised because of the shortage of men. Offices, mills, etc. were conveniently empty of workers since it was a holiday. Downriver from O'Connell Bridge, de Valera had easily taken Boland's by ejecting the bakers who had just put a thousand loaves of bread in the ovens. Upriver, the Four Courts, under Commandant Edward Daly, was taken with equal ease. To the south, Jacob's biscuit factory under Commandant Thomas MacDonagh was taken, as was the old workhouse, the South Dublin Union, under Commandant Eamonn Ceannt.

Constance's company, the Citizen Army under Commandant Michael Mallin, had marched up to St Stephen's Green and with difficulty persuaded the people drifting among the trees that they needed the park for a revolution. Another detachment of the Citizen Army had marched up Dame Street to Dublin Castle and the City Hall next to it. A half-hearted attempt was made to seize the Castle. The first casualty of the week, Constable O'Brien, was shot as he stood at the gate. The rebels entered, bound some soldiers hand and foot in the Upper Yard, and then withdrew. They did not know it, but the Castle was theirs for the taking. Only two officers and twenty-five soldiers were in the barracks at the time. It could be supposed that seizing the Castle was never part of the plan. But it seems that bewilderment on the part of the revolutionary rank and file as to how far they were meant to go and disbelief that this was for real was the reason for the retreat. It would be practically impossible to defend the straggling complex of buildings that the Castle comprised, but on the other hand, holding it even for a short time would have been of major tactical importance. It was the centre of military telecommunications, and news of the rising might not have permeated to the outside until all positions had been strengthened.

The withdrawal to City Hall overlooking the Castle seems to express the symbolic character the rising had assumed. The leaders knew victory was impossible. 'We are going out to be slaughtered,'[2] Connolly had whispered to a friend as he led his men out of Liberty Hall. In the street that morning, as she was coming from Winifred Carney's in Belvedere Place where she had passed the night, Constance had met The O'Rahilly who was of the same opinion. Yet he had done an about-turn from his countermanding activities in Kerry and travelled through the night to be there. 'It is madness' he told her, 'but a glorious madness and I am with you.'[3] All they cared about now was that the drama to which their lives in the last year had been a prologue was begun.

Dr Lynn's open-topped car, driven by Mark Cummins, arrived at City Hall with Constance in her characteristic high spirits, standing up and waving her plumed hat, and calling 'Go at it boys' to her old Fianna graduates. Here Dr Lynn was dropped off – 'me and my medical traps'[4] – and Constance and the driver drove on to carry out liaison duties between the different positions. Most of the women of the Citizen Army lacked Con's grand daring in wearing breeches and had ripped their long skirts when they climbed over the iron gates of City Hall. Inside, Helena Molony was in charge of the commissariat in the caretaker's kitchen and the Red Cross station, while men had scaled the roof and were exchanging fire with the military in the Castle Yard. From this vantage, they controlled the entrance to the Castle, so the place was effectively under siege, if not incommunicado.

It was on the roof of City Hall that the revolutionaries had their first casualty. He was Sean Connolly, an actor at the Abbey, and would be immortalized by Yeats some months later as 'the player Connolly' in the poem '1916'. By the time Dr Lynn had crawled across the bullet-pocked roof to where Helena was cradling his head on her lap, he was dead. The others went on to Jacob's, Constance calling out exuberantly when they got there, 'The Citizen Army are taking the Green, Dublin Castle is falling.'[5] They went on then to Stephen's Green, driving the car boldly inside.

Much has been made of allegations that here Constance was responsible for the shooting of Constable Michael Lahiff, who would die later that day in the Meath Hospital. They would seem to be entirely unfounded, the evidence differing hugely on such crucial matters as the time of the shooting, its location and the dubious nature of an account by the purported eyewitness, a nurse called Geraldene Fitzgerald. The DMP placed the time of the shooting for instance at 12 pm, while Miss Fitzgerald's account puts it as occurring at 1 pm at the earliest. If noon is correct, which is the most likely, it occurred when Constance was at City Hall.

And it took place at the main entrance to the Green, the Fusiliers' Gate when the revolutionaries were entering the Green, while the eyewitness locates it on the west side adjacent to Harcourt Street. There are other aspects too of the so-called evidence that cast serious doubt on its truth.[6]

Of course in any case the purpose of taking the Green was to prevent the police and soldiery from making their way to the other fortified positions in the city centre and since this was not a dress-rehearsal for a revolution but for real, it was the duty of a soldier on either side to do his or her duty. However, considering her actions on not dissimilar situations over the next few days – one of them involving another policeman, Sergeant Hughes, whom she released unharmed (though he was shot and wounded by a sniper as he left the Green) – it would be more characteristic of Con, if she had been there, to take Constable Lahiff prisoner.

The revolution here, apart from this incident, was proceeding in a relatively playful and decorous manner. Mary Hyland and Kathleen Cleary had taken over the summer house for their commissariat and had laid out a tasteful array of sandwiches, hams, cheeses and cakes. Madeleine ffrench-Mullen had taken the glass conservatory as her first-aid shelter. Inside the railings that bounded the Green, men were busy digging trenches in the fashion of Flanders. On her arrival, Constance was told by Commandant Mallin, silk-weaver and musician in his everyday life, that she could not be spared as a liaison officer but must take her turn as a sniper. To this, she was proud to assent. Soon, Mallin appointed her his second-in-command.

For some time, to the bemused audience squinting through the railings, the scene had the appearance of a charade. The women laying out the picnic-teas, the men digging with the warm sun on their backs; the air laden with the scent of spring flowers and the hum of insects; and Mallin and Markievicz, guns at the ready, authoritatively pacing around. It was soon apparent that the tactic of possessing the Green was a bit of a mistake. Tall houses overlooked it on three sides and the fourth was dominated by the massive structure of the College of Surgeons. Once the military got through, as they must, and took over the buildings on the perimeter, the rebels pinned inside the Green would be sitting targets.

Commandant Mallin, Constance and a small party therefore sallied forth, commandeered some houses and placed men inside them.

The Shelbourne Hotel, the highest and most commanding building, could have been taken but strangely it was not. Instead, snipers contented themselves with taking pot-shots at its decorative facade whenever a figure in khaki appeared in a doorway or window. Some British officers lunching there – the Shelbourne was a favourite watering-hole for officers and gentry – gamely opened fire with their revolvers and were outraged to see a woman, who would be later identified as the Countess Markievicz, emerge from behind a tree at intervals and expertly return their fire. To block the progress of troops who could be expected on any of the ten approaches onto the Green, barricades were constructed at four key positions. Carts, bicycles, furniture and cars were seized at gunpoint and piled in the roadway. At this point, the writer James Stephens, returning meditatively from lunch to his office in Merrion Square, inquired of a man why groups of people stood so silent in the street and gazed with such steadfastness in the direction of the Green. 'Don't you know?' the man replied. 'The Sinn Féiners have seized the city this morning.'[7]

Stephens ran to the Green. He saw men inside with guns over their shoulders. He saw abandoned trams pushed over on their sides, and the barricades constructed from anything to hand. Cars bowling citywards were held up, their drivers were saluted and removed as politely as their protestations allowed, and the cars were driven into the mounting barricades. Stephens saw that many of those with revolvers were mere boys and was struck by the fevered and abstract expression in their eyes. During the afternoon, Constance, with two women and four men, emerged from the gate on the west side of the Green and crossed the street to the College of Surgeons. She ordered that the caretaker and his wife be locked in their rooms for safety and then the building was searched. They found skeletons and human organs embalmed in jars, but nothing living. The men stayed there as a holding force and the women returned to their positions on the Green.

Constance had a sister sniper in Margaret Skinnider, who had brought the detonators from Glasgow at Christmas and had been lately summoned by Con as promised. It was Margaret who later crossed the road again with a tricolour, which was hoisted on the roof of the college. Other posts had not got off so lightly. A troop of cavalry of the 5th and 12th Lancers was returning, quite innocent of the morning's events, to barracks from the North Wall with a routine convoy of ammunition, when they ran into the rebels holding the Four Courts. Six were killed at once, and the rest blundered under fire around the small streets behind the Four Courts. At the South Union, there was fierce fighting throughout the day, with heavy casualties suffered by the 3rd Royal Irish and outnumbered Volunteers alike. A handful of de Valera's men commandeered a number of houses, including Clanwilliam House on Mount Street Bridge, by evicting the occupants with as much politeness as the situation allowed and with assurances of compensation for damage by the republican forces.

Rebels, in the early days at least, were determined to protect the honour and good name of the nascent Irish republic. This sense of honour of the men in the GPO was affronted by the dwellers of the slums and tenements, which pressed close around Sackville Street. Seeing at once the possibilities presented by the suspension of everyday life they were braving the flights of lead to indulge in a delirium of looting. Nobletts confectioners, Saxone shoes and Lawrence's toyshop were broken into, offering a delightful junket for people who passed them by every day but who rarely or never had the wherewithal to buy anything. They arrived with handcarts and piled them with incongruous heaps of merchandise. A dead horse lay in the road, a forlorn reminder of the incursion of a troop of cavalry earlier in the day; and women sat on the dead horse, with evening dresses under their shawls and munching luxury confections while their children ran about in silk top hats firing airguns in imitation of the rebels who watched helplessly. The rebels thought it all abject and degrading to the revolution but how could it be stopped? It was clear they would have to shoot the people. Commandant Connolly refused to take this step.

As shops were looted, they were set alight. A woman was trapped on a top storey. People could be seen walking around their upper rooms, unaware of the fires spreading below them. A fire engine arrived to fight the first of a never-ending series of fires. At five o'clock, as the shadows of the trees lengthened on the pavements, Stephens returned to the Green. A crowd stood watching as before. He saw a man who attempted to remove a cart lodged in one of the barricades fall dead as 'a rifle spat at him'. 'There was a hole in the top of his head,' wrote Stephens, 'and one does not know how ugly blood can look until it has been seen clotted in hair.'[8] At that moment onlookers hated the Volunteers.

However, most Dubliners did not know what to think of the day's events and the audacity of the Sinn Féiners, or Shinners as the revolutionaries were known colloquially. Many of them would, by tradition, support in theory, a rebellion – but when it was for real, and inconvenient and dangerous. Others, the South Dublin middle class, for example, were, with exceptions, outraged, and trusted it would be quelled with all haste and firmness. Very few, apart from the participants, were actually keen on it. As dusk drew on, people re-entering the city from their day out with tired, whimpering children in tow, were irate to find the trams not running – the stations had been seized and the lines ripped up at some points to hinder the movements of troops – certain streets impassable, and the city preparing for siege. In the following days, as the shops remained closed and food and milk deliveries were interrupted and rumours spread and tales were told of uninvolved citizens getting shot and killed, they grew more irate still.

Behind the barricades, the first day of the revolution ended in euphoria. All attacks had been valiantly repulsed. In holding Dublin for a day, this revolution had already gone farther than any of its time-hallowed predecessors. Robert Emmet's, after all, had lasted for only two hours. And there was the persistent if ill-founded belief that the Germans would soon arrive with reinforcements. The military seemed in disarray.

German aid would not come. And the military, after its initial astonishment, had rapidly organized. Troops were arriving by train from the Curragh military camp at twenty-minute intervals. An entire division was on its way from England. And Birrell, distraught at the errantry and betrayal of his charge, and at his ruined career, was preparing to return to Dublin. Inside the Castle, his under-secretary, Sir Matthew Nathan, though besieged, knew things were again under control. Reinforcements were able to enter the Castle by the gateway on Ship Street, without running the gauntlet of the snipers on the roof of City Hall. All the same, the scene in the Castle Yard was 'a strange and awful one' according to a Castle official, Hamilton Norway: 'The yard was lit by torches and crowded with men and soldiers. Among them from time to time a woman was carried in, caught in the act of carrying ammunition to the rebels and fighting like a trapped cat.'[9]

There were about 120 revolutionaries of the ICA in St Stephen's Green on the first morning, of which about fifteen were women. They were joined by several Volunteers who had missed their mobilization orders or who couldn't make it to their own posts. A Professor of Romance Languages at the National University, Liam O'Broin, and a friend were wandering around in search of a rebel company to join, propped their bicycles against the railings of the Green on the urgings of those inside, and climbed over. The revolutionary forces numbered about 1000 in all. The night's discomfort was mixed with a sense of triumph and expectation. On the morrow, they would meet a renewed cavalry and bayonet charge, but today they had acquitted themselves well. Many were nervous and tense, not having fired a gun before, certainly not at a human target, an inexperience they shared with the khakied war recruits who would be their opponents. Many had had no access to food during the day and few of those who had were able to eat. It was a cold night to spend huddled on roofs and parapets and on the lawns and benches of the Green. Constance climbed into Dr Lynn's car, curled up on the upholstery, and fell asleep.

During the night, a hundred soldiers and a machine-gun crew moved stealthily out of the Castle, down Dame Street and up Kildare Street, and arrived at the Shelbourne without incident. The hotel was occupied, the machine guns placed on the fourth floor and, by four in the morning, the dozing occupants of the Green were under fire. One man died at once and another was wounded. The dawn battle raged for nearly three hours. Constance lay in a trench with Michael Mallin opposite the hotel, and twice her aim resulted in a temporary cessation of machine-gun fire. The insurgents were forced, however, to retreat to the south-west corner where shrubberies, tall trees and a mound of earth offered protection. But this too proved inadequate and they soon decided to abandon the position and retreat to the College of Surgeons.

Crossing the road under fire was hazardous, especially for the nurses who were easily targeted in their white hobble-dresses. One girl got her skirt ripped by a bullet, another had the heel of her shoe torn off. But the retreat was accomplished in twos and threes without serious mishap. Five bodies were left behind in the Green.

A rebel on the roof of the College, Michael Doherty, had lain slumped over the parapet since dawn, his blood staining the facade. Captain Joseph Connolly, brother of Sean who had died at City Hall, courageously went up and brought him down, still alive. By 7 am the erstwhile defenders of the Green were assembled in the College of Surgeons. After the sunlit lawns and foliage, it seemed to them an unwelcome and inhospitable place.

The huge cold rooms smelled of formaldehyde and they did not like the brooding presence of the glass cases and jars containing strange objects and pickled organs. Worst of all, they had been obliged to leave their provisions, the hams and pies and cakes, behind in the summer house. Most of them rolled up in rugs and carpets and fell asleep at once on the floor.

Food was a problem for insurgent and citizen alike. Many of the rebels, hidden away on roofs and in isolated outposts, did not eat for days on end. Mothers and sisters turned up at back entrances to present food parcels. In Boland's, they had any amount of bread and flour and fruit cake. In Jacob's, they had the cream crackers and the ham all battalions seem to have stocked up with, and some 'chocolate slab stuff'[10] they used for cocoa. In City Hall, Helena Molony found some oatmeal and made porridge. The rebels occupying the Pillar Cafe in Sackville Street had bacon and eggs for breakfast every day. In Jacob's, they had a 'great stew' when a side of beef was commandeered – Maire ni Shiubhlaigh sent out 'a great-little fellow Bob Donohue' to find some onions.

Often food supplies travelling about the city were requisitioned by the rebels who ventured into the streets, usually on bicycles, to waylay the carts. In Stephen's Green, two young Citizen Army women, Lily Kempson and Mary Hyland, held up a milk float at gunpoint. Three women arriving at the College from the GPO with some ammunition also had bread, cheese and OXO cubes, bought with money James Connolly gave them for provisions. Hanna Sheehy-Skeffington brought bread, potatoes and oxo cubes, with which they made bouillon. But hunger was endemic, especially in the GPO. As the week went on, rebels began to hallucinate, to imagine things, to see faces in the sky, and to fall asleep at their posts.

On Tuesday, Trinity College, skeletally defended by the Officer Training Corps the day before, was reinforced; and with the British now in command of the Castle and Trinity, the rebel outposts were cut off from their headquarters at the GPO. All outposts expected attack at any moment. They expected this to take the form of a bayonet charge. The wait would prove interminable. That night, an exchange of intensive fire broke out between the Shelbourne Hotel and the College of Surgeons. A party was sent meanwhile to dig through the houses next to the hotel and set fire to the buildings on that side. But after some time, Constance made her way through the tunnels to say the exploit was to be abandoned.

Margaret Skinnider was a despatch rider and used to change from her uniform into a demure grey dress and hat for her cycling trips to the GPO. She found 'an exalted calm' there. By Wednesday, she was thirsty for action and suggested that she and Joseph Connolly should ride up to the Shelbourne on bicycles and hurl bombs through its windows. Instead, she was sent on a less suicidal mission to the Russell Hotel, on the corner of Harcourt Street and the Green, to get rid of a sniper on its roof. Her patrol came under fire from Harcourt Street, from the Sinn Féin headquarters now occupied by soldiers. One of the party was killed at once and Skinnider was severely wounded. William Partridge carried her back to the College; and she cried only when the coat of her uniform, which Constance had given her, was cut away to get at her wounds. Then Constance and William Partridge went up Harcourt Street, Margaret remembered, and 'cleared out' her attackers.

Margaret developed a fever and was nursed by Constance, a 'natural nurse'. She grew delirious; and when she heard some time in the afternoon the boom of great guns, she thought 'Everything's all right now, that's the Germans attacking the British.'[11] It was, of course, the British attacking the Irish. Two nine-pounders were newly mounted on the roof of Trinity. When they opened fire, the boom shook the walls of the GPO and the College itself, and every pane of glass in the area shattered. Every half-minute a shell was lobbed through the windows of Kelly's fishing-tackle shop on the corner of Sackville Street – Kelly's was a rebel outpost – but by the time the nine-pounders were at work, the snipers had broken their way through its walls into the shop next to it and from there to the next one. James Stephens used to walk around the city each day to observe the revolution. He watched the bombardment of Kelly's and saw the six strategically placed machine-guns firing into Sackville Street. He knew then that the street was doomed.

Earlier that day the gunboat *Helga* had come up the Liffey and dropped anchor opposite the Custom House. The *Helga* then opened fire on Liberty Hall in the belief that hundreds of insurgents were holed up inside. Only the caretaker, Peter Ennis, was and as the bombardment commenced, he darted into the street and got away. When the *Helga* ceased its pounding, Liberty Hall still seemed to be intact. The walls stood, but its interior was blown completely away. The arrival of the artillery was a great blow to the rebels. It was something they hadn't considered – that they might be fired on with such force and from such a distance that they could not fight back. They had envisaged charges of infantry, in which the enemy would present themselves in great numbers and they would engage them in a glorious fight with bayonet and rifle and hand-to-hand combat.

Apart from the foray in which Margaret Skinnider nearly met her death, the Green was relatively quiet. A dead horse lay in the road. Bandoliers and rifles lay abandoned in the park and urchins braved the fire of snipers to retrieve them. Sniping broke out periodically from roofs and windows. James Stephens found the crowds that gathered near the flashpoints though voluble, strangely reticent in expressing opinions on the whole affair. The women, he wrote, tended to be more hostile and more forthright than the men. 'They ought to be all shot,' they would say, 'I hope every man of them will be shot.'[12] While they exchanged information and rumour and news, they offered little comment. They also displayed a foolhardy insouciance in spite of the bullets whistling around their ears and the roar of the great guns, gathering where these were heaviest and as regardless of them as of the flight of birds. Civilians inevitably died – shot at street corners, in doorways, watching from windows; here, a stray bullet caught a woman as she walked home with a can of milk, there, a man as he mounted his own stairs. And yet, Stephens detected an element of pride in the reactions of Dubliners to the revolution, a feeling of gratitude for 'holding out for a little while', for saving them the humiliation of being quickly beaten. And, he wrote, Dublin curiously 'laughed at the noise of its own bombardment and made no moan about its dead' – in public at least.

There was one group of women who were vituperative in their hostility to the rebellion – perhaps the women Stephens heard speak out against it in the streets. These were the so-called 'separation women', the wives of Irishmen who had joined up for the duration of the war and who were fearful that the rebellion would jeopardize their 'separation allowances'. One such woman who attacked a Volunteer reporting to Jacob's on the first day of the rebellion was shot dead in front of Stephens. The starkly differing reactions of the Dublin populace astonished the military who were new to Ireland and did not know what to expect. On Wednesday, two battalions of the Sherwood Foresters landed at Kingstown (now Dun Laoghaire) and were marched towards Dublin about eight miles away. Along their route, maids emerged from fine houses carrying jugs of orangeade and trays of sandwiches while their mistresses proffered cups of tea. These boys had come to their rescue. At Mount Street Bridge, one of the battalions ran into an ambush. Two houses at the bridge were occupied by a handful of Volunteers, and from this advantageous position they routed the oncoming tide of khakied soldiers in a terrible battle lasting nine hours. Over 230 Foresters were killed or wounded while a number of Volunteers incredibly escaped with their lives. It was modern Ireland's Pass of Thermopylae. And all week, the occupiers of the College of Surgeons, Boland's Mills and Jacobs' hoped for a frontal assault like it, when their guns would burn in their hands and their heroism could be truly tested. Constance fretted that she did not have the weapons that were appropriate to the combat. 'I'll have to get a bayonet or a sword or something' she is said to have told Michael Mallin.[13]

All week it was perfect weather. For years afterwards a hot sun in a blue sky was described as 'rebellion weather'. Through it all most of the Irish Citizen Army was cooped up in the cold shadowy spaces of the College of Surgeons, increasingly bored and very hungry. For some days there was nothing to eat. An outpost sent a request for food to Nellie Gifford who was in charge of the commissariat, but she could muster only a little rice. At intervals potshots were exchanged with the Shelbourne Hotel and surrounding houses. At night they gathered in a lecture-room to sing rebel songs and recite the rosary.

The British, under General Lowe, had decided to concentrate their efforts on the GPO. Their resources were now formidable. The initial force of 2500 men had swelled to over 5500, all with some training as soldiers and well equipped. The cordon drawn around Sackville Street grew ever tighter. By Thursday Abbey Street was ablaze. Soon, Bolton Street to the north and Lower Sackville Street were also ablaze and flaming so brightly that the night sky glowed with a phosphorescence paler than daylight. Constance stood on the roof of the College and watched Dublin burn. Inside the GPO the heat was almost unbearable. James Connolly had an arm wound and had had his ankle shot away. He was in great pain but still directed operations from a bed, his incisiveness and cheerful calm inspiring confidence in everyone.

On Friday morning Sackville Street was a wasteland, palled in smoke and dust. Every now and then, there was the awful rending sound of collapsing masonry. An acrid smell hung over the city. That evening, an incendiary shell landed on the roof of the Post Office, setting it on fire, and the building quickly began to burn uncontrollably. At 7 o'clock in the evening, Headquarters was evacuated to neighbouring streets and houses. At 9 pm the General Post Office collapsed in ruins. At 9.50 pm the flagpole bearing the tricolour fell from its position into the street. The wounded, including Connolly on a stretcher, were carried with difficulty through the maze of tunnels and holes that connected their former HQ to adjoining shops on its western side. They spent the night, with the battle raging in their ears, in O'Hanlon's Fish Shop at 16 Moore Street. The O'Hanlon family retreated to the cellars for safety leaving their shop upstairs to be the last headquarters of the Provisional Government of the Irish Republic.

On the following day at noon, the decision was taken to surrender. Elizabeth O'Farrell, a nurse, walked into the devastated street carrying a white flag and was brought to General Lowe. At half past three, Patrick Pearse handed his sword to General Lowe in the unconditional surrender the general had demanded. Pearse issued a communiqué to be despatched to all remaining outposts. It read:

> 29 April, 3.45 p.m. In order to prevent the further slaughter of Dublin citizens, and in the hope of saving the lives of our followers now surrounded and hopelessly outnumbered, the members of the Provisional Government present at Headquarters have agreed to an unconditional surrender, and the Commandants of the various districts in the City and Country will order their commands to lay down arms.
>
> P.H. Pearse.

The surrender was countersigned by James Connolly on behalf of the Citizen Army: 'I agree to these conditions for the men now under my command in the Moore Street District and for the men in the Stephen's Green command. James Connolly.'

By nightfall 400 revolutionaries, many of them with begrimed and ravaged features from the rigours of the week, were herded into Sackville Street. They passed a cold, hungry and apprehensive night huddled together with ruins all about them and the air heavy with the stench of rotting horseflesh. In the morning, they were marched to Richmond Barracks. Also in the morning – it was now Sunday – Elizabeth O'Farrell was driven up Grafton Street. From there she walked the short distance to the College of Surgeons bearing her white flag and copies of the order to surrender. Michael Mallin was asleep and she met Constance as second-in-command. The College erupted in confusion at the news. Some refused to believe in the order to surrender but Constance repeatedly insisted, 'I trust Connolly. We must obey.' At one point, a British soldier entered the hall, under the impression that the surrender was effected, 'unarmed, bareheaded, smoking a cigarette'. An insurgent lifted his revolver to shoot but Constance stopped him with, 'Don't Joe. It would be a great shame now.'[14]

Captain de Courcy Wheeler, King's Royal Rifle Corps of the Anglo-Irish Ascendancy and a relation by marriage of the Gore-Booths, received the surrender from Commandant Mallin and Lieutenant Markievicz at the side door of the College. Before handing up her gun and Sam Browne belt Constance 'reverently kissed' her weapon, saluted the Captain, and said 'I am ready'. The Captain's gallantry demanded that he offer to drive her in his car to the prison, and of course her gallantry demanded that she refuse. She marched off with her Commandant at the head of her fellow, and sister, revolutionaries. On the way, she and Mallin discussed the one questionable aspect of their futures. Were they to be shot or hanged?

NOTES

1. See illustration no. 17.
2. Connolly said this to the Labour leader, William O'Brien. *Constance Markievicz* , Van Voris, p. 188.
3. *The Sunday Independent*, May 1966.
4. Bureau of Military History Records, WS Lynn.
5. *The Splendid Years*, ni Shiubhlaigh, p. 168.
6. See Author's Introduction.
7. *The Insurrection in Dublin*, James Stephens (Scepter, Dublin, 1965) p. 17.
8. *Ibid.*, p. 25.
9. *Ibid.*, p. 87.
10. Rough draft of Maire ni Shiubhlaigh's memoirs in the National Library, Dublin.
11. *Doing My Bit for Ireland*, Skinnider, p. 206.
12. *The Insurrection in Dublin*, Stephens, p. 38.
13. *The Easter Rebellion*, Max Caulfield (Muller, London, 1964) p. 319.
14. Recounted by Professor Liam O'Broin in the *Capuchin Annual 1966*.

ELEVEN

'DEAD HEARTS, DEAD DREAMS, DEAD DAYS OF ECSTASY'

YOUNG REBEL and medical student Brighid Lyons spent the last night hours of the rising in the Four Courts, wrapped in the ermine and sable robes of the judges. On Sunday morning, she and some other women were loaded into an army truck going to Richmond Barracks, and that evening when they were lined up for the march to Kilmainham Prison, she found herself beside Countess Markievicz in her elegant uniform. The rebels were glad, for once, of their military escort because, as they left the Barracks, they were met with a clamour of insults from the 'Separation Women' who had not been paid that week due to the cessation of normal life and its bureaucracies and feared they would not be paid again. A lot of the hatred, said Brighid Lyons, seemed to be directed at the Countess's breeches.[1]

Kilmainham was awful, as dark and as wretched as any prison of the time; but for a fervent revolutionary, to be incarcerated there had a certain *éclat*. It was Ireland's Bastille and figured in her rebel songs and stories because many of the illustrious had spent time there – Napper Tandy from 1798, Robert Emmet and Anne

Devlin from 1803, William Smith O'Brien from 1848.

Fenians from 1867 had been there, such as O'Donovan Rossa and John O'Leary, and, later, Charles Stuart Parnell. The pride Constance must have felt at joining this roll of honour was undermined by being placed in a single cell, isolated both from the other women and from the male leaders of the Rising who were kept on the same corridor but with whom she was unable to make any contact. Some of these men had, for the time that remained to them, at least the consolation of each other's company.

Liam O'Broin, for instance, from the College of Surgeons, was placed in a cell with Joseph Plunkett, Willie Pearse, Tom Clarke and Thomas MacDonagh. Liam had a blanket, which he had brought from the College and he was asked to let Plunkett have it because he was very ill and was lying racked with pain on the floor. For the next few days, Plunkett, still in his smart uniform and boots, used the blanket, sometimes as a bed, sometimes folded up for a pillow. Tom Clarke, Liam O'Brien noticed, was just as he used to be in his tobacco shop – still wearing the same clothes and smiling to himself occasionally. He seemed to be very satisfied, thought Liam, with himself and with the situation. He saw Sean MacDermott fall asleep with his head on Clarke's chest. Constance was entirely alone.

Dublin, indeed Ireland, spared the rebels little sympathy. The Separation Women were by no means the only element to feel outrage and anger. The city had suffered great discomforts and inconveniences. It was still suffering the indignity of the martial law imposed during the week. About 250 civilians were killed, as against sixty-eight insurgents, and many more were among the 2217 wounded. Many had relations among the 132 members of the crown forces killed and almost 400 wounded. The beautiful main street of their capital city was in ruins. It was estimated that damage to property amounted to £2,500,000. On the Friday, General Maxwell, late of the Egyptian campaign, had arrived in Dublin to take charge of the situation and announced that 'In view of the gravity of the rebellion' he found it imperative 'to inflict the most severe sentences on the organisers of this detestable Rising.'[2] The newspapers, by and large, couched the hope that he would do so in more extreme and judgemental form.

Yeats' sister Lily provided her father, Jack B. Yeats, who was living in New York, with a running commentary on its aftermath: 'Sackville Street is gone. The Pillar stands up alone in a rugged plain. You cannot find Abbey Street or Earl Street. The RHA is gone. Some of it is smoking still.'[3] Her comments suggest the remoteness and relative peripherality to many Dublin people of the political movements that had brought about the devastation. And her Sligo connections meant she was both preoccupied with and disparaging about Constance:

> What a pity Madame Markievicz's madness changed its form when she inherited it. In her father it meant looking for the North Pole in an open boat. Very cooling for him and safe for others. Her followers are said to have been either small boys or drunken dock workers out of work, called the Citizen Army. I don't think any others could have followed her. I would not have followed her across the road.[4]

Patrick Pearse was, like Constance, in solitary confinement. On the third morning Constance heard a volley of shots from the court-yard at dawn. She supposed they represented the executions of some insurgents but did not know who. They were Pearse, MacDonagh and Clarke. On the fourth morning, there was the same awful volley. This time four men were shot, including Pearse's brother Willie, and Joseph Plunkett. On that day Constance was taken from her cell and brought, as those executed had been, to stand trial before a secret military tribunal. The judge, she wrote contemptuously, was 'a fuzzy little officer with his teeth hanging out to dry'. The principal witness was a page boy at the University Club in St Stephen's Green who described how he saw her aim at the club from behind a monu-ment in the park, and fire: 'I ran upstairs,' he said, 'and saw where the bullet struck. After firing she walked up towards the Shelbourne Hotel dressed in knickers and puttees.'[5]

Legal advice was not permitted but Constance cross-examined the boy, reduced him to tears, and caused him to change his evidence when she adopted a high moral tone and asked him whether he had been put into the industrial school for thieving. A few hours later, her court-martial took place. The accusation was that she:

> 1) Did an act to wit did take part in an armed rebellion against his Majesty the King, such an act being of such a nature as to be

calculated to be prejudicial to the Defence of the Realm and being done with the intention and for the purpose of assisting the enemy. Did attempt to cause disaffection among the civilian population of his Majesty.

She admitted both charges: 'I told the Court that I had fought for the independence of Ireland during Easter Week and that I was as ready now to die for the cause as I was then.'[6]

Another story often told against her is that this account she gave was not true and that in fact she 'whimpered' and curled up 'like a cat' and begged for mercy, saying 'You can't shoot a woman'. But this appears nowhere in the court transcripts. The first report of it appears in a memoir, written years later when Constance was dead, by William Wylie, a British army officer and prosecutor at the court-martials and a man not biased to say the least in favour of rebels.

On the fifth day at dawn, the volley of shots rang out again. To the prisoners in Kilmainham, the realization of what these daily volleys meant came only gradually, but then with shattering force. Brighid Lyons said, 'For months afterwards I always woke at that hour and I've never forgotten those volleys, never.'[7] That evening, a kind English soldier on guard came to sit with Con in her cell, offered her a cigarette and told her that Pearse, Clarke and the others had been joined that morning by Maud Gonne's estranged husband, John MacBride. The following day, as she stood on the table in her cell attempting to see out through the high barred window, an officer came in to read to her the results of the court-martial: 'Guilty. Death by being shot. The Court recommend the prisoner to mercy solely and only on account of her sex.' The Confirming Officer, General Maxwell, had then added: 'Confirmed. But I commute the sentence to one of Penal Servitude for Life.'

To Constance, then, it seemed the worst possible outcome. Her comrades in the heroic act, who had become dearer to her than life itself, were dead or soon would be dead; while she, as a result of one of those random privileges offered to her sex, must face the contemplation of their failure alone, and in ignominy. It was a privilege she did not want. 'I wish,' she told the officer who brought the news, 'you had the decency to shoot me.' Esther Roper wrote of how Constance had inveigled another prisoner,

Maire Perolz, into her cell, by asking for the loan of a comb but really because she wanted to tell her, 'Oh, Perolz, did you hear the news. I have been sentenced to death.' And when a priest brought her clothes to wear in Kilmainham, she refused them, saying gaily 'I'll die in the clothes I fought in.'[8]

Her family had been working for a reprieve, Eva, frantically, in London, and Sir Josslyn, more soberly, in Ireland. Some of her acquaintances were not at all sympathetic. Sir Horace Plunkett wrote in his journal that the Countess Markievicz 'is deeply dyed in blood but her motives were as noble as her methods foul. I met Powerscourt (Lord Powerscourt) and he was, he told me, begging the authorities to shoot her.'[9] Éamon de Valera also had his death sentence commuted, probably because he was of American birth, as had Thomas Ashe, for reasons that are less clear.

For two days dawn passed without the dreadful reverberations from the courtyard. On Monday 8 May they came again, despatching Con Colbert and Sean Heuston, old Fianna boys, and Eamonn Ceannt and Michael Mallin, Constance's commander in the Green. On the 11th Eva and Esther Roper crossed to Dublin on the night mail that also carried Asquith, the Prime Minister. Asquith left London with the knowledge that James Connolly was now deemed fit enough to face the firing squad and would be executed at dawn. When the boat docked at the North Wall, Connolly was dead. His gangrenous leg meant that he could not stand to face the guns and had had to be shot sitting down, tied onto a kitchen chair, to keep him upright. Eva and Esther – and Asquith – disembarked to find the news shrieking from every hoarding in the town: 'Execution of James Connolly'; 'James Connolly shot this morning'.

By now Constance had been transferred to Mountjoy Jail on the north side of the city so was spared the relentless morning chorus. Eva and Esther went straight there, through streets that looked newly 'muddled and desperate', Eva wrote, 'as if everybody, even the very houses, were crouching down, hiding from something'.[10] A rumour had circulated in London that Constance's body had lain in the Green for several days, and Eva was immensely relieved to be able to discern her sister's face, shadowed though it was by bars, across the passage and two small barred windows that divided them. A warden paced up and down the passage as they spoke. To Eva, she seemed calm and smiling despite her odd prisoner's cap.

The first enquiry Constance made was for James Connolly. As she read the truth in their faces, tears ran down her cheeks as she said 'You needn't tell me. I knew. Why didn't they let me die with my friends ?'[11] She rallied quickly and began to talk very fast of her adventures, of the week she had passed in the College of Surgeons. 'But why on earth did they shoot Skeffy?' she wanted to know. 'After all, he wasn't in it. He didn't even believe in fighting.' The death of pacifist Francis Sheehy-Skeffington was one of the random excesses of the week. During the Rising, a British army officer, Captain Bowen-Colthurst from Cork, had ordered the shooting of a number of innocent civilians in a kind of irrational private campaign. They included two loyalist journalists and Skeffy, arrested as he walked home from pasting up anti-looting posters.

Constance was also preoccupied with the welfare of Michael Mallin's widow, who was expecting a baby, and begged Eva to find her. Four days later on 16 May, Con wrote a letter to Eva that shows her at her most splendid. She faced a lonely and squalid future but she did not brood or betray any self-pity at all. The letter is brisk, resilient and optimistic, and is also interesting because it shows her domestic side that co-existed happily with her abstract and idealistic nature. Kathleen Lynn would later say that while 'you might gather from her manner that she was fantastic she was full of sound sense and was quite practical'.[12]

> Dearest old Darling, It was such a Heaven sent joy seeing you, it was a new life, a resurrection, though I knew all the time you'd try and see me, even though I'd been fighting and you hate it all so and think killing so wrong. ... Now to business. ... [she wanted all her furniture stored since she had been relieved of the tenancy of Surrey House] There is a lot – I don't want anything thrown away. ... Don't store furniture with Myers, he was a brute to the men in the strike.

She wanted Eva to see about letting the house in Frankfort Avenue and to pay various household bills. 'You dear old darling, it's such a bore for you. I feel rather as if I was superintending my own funeral from the grave.'

She wondered about her bike, and Poppet and Mrs Connolly's welfare. And she wanted Bessie Lynch who was 'a beautiful laundress' set up in business somehow: 'You could let her know I haven't forgotten her and that the 10/– a week is only to keep her safe and happy till something can be arranged. It's much better for people to earn their own livings if they can.' She wanted 'poor Bridie Goff my servant' to get a month's wages at least and the rent to continue to be paid on 'the little hall in Camden Street'. There is a little of 'noblesse oblige' about the letter – but it basically displays Con's sense of responsibility and her wish to make reparation for the difficulties brought about in peoples' lives as a result of her actions:

> I feel I'm giving you such a lot of worries and bothers, and I feel too, as if I hadn't remembered half. Anyhow it's very economical living here! And I'm half glad I'm not treated as a political prisoner as I should feel so greatly tempted to eat, smoke and dress at my own expense. In the meantime I live free, all my debts will be paid. ... Now darling don't worry about me, for I am not too bad at all; and it's only a mean spirit that grudges paying the price. Everybody is quite kind, and though this is not exactly a bed of roses still many rebels have had much worse to bear. The life is colourless, beds are hard, food peculiar, but you might say that of many a free person's life, and when I think of what the Fenians suffered and of what the Poles suffered in the sixties I realise that I am extremely lucky.[13]

In fact, Surrey House had by now been looted both by military and citizens. Books, pictures and furniture were smashed or carried away. A box of lantern slides was wantonly trampled on and the hand-press that was used to foment revolution was broken up. When Margaret Skinnider visited the house in August, she thought it had 'that peculiar look of bereavement some houses wear'.[14]

Eva and Esther returned to London some days later. In the following weeks as Constance languished in the Joy (as Mountjoy Prison is known in Dublin) surrounded by familiar things – 'seagulls and pigeons, which I had quite tame ... little boys splashing in the canal ... a most attractive convict baby with a squint, and soft Irish voices everywhere'[15] – Ireland experienced a change of heart. The official executions ironically achieved what the Rising had not. In the centuries-old manner they created niches for martyrs and heroes. Liberal opinion, disturbed by the rapidity and vindictiveness with which the executions were carried out, soon became convinced they should not have happened. The people began to revere the dead as they did saints and martyrs of the Church.

John B. Yeats wrote to Lily from New York on 12 May with a radical change of tone from his previous missives: 'Those poor heroes, for they are heroes and martyrs even though their attempts were folly. And yet these feather-headed enthusiasts have perhaps done more for Ireland than years of politics would do.'[16] Lily, formerly so caustic, wrote to tell her father of how General Maxwell – 'in fact the public executioner' – turned up with Lady Fingall at a party:

> He came with Lady Fingall very late, about 20 to 11 o'clock. There was a silence and a gasp when he came in. If he had not been in uniform the shock would have been less. I felt myself looking at his boots for bloodstains. James Stephens turned a yellow green and looked as if he would be sick. Susan Mitchell left at once. ... He is a short stout ruddy man, looking as many of the men in uniform do, rather unwashed and overheated.[17]

Stories abounded of the nobility of heart and mind of the dead. How James Connolly, whom many believed to be an atheist, had gone to his death with a priest by his side; how Joseph Plunkett and Grace Gifford were married in Plunkett's cell by candlelight the night before his execution; of the defiant and well-made speeches they delivered before they died. In June, Maxwell was forced to write to Asquith that it was true there was 'a strong recrudescence of Sinn Féinism. Young priests and militant women – of them there seems to be a strong contingent – encourage this in every possible way.'[18] Then, and for a long time afterwards, it was women who made up the national movement and who developed its revolutionary character. The men were dead, imprisoned, or interned. About 2000 of them, among whom were many whose connections with the movement were tenuous, were rounded up, deported, and incarcerated in a prison camp in Frongoch in North Wales. Tom Clarke had left the IRB fund, amounting to £3100, to his wife Kathleen – who was as fiercely republican as he was – to set up a Volunteers' Dependents Fund. This provided a focus and a purpose for Cumann na mBan, many of whose members were still at liberty.

As pictures of the dead began to appear like icons in shop windows and postcards bearing their likenesses were sold on the streets, Cumann na mBan kept up a consistent campaign to ensure they were not forgotten. Every month there were Remembrance Masses where printed handbills were distributed. Nora Connolly, Nellie Gifford and Margaret Skinnider were among a group of women who went to America on a propagandist lecture tour. By June, Maxwell was writing to the Home Office:

> It appears to be desirable that the Countess Markievicz should be removed from Mountjoy Prison, Dublin to some prison in England. From censored letters it appears that sympathizers know how she is getting on in prison and that in some way information is leaking out. This would be quite possible through the Visiting Justices ... eight of whom are elected by the Dublin Corporation which, it is well-known, has strong Sinn Féin sympathies. ... This lady is the only prisoner convicted for rebellion who is now in Ireland.[19]

And Con wrote a hurried note to Eva on lavatory paper:

> Darling. I am alas! going into exile. Make a point to try to get in to see me. I believe you could by influence. Remember, I don't mind being in jail. ... My only desire is to be of use to those outside in the long tedious struggle with England. I am going to Aylesbury. Shall be quite amiable. ... My family must be quite amusing about my latest crimes. ... I told you to write to Casi and try and get the news through.[20]

Another smuggled note said 'If it's better for the cause to leave me in just leave me ... I am glad that M(aeve) was amused and not shocked. Best love and many kisses and hoping we may someday meet again ...'[21] Whether Maeve was indeed 'amused' or not we can't be sure. Eva may have used the phrase to reassure Constance – or to reassure Eva, Maeve may have put a brave face on it and affected amusement. In 1916 Maeve was at a boarding school in England and to be revealed as having such a scandalous revolutionary for a mother and called 'the rebel's daughter' can't have been entirely amusing.

With her own characteristic courage, Constance presented a smiling face to her sister and those around her. But a poem she wrote in memory of James Connolly at this time betrays her inner anguish – and also shows that she was steeling her courage to her 'stern destiny'. There is often speculation as to whether she and Connolly were lovers. He often stayed in Surrey House and pre-revolutionary Ireland did not have the puritanical attitudes towards sexual love it would later assume. Certainly the tenderness of her words in this poem could imply that they were perhaps more than comrades. But the poem may simply be revealing that the most intense emotional bond she knew, in recent times at least, was with her brothers in arms, especially Connolly, and all the more now that he was dead. That Con gave the poem to a warden before she was removed to England would suggest this as the most probable interpretation:

> You died for your country my Hero-love
> In the first grey dawn of spring;
> On your lips was a prayer to God above
> That your death will have helped to bring
> Freedom and peace to the land you love,
> Love above everything.

The weeks in prison and their deaths had not cooled her ardour or killed her hopes, on the contrary:

> For the woman you found so sweet and dear
> Has a sterner destiny -
> She will fight as she fought when you were here
> For freedom I'll live and die.[22]

She enjoyed the sea-crossing to England, 'a sunny porthole and a fresh breeze'[23] and the sight of an airship.

Among the Irish rebels, Con's period of imprisonment in Aylesbury Jail was unique. The men, imprisoned at Dartmoor and Reading and interned at Frongoch, were together, enjoyed relatively free association and had, according to one internee, 'the life of Riley'.[24] They played football, organized singsongs and concerts and Irish classes – and most importantly, furthered their revolutionary education. They drilled, trained themselves in the military arts, and plotted and planned for the guerilla war that would ensue in Ireland. Constance, as the only convicted woman prisoner, was placed among women convicted of ordinary criminal acts – prostitution, abortion, infanticide and theft. Most of them had no interest in politics, certainly not Irish politics.

Helena Molony was also at Aylesbury, along with Nell Ryan and Winifred Carney (who had been in the GPO), but as internees they were in a separate section reserved for those suspected of espionage. They had no contact with Con, apart from the exchange of significant glances with her in chapel on Sundays and an occasional surreptitious note; and twice a day, they stood on a high step and waved to her across a dividing wall as she made her way across a yard to the wash house. In the autumn the three women presented an unprecedented request to the Home Office. They asked to be allowed to live as convicts in Constance's section and agreed to forego, if this request was granted, their privileges as internees: the food, visits, letters, and even their 'right' to communicate illicitly with the outside world. The request was refused.

Prison conditions in 1916 were truly punitive. As well as loss of liberty, prisoners were subjected to a regime of near-starvation, a dangerously squalid environment and a gruelling routine of hard labour and absence of intellectual stimulus. At Aylesbury, they rose at 6.30 am and had breakfast alone in their cells – lukewarm tea and two ounces of bread. At noon, they got two ounces of meat, one potato, two ounces of vegetables, usually cabbage, and six ounces of bread. On Fridays, they were given boiled fish. At half past four, they had a supper of a pint of cocoa or tea and four ounces of bread. Constance found the red coarse meat impossible to eat and Eva finally succeeded in persuading the Home Office to allow her a glass of milk each day instead. She became extremely gaunt and the governor accused her of untidiness as her prison clothes became too big and had to be hitched up. She was always hungry. She told Eva and Esther one day that 'All prison does for people is to teach them to use bad language and to steal. I was so hungry yesterday I stole a raw turnip and ate it.'[25] She later wrote that the necessary preoccupation with food did give a certain desperate dynamism to days that might otherwise have been unbearably dreary: 'We had a certain community of hatred that gave one mutual interests and the mutual sport of combining to pinch onions, dripping or rags. Doesn't it sound funny and mad? But it kept one going.'[26]

At first, Constance worked in the sewing room where nightgowns and underwear were made from hard unbleached calico for the prisoners. It was a posting envied by the other inmates because it was warm and dry in comparison with other areas in the cold, damp, run-down jail. But she soon chafed at the inactivity and asked to be transferred elsewhere. She was sent to the prison kitchens and later described what the work there was like:

> The dinners were served in two-storey cans, used indiscriminately among 200 women and, more, some of the cans were very old and musty. A great many of the women were known to be suffering from venereal disease and at the time an attempt was made to keep their tins separate. This was dropped after a while. There was no proper accommodation for washing these 400 tins. I used to do 200 with another convict. We did our best to get them clean in a big terra-cotta bowl on the kitchen table and to dry them on two towels. Sometimes the water would not be hot, sometimes there was no soap or soda, and then you could neither dry nor clean the tins. Many of the tins were red with rust inside.[27]

She described the alarming lack of hygiene, which pervaded throughout the prison; how the porridge ladle was 'left for the night in a dirty pail with the brush which was used to sweep the lavatory'; how the dress she was given on entry 'was so dirty that I cannot describe it', and her shoes, discarded by a convict who had been released, were 'full of holes, which let in the ice and snow'. The one horror 'always hanging over the prisoners' heads', she wrote, 'was the fear of catching loathsome diseases'.

The long weeks of privation and hard labour scrubbing pots and pans and kitchen floors were broken by Eva's monthly visits and by occasional, though often less welcome, visits from old friends of her debutante days who interested themselves in her plight. Sir John Leslie, who had brought her out on the lake on the velocipede when she stayed at Castle Leslie, came. He was as affectionate towards her as ever and wrote to Eva that, since he was serving as an officer in Ireland after the Rising, he wondered 'what the dear child would say if she knew I was commanding the garrison here, defending bridges and controlling the district'.[28]

A more patronizing visitor was the Dowager Duchess of Bedford who made it clear that she regarded Constance as an unfortunate sinner. When the Duchess asked her if she were saying her prayers, Con got her own back by opening her eyes wide and replying, 'Of course. Why, don't you?'[29]

She was indeed saying her prayers – though not of a kind perhaps which the Duchess would have entirely approved. She had decided to become a Catholic and was taking instruction from the Catholic chaplain to the prison. She later described to Esther Roper how 'a vision of the Unseen' had come to her on the last night in the College of Surgeons as her assembled companions knelt as usual to pray. From then on, 'things seen became temporal and things unseen eternal'. Life, she said, changed for her then.[30] In Mountjoy she had written of this epiphany in a verse dedicated to William Partridge who had been a source of strength and courage to everyone throughout that week:

> The great hall fades away into the gloom,
> As tremulous night falls slowly from above,
> Merging us each in each in tender love:
> One shadow marching onward towards one doom.
> On our rough altar white flowers shine and bloom
> Intensifying dusky waves that move
> Around the tall black Cross. One hope, one prayer
> Filled all our hearts, one perfect holy Faith
> Lifted our souls. As we knelt humbly there,
> Your silvery voice, soft as a dying breath,
> Was answered by a hundred strong and clear,
> Craving a grace from her whom all hold dear
> Mary! be with us at the hour of death.[31]

This religious awakening removed a barrier that had divided her from the majority of her soulmates in revolution, and was probably only obvious to her for the first time with those late-night vigils in which she could not share. At the same time, it cut her off irrevocably from the culture of her background.

To Protestant and Catholic alike, one's religious affiliation was a badge of one's political and social identity; and to forsake the belief of one's birth aroused hostile reactions. A Clareman wrote of his daughter who had converted to Catholicism:

> If she persists she passes out of our life for I must protect my younger children from such influence within their home and by reason of the bitter shame she will put on her mother and myself, and these are as nothing to the scandal which will be caused in these parts by a child of mine deserting their Church.[32]

The reaction of Con's family was not at all as severe, but they would have regarded her 'turning' as a further, perhaps final, rejection of all that they stood for.

Prisoners were allowed to write one letter a month and it seems Con always wrote hers to Eva, her natural ally and confidante. Con's new religious awareness may partly explain the strange quality Eva found in these letters. On receiving the first letter, Eva wrote to their cousin Jane L'Estrange in Wicklow, that Con 'has developed a queer dreaming faculty, she dreamt all the circumstances of Father Walter's death in the beginning at Mountjoy and she is always dreaming odd trifling things about me queerly correct'.[33] Of course, since letters were censored and so many subjects of immediate interest to the prisoner could not be written about, it is not surprising that Con seemed exceptionally remote from her surroundings. She could not write about politics or prison conditions – but a couple of fragments she managed to have smuggled out uncensored show an incisive, typically rebellious and down-to-earth attitude towards the miseries of prison life:

> Let me know the Trade Union conditions for workroom temperatures. The T.U. should have a visitor or inspector here. They should start jail reform. The people are all poor people, and they should see to them ... . These questions should be asked me and all political prisoners at a visit: What do you weigh? What was your normal weight? What do you get to eat? Can you eat it?
> How much exercise do you get per day?
> How often do you get clean underclothes?
> Are you constipated? Can you get medicine?
> What temperature is the room you work in?
> What is your task? How much do you do in a week?...
> If they won't let me or any of the others answer, push to get answers by every possible means.[34]

Con's letters to Eva reveal her confidence that they would be received with absolute acceptance and understanding. They reveal as well the bond of affection and mutual respect between the two sisters that had thrived despite their differences in temperament and ideas and the years they had spent apart. After Eva's death Maeve destroyed in a moment of anger and distress, according to Esther Roper, her side of the correspondence. But Con's letters, which survive, are an indication of how engaging and admirable her nature was, and how unconventional – which may explain why she aroused an antipathy in others more staid. Her letters are full of her originality, her vigour and her spontaneity. At forty-eight, she was girlish in the best sense of the word – questing, proud, defiant, irrepressible and resilient.

She used to greet Eva as 'Dearest' or 'Beloved old darling'. She described her thoughts and her dreams – 'Look it up in a dream-book' and she always made her letters as buoyant and humorous as she could, thus relieving Eva of worry about her emotional welfare at least. And, while she may have got religious, she never became pious or 'holier than thou': 'I am quite patient and I believe every-thing will happen for the best. One thing I should enjoy getting out for and that would be to see the faces of respectable people when I met them! I don't like to send anyone my love for fear that that most valuable offering would be spurned.'[35] There was 'a great crop of carrots ... which we pass every day, going to exercise round and round in a ring like so many old hunters in a Summer'. She enquired about family, friends and the 'rebelly crew'. She especially hoped for and expected news of Casi and wanted pictures of Eva and Maeve.

That summer Eva was also preoccupied with the fate of another prisoner, Sir Roger Casement, who was tried for treason, convicted and sentenced to death. Despite Eva's and many others' efforts to obtain a reprieve, he was hanged in early August. Con's plight, in comparison with the finality of death, may not have seemed so terrible. There was after all always the possibility of release at some time in the future.

Con and Eva were not above sisterly competitiveness. Con sent poems she'd written to Eva, the poet, and Eva in turn took up drawing. Their respective comments were critical but supportive. Constance used to insist that she knew she had no talent for poetry. 'I am now going to lapse into verse. I want you to criticize. Tell me something about metre and what to aim at. I am quite humble and I know I'm not a poet but I do love trying...' She transcribed some lines, overly reminiscent of Wilde's 'Ballad of Reading Gaol' perhaps, but powerful all the same, and deprecatingly added, 'Of course, I know it's only jingle:'[36]

High walls hang round on every side
A cage of cruel red,
The sickly grass is bleached and dried,
As brick the flower bed.

The fierce rays of the sun down beat,
The burning flagstones scorch our feet,
As in the noonday's blighting heat
We walk with weary tread.

The poems and drawings she worked on at Aylesbury are contained in a prison-issue notebook, a large-leaved lined hardcover folio.[37] Each of its ninety-four pages was numbered to prevent its use for illicit communications and the prisoner was sternly reminded that 'entries respecting prisoners or the prison administration are not permitted'. Unable to make any reference to her immediate surroundings, Constance filled the pages with fanciful images.

Her confinement in small spaces behind bars and weeping stone made her long for light and the unbounded freedom of sea and sky. She drew scenes from her Sligo childhood and peopled them with characters from the distant heroic past – Cúchulainn and Fergus; Maedhbh, bearing a strong resemblance to her own daughter Maeve; Deirdre and Naoise ... Her themes are often allegorical, perhaps to fox the censor. A bound figure lying on the ground she calls 'The Curse of Cromwell'. 'Where I Would Like to Be' portrays a barefooted, timeless figure seated on rocks by a bay and gazing over the placid water. The trees in these landscapes are always the twisted storm-stunted bushes of the west of Ireland and the mountain in the background is generally Ben Bulben. This was the past that Con and Eva shared most vividly; and now when they thought of each other each evening at a time they had fixed, it was perhaps there they went imaginatively together, where, as Eva wrote 'waves break dawn-enchanted on the haunted Rosses shore, / And clouds above Ben Bulben fling their coloured shadows down, / Whilst little rivers shine and sink in wet sands at Crushmor.'[38]

The prison authorities considered the Countess de Markievicz, on the whole, a well-behaved prisoner. In prison, she found a quiescence and abnegation that flatly contradict the common perception of her as a histrionic and attention-seeking self-publicist. She wrote to Eva:

All my life in a funny sort of way seems to have led up to the last year, and it's all been such a hurry-scurry sort of life. Now I feel I have done what I was born to do. The great wave has crashed up against the shore and now all the bubbles and ripples and little me slip back into a quiet pool of the sea ... I am often afraid that you are much more unhappy than I am. I feel a quiet, peaceful, a *nunc dimittis* sort of feeling.[39]

Once only did she feel called on to make a political protest. At a time when the Germans were making headway in the war, the convicts were brought to the church to pray for British success. Constance refused to go, as did a German spy, and another prisoner of Irish birth, the colourful May Sharpe, known as Chicago May, who was serving a fifteen-year sentence for swindling and other nefarious activities. In her memoirs, Chicago May described how the guards, in retaliation, made the three women

carry enough gruel around the prison to feed the entire two hundred convicts. We had to carry immense heavy cans up winding stairs. While we were doing this, the Countess recited long passages in Italian from Dante's Inferno. The place looked like hell all right, with the lights dimmed and musty-smelling bags tacked across the windows, as a precaution against bombing.[40]

Chicago May greatly admired Con's spirit and they became firm friends. Constance also sought to make friends with one Alice Wheeldon, a woman of about Con's age and a socialist, who was serving a ten-year sentence for attempting to poison Lloyd George with a phial of curare. Alice Wheeldon always denied the charge and when Constance greeted her in the passage with an equable 'Oh, I know you, you're in for trying to kill Lloyd George', Mrs Wheeldon protested 'But I didn't'.

On the first anniversary of the Rising, Easter Week 1917, Constance wrote a verse:

Dead hearts, dead dreams, dead days of ecstasy,
Can you not live again?
Nay, for we never died ...[41]

As far as she knew, her future contained only dreams, deathless though they might be. But the past year had not been uneventful in the world outside. As the British, in the shape of General

Maxwell, hardened their hearts against the rebels, public opinion in turn hardened against Britain. Sinn Féin and Cumann na mBan increased in strength. Seditious and revolutionary talk became the norm in all strata of society. In August Cumann na mBan elected Constance as its President *in absentia*. A Friends Committee, that included two Aldermen as well as Madame O'Rahilly and Mrs Pearse, was working to win her political status and succeeded in persuading local authorities etc. to pass resolutions of protest in her favour. She was especially pleased by reviews of *The Death of Fionavar*, a verse-play of Eva's, which Constance illustrated and which came out during 1916.

The play describes how Maeve, the Warrior Queen, was chastened by the death of her compassionate daughter, Fionavar, and sought the life of a contemplative. Written in Eva's characteristic mystical vein, it ends: 'The winged Horse shall be harnessed to many ploughs, but in the end there is freedom and the aether vibrates to the rhythm of unseen Light.' Con's illustrations suggest an idealized Sligo, the land of Faery, of winged horses, bubbling torrents, flowers and birds and serpents and stringed harps. In September, the *New York Times* devoted an entire page to the book and the Gore-Booth sisters. Its approach to Constance's activities, echoing American opinion generally on the Irish question, and which the British government could not much longer ignore, was approvingly partisan. 'It is said,' claimed the reviewer, 'that the clocks at Lissadell are kept running at English time instead of Irish' – Ireland still kept its own time, about half an hour behind Greenwich Mean Time – and he described her drawings for Fionavar' as 'cabalistic'.

By Christmas the 600 internees at Frongach had been released, and returned home to find themselves heroes. And on 23 December the remaining Irish women confined on the other side of the wall at Aylesbury, Winifred Carney and Helena Molony, were allowed to leave. The revolutionary movement was not long in re-grouping. In the spring of 1917 Sinn Féin put up two candidates in by-elections, one of them an IRB man imprisoned in Lewes Jail, and won both of them. In April the United States entered the war as Britain's ally – one result of which was increased pressure on Britain to display magnanimity towards the Irish problem. Constance, among the 122 Irish still in prison, continued to make the best of things. Nowhere is her capacity to live and find intensity in the present moment more evident than in her final letters from Aylesbury. A request to 'Please ask Joss to give Maeve £1 to buy an Easter egg' is juxtaposed with comments on the bird she tamed enough to come to her windowsill for scraps: 'The B.B. will have finished pecking at her evening meal by now and is probably preening her feathers and wondering what I am doing ... The one thing I am learning here is to watch everything closely, whether it is trees or blackbeetles or birds or women.' But there are also suggestions of profound boredom and of desperation kept firmly at bay. To the flowers in her cell that well-wishers had sent, she talked 'nonsense ... and they are great company ... The hours slip by, like rosary beads of dragon's teeth, with a big glowing opal bead to mark the rhythm of your visit ...'[42]

On 15 June Bonar Law, Leader of the House of Commons, announced that all participants in the Rising would be shortly released, and that he had arranged for a Home Rule convention to take place in July. On 17 June Eva was informed by the Home Office that she could go to Aylesbury next day to take her sister away. And next day, Constance, 'thin but beautiful again in a blue dress' that Eva had brought for her, arrived in London, at the flat in Fitzroy Square which Eva and Esther shared. It was the centre of wild celebrations; there were flowers and messages and well-wishers including Helena Molony and Maire Perolz who had come over from Ireland to greet her. Next day, she visited sympathizers at the House of Commons and provocatively took tea and a seasonal plate of strawberries and cream on the terrace.

NOTES

1. *Curious Journey*, Kenneth Griffith and Timothy E. O'Grady (Hutchinson, London, 1982) p. 78.
2. *The Damnable Question*, Dangerfield, p. 209.
3. *Prodigal Father. The Life of John Butler Yeats*, William M. Murphy (Cornell University Press, Ithaca, 1978) pp. 253–4.
4. *Ibid.*, p. 450.
5. *Prison Letters*, Roper, p. 25.
6. *Freeman's Journal*, 19 June 1917.
7. *Curious Journey*, Griffith and O'Grady, p. 84.

8. *Prison Letters*, Roper, p. 97.
9. *Horace Plunkett*, Margaret Digby (Basil Blackwell, Oxford, 1949) p. 27.
10. *Prison Letters*, Roper, p. 46.
11. *Ibid.*, p. 48ff.
12. *Ibid.*, p. 137.
13. *Doing My Bit for Ireland*, Skinnider, p. 206.
14. *Prison Letters*, Roper, p. 149.
15. *Prodigal Father*, Murphy, p. 632.
16. *Ibid.*, p. 452.
17. *Leaders and Men of the Easter Rising, Dublin 1916*, Martin: 'Markievicz and the Women of the Revolution' by Brian Farrell, , p. 236.
18. *From War to Civil War in Ireland*, F.S.L. Lyons (Weidenfeld & Nicholson, London, 1973) p. 83.
19. *Constance Markievicz*, Van Voris, p. 217.
20. *Ibid.*, p. 217.
21. In the National Museum, Dublin.
22. *Prison Letters*, Roper, p. 150.
23. *Curious Journey*, Griffith and O'Grady, p. 93.
24. *Prison Letters*, Roper, p. 70.
25. *Ibid.*, p. 196.
26. 'Conditions of Women in English Jails' in *New Ireland*, 15 April 1922.
27. *Prison Letters*, Roper, p. 42.
28. *Ibid.*, p. 66–7.
29. *Ibid.*, p. 106.
30. In the National Museum, Dublin.
31. *Politics and Irish Life 1913–1921*, David Fitzpatrick (Gill & Macmillan, Dublin, 1977) p. 54.
32. Letter in private collection.
33. *Prison Letters*, Roper, p. 145.
34. *Ibid.*, pp. 150–1.
35. *Ibid.*, p. 154.
36. In the National Museum, Dublin.
37. *Poems of Eva Gore-Booth*, Introduction, E. Roper (Longmans Green, London, 1929).
38. *Prison Letters*, Roper, pp. 157–8.
39. *Constance Markievicz*, Van Voris, p. 220.
40. In the prison notebook.
41. *Prison Letters*, Roper, p. 172.
42. *Ibid.*

TWELVE

THE CONVICT'S RETURN

WHEN SHE LEFT for Ireland later that week, the platform at Euston was crowded with fans singing 'The Soldier's Song', an old Fianna song and fast becoming the hymn of the republic. As they finished, Con, like a true *prima donna*, scattered her bouquet of roses among them. On the boat, the ex-convict turned hero was feted with smiles and grapes and peaches. Her arrival in Dublin was triumphant: 'The Countess entered Dublin in the midst of a long procession with banner after banner and brass band after brass band; with riders on horseback; with running boys waving branches; with lumbering floats drawn by slow-footed good-natured Clydesdale horses,'[1] ragged urchins, public figures in uniform and trades guilds. Some of it was orchestrated by the thriving post–1916 movement, and much of it was a spontaneous display of the love and respect she had inspired among the people. It was a love she would not lose.

Surrey House being no longer hers, she went to stay with Dr Kathleen Lynn for a time to recuperate. And a week after her return, she was received formally into the Catholic Church by Fr Matthew MacMahon, Dean of Clonliffe College. Her family responded to the snub, as they saw it, by privately deciding that

Con took this step to ensure that she would be privy to whatever plots and plans her fellow revolutionaries but not, by and large, her co-religionists were hatching. Con however was far too honest to take such a serious step solely for that reason. We need not be sceptical about her account of her religious awakening, because it does harmonize with the quasi-mystical side of her nature; the part that empathized with nature, that had fallen so naively for the idealistic, reverential nationalism of the pre-Rising, the part of her that her skittish ebullience tended to hide. She shocked a priest somewhat, for instance, by referring mischievously to the Devil as 'a good rebel'. But while she had no interest in arguing about the dogmas of the Church, declaring simply that she believed it all, she kept scrupulously to its rules. And some years later she wrote a closely worked little treatise on the Church and socialism.

A year after Easter Week the various nationalist groups had sunk their differences by consensus into one movement. This umbrella movement shrewdly took the name Sinn Féin, as the media had made the revolution famous under the soubriquet of the 'Sinn Féin rebellion'. As Sinn Féin clubs, accommodating with a new spirit old Sinn Féiners, Volunteers, the IRB etc., sprang up countrywide, Madame Markievicz was treated as a celebrity. In the autumn of 1917 she addressed meetings at Kilkenny, Clonakilty, Ennis, Carrick-on-Suir and several other towns. She travelled to Sligo to receive the freedom of her home town, but did not venture as far as Lissadell. As a kind of counterpoint, she did go to visit the convent of the Ursuline nuns there. Everywhere, there were crowds and cheers and bouquets. Sometimes she looked demure in a feminine dress and hat; sometimes she wore her Citizen Army uniform. She always wore as a bracelet rosary beads, which William Partridge had given her in the College of Surgeons. Michael Collins, on behalf of the Irish National Aid Association sent her money. She wrote to say it was 'most useful' as 'I was left with no clothes and could not get at my own money'.[2] A photograph of her in uniform in 1917 is a sad illustration of how damaging to her health her stay in prison had been. She looks thin and worn and aged, her teeth ravaged.

It was an emotive period. In July, Éamon de Valera, ex-commandant at Boland's Mills and newly released from prison, won a by-election in East Clare. Constance went down to Clare to canvass for him. In August, another by-election victory by a released penal servitor, William Cosgrave, evoked such seditious rhetoric that Thomas Ashe was imprisoned in Mountjoy. Ashe sought the status of a prisoner of war, went on hunger strike, and died as a result in late September. His huge funeral was engineered in the tradition of mass-demonstrations by the IRB. Tom Clarke, Pearse and the others who had been shot in Mountjoy would have approved of the funeral oration given by Michael Collins: 'That volley which we have just heard,' he said, 'is the only speech which it is proper to make over the grave of a dead Fenian.'[3] Disaffection was clearly mounting. The government feared revolution and made hapless attempts to head it off. An Irish Convention was called, which was boycotted by the new Sinn Féin and Labour, and exposed the yawning differences in aspirations between the northern unionists, southern unionists and nationalists.

In October Sinn Féin held its convention. The constitution adopted by the 1700 delegates and the executive they selected reflects the anxiety to reconcile all shades of opinion, moderate and radical alike, in the new movement. It also showed the shift in consciousness that had occurred since the Rising. It asserted that the republic claimed by the Proclamation of 1916 was now established – 'Sinn Féin aims at securing the international recognition of Ireland as an independent Irish Republic. Having achieved that status the Irish people may by Referendum freely choose their own form of government.' During the election of members to the executive, Constance displayed the intransigence that was to become the hallmark of political women in the 1920s. When Eoin MacNeill was put up for election, she opposed his candidacy since, she said, in the crucial days before Easter 1916 he had proved himself not trustworthy. De Valera, who was now President of Sinn Féin, spoke for MacNeill, saying that MacNeill 'did not act otherwise than as a good Irishman'. He was duly elected, top of the poll. Constance's objection rose from the integrity of a political innocent; she lacked the native astuteness of a politician who would have recognized that MacNeill still commanded enormous support. But she was elected to the 24-member executive, the fifth to be elected behind MacNeill. The other women elected were Dr

Kathleen Lynn, Mrs Clarke and Grace Gifford, now Mrs Plunkett.

Con proceeded, as before, to spread her energies widely. She was also President of Cumarin na mBan, a major in the Irish Citizen Army, Chief Scout of the Fianna, and was recognized as the spokeswoman for Labour and disciple of James Connolly, in which capacity she stood on many platforms, including one in Manchester. In the spring of 1918 she was in Dungannon to speak in support of the Sinn Féin candidate in the East Tyrone by-election. This was a very disorderly meeting because Sinn Féin was strongly opposed by the Redmondite Irish Party represented in Ulster by the Ancient Order of Hibernians who were able to marshal great numbers of supporters and used quite rough methods. Seamus O'Connor, a Sinn Féiner wrote that the AOH supporters 'kept up a barrage of shouting and throwing stones, potatoes and eggs (which they were buying at sixpence each) at the speakers'. He described how the Countess Markievicz, in a trench coat, having been hit several times with potatoes and eggs exclaimed, 'in what to me was her peculiar accent, "I care no more for your stones than I cared for the bullets of Easter Week."'[4]

The new Sinn Féin was a radically different organization than the previous one of the same name. Along with the moderacy of Arthur Griffith, Vice-President in 1918, and Eoin MacNeill, it accommodated a militancy and a practical sense of its own autonomy that had not existed before. The revolutionary spirit of 1916, which seemed rather mad then, and was certainly marginal, now extended everywhere. By early 1918 Sinn Féin could boast 81,000 members in 1025 clubs and each club was attached to a company of Volunteers, committed to physical force when the time came. Its leaders, notably de Valera, spoke in public of the feasibility of physical force and condoned the forcible division of land. The demand for land, which had smouldered since the Land War and was not satisfied by the measures of the Land Acts, now resulted in bodies of men, carrying Sinn Féin flags, marching onto grazing land and forcing the owners to let the fields to those with ten acres or less, at an annual rent of £4 per acre. Where the owner was unwilling, cattle drives, involving the scattering and houghing of cattle, often ensued. In Clare, the situation became so anarchic that an especially strict form of martial law was imposed.

Britain meanwhile was facing on its western front greater problems than these comparative irritations. The German breakthrough under Ludendorff was proving dismayingly successful and the Allied forces seemed to face defeat. Partly out of necessity, partly out of resentment at the recalcitrance of the Irish, it was deemed by the government that conscription, long-threatened, should now be applied to Ireland. In April 1918 a Manpower Bill was passed, which provided for the extension of compulsory service to Ireland, enforceable by an Order in Council at any time. The Irish Party bitterly opposed the Bill and Ireland was outraged. It completed the making of Sinn Féin.

A defence fund was set up and a pledge to resist conscription by any means was taken by all parties. The Bishops, persuaded by de Valera, a white-headed boy in ecclesiastical circles, issued a manifesto to the same effect. The Trades Union Congress called a twenty-four hour general strike, which was effective everywhere except Belfast. Constance addressed several meetings on the question and, through Cumann na mBan and the IWFL, pledged women to a firm stance against conscription. Ireland withdrew, in effect, from the United Kingdom.

The government was not oblivious of the danger this state of anarchy presented. Just when it was hard-pressed in Europe to the degree that men of fifty were now being sent to the front, a revolution much more troublesome than that of 1916 seemed about to occur at any time in Ireland. The quelling of an Irish revolution could mean defeat in the war. To avert this danger, it was decided that the Sinn Féin leaders would have to be removed. It was agreed that the more vociferous among them should be interned, and to justify this action evidence of an Irish-German intrigue was concocted. A young man called Michael Collins, who was on the Sinn Féin executive, was already involved in the intelligence activities which were later to prove so decisive and, through a 'friend', a detective in Dublin Castle, he learned of the impending arrests and warned the leaders. They decided that their best tactic was not to go on the run but to submit to imprisonment. Between 17 and 18 May seventy-three people were arrested and interned in English prisons.

On the evening of 17 May Constance was walking home along Rathmines Road, having called on Maud Gonne MacBride in her flat on Stephen's Green to warn her of the arrests, when an armed car drew up alongside. She was taken in and next morning brought to Kingstown and placed in the hold of a gunboat. As the day passed, she was joined by more internees. When the gunboat docked in Holyhead that night, the men were sent to Usk and Gloucester Jails and Constance was sent on the train to London. She was delighted to be met on the platform at Euston by Eva and Esther. Esther, uncharacteristically, had had a premonition of Con's arrival and insisted that she and Eva go to Euston to meet the train. Poppet, the dog, had also come this far, and even accompanied Con to Holloway Jail but was despatched to Fitzroy Square by taxi within a few hours, from where he may have been collected by Dulcibella Barton and brought back to her house at Annamoe. 'Whenever Con went to gaol,' Dulcibella said, 'her dog always came to me.'[5]

Constance's incarceration in Holloway was quite different to her prison term in Aylesbury. This time, she was an internee, not a convict, and this distinction was reflected in the conditions there. For one thing, she had for company two political sister-stalwarts, Maud Gonne MacBride and Kathleen Clarke. The three women were confined on a landing to themselves and were allowed free association. They were able to wear their own clothes and could send out for foodstuffs to supplement the prison fare. Con speaks of pickles, anchovies, strawberry jam and vegetables – including some that seem to have been sent by her mother – a box of chocolates sent from Ireland, and other delicacies. Only visitors were disallowed – this because the internees, especially Constance, refused to submit to the requirement that politics must not be discussed with visitors. This time too of course there was no hard labour and Con was able to spend much of her time painting watercolours.

Nevertheless, she chafed more at this imprisonment than she had at her arduous term in Aylesbury. She had lost her 'dreaming faculty' and was energetic instead, and therefore restless and impatient. 'Just at present,' she wrote to Eva, 'I wish I could challenge King George to mortal combat, box the Censor's ears, ask many questions of L. George in the English Parliament, publish a newspaper in America and kiss you!'[6] She also complained of boredom, and about the fiction of the 'German plot'. The 'plot' does indeed seem to have been a fiction, although from the English point of view it was a plausible one. The Irish revolutionaries traditionally sought the discomfiture of England and help for their cause by appealing to her enemies. In the old days they looked to France, in 1916 they had looked to Germany. But no evidence of a conspiracy in 1918 has come to light. Con therefore felt a righteous indignation at her imprisonment which she had not felt in Aylesbury.

A philosophic mind was not induced by the presence of Mesdames MacBride and Clarke. They reacted very badly to their imprisonment; they both became ill and worried so terribly about their children that they could not eat or sleep. Kathleen had left five bewildered children behind, while Maud was haunted by her last glimpse of her young son, Sean, running after the receding Black Maria that carried her away.

'My companions,' Con wrote, 'I think of as "Niobe" and "Rachel" as they are the two most complete and perfect – though now, alas! mournful – mothers that I ever met!'[7] Their grief may have discomfited her since she had accepted with *sang froid* the absence of her daughter. She was perhaps forced as well to engage in the kind of intimacies and the examination of questions about her role as mother that she preferred to ignore or suppress. Maude Gonne wrote that they spoke of 'these things' when they were together in Holloway and

> that Constance loved children and it was a great sacrifice when she sent Maeve to be brought up by her mother because life's evolution had made things too strenuous for the child at home ... Only people who knew her very closely and intimately knew how deeply she felt, for with all her open exuberant manner and frank way of speaking she was very reserved about her personal feelings and kept things deep hidden in her heart.

Maud said she thought it would have been 'better spiritually for Maeve to be more with Constance even though life would not have been so great and comfortable for her ... [but] Constance felt she was doing the best for her and never considered herself on the matter.'[8] Constance could certainly argue that it was better to provide Maeve with a means of choosing her own future and lifestyle rather than imposing on her the Bohemian and marginalized culture she herself had adopted.

As Constance kept herself busy with her painting – she did horses and landscapes and heroes as usual – Maud paced her cell 'like a caged wild animal ... a tigress prowling endlessly up and down'.[9] Maud disclaimed it afterwards, but there was quite a bit of friction between herself and Con; they were both natural competitors. Kathleen Clarke said they both walked up and down the prison yard arguing as to which had the better claim to aristocratic status. Maud, said her son Sean, liked to say she was a better painter than Constance. We can imagine her communicating somehow her disdain for her cell-mate's work, while perhaps also envying Con's ability to immerse herself in painting. When the women were offered the opportunity to apply to the Sankey Commission for release, Maud declared in desperation that she was going to apply. Con, according to Kathleen Clarke, advised her: 'If you do that, you need never come back to Ireland.' Maud tore up the application. In the following months, Maud heard of the deaths of her former lover, Millevoye and of her sister and became quite ill – although Kathleen Clarke remarked that she may have 'feigned sick ... She was such a good actress that you couldn't tell.'

Constance, always attracted to the vulnerable, fussed over Kathleen who did not succumb very willingly to her ministrations. When Con said to her, patronizingly in Kathleen's view, 'I can't imagine why they arrested you, such a frail, inoffensive little thing as you are,' she rounded on her at last: 'Little and inoffensive I may be, but my charge-sheet is the same as yours.'[10] Constance did respect Kathleen Clarke and referred to her often in letters to Eva. She had, she wrote, a 'hero's soul ... She makes the best of everything and is an ideal jail-bird.'[11] She did not include Maud Gonne in this compliment. The three women were joined briefly by Hanna Sheehy-Skeffington who was arrested on her return from a lecture tour in the United States. She went on hunger strike at once and was released within a few days. In October Maud was released to a sanatorium because of her ill health.

There were two big events in that year, 1918. In February, women over thirty were given the right to vote; and on 11 November the First World War came to an end. As a result of the latter, the election planned for December became definite. The election was contested in Ireland by the Irish Party, the Unionists and Sinn Féin. The Irish Party's manifesto called for Home Rule, while Sinn Féin's called for an Irish republic. Sinn Féin enjoyed the support of Cumann na mBan – it had been persuaded to insert as a final clause in its Constitution: 'That the equality of men and women in this organisation be emphasized in all speeches and pamphlets'[12] – and now agreed to put up two women candidates. They were Winifred Carney, who was in the GPO during the Rising, standing for the Victoria Division in Belfast; and Countess Markievicz, standing for St Patrick's Division in Dublin. Constance's candidacy was seen to straddle several platforms. She was President of Cumann na MBan and approved of, for the most part, by the IWFL. She was regarded by the Labour Party – which was not contesting the election so as to ensure maximum support for Sinn Féin – as Connolly's inheritor and a voice for the interests of labour. And she was standing on the Sinn Féin ticket, for which her republican credentials were impeccable.

Her election messages from prison were necessarily brief but they display her developing political acumen as well as her interest in all three causes. To the IWFL she wrote: 'One reason I'd love to win is that we could make St Patrick's a rallying ground for women and a splendid centre for constructive work by women. I am full of schemes and ideas.'[13] Of Sinn Féin she asked that 'Where Irish resources are being developed, or where industries exist, Sinn Féiners should make it their business to secure that workers are paid a living wage.'[14] And in her address to the constituents of St Patrick's she wrote: 'I stand for the Irish Republic, to establish which our heroes died ... There are many roads to freedom, today we may hope that our road to freedom will be a peaceful and bloodless one; I need hardly assure you that it will be an honourable one.'[15] The hope that the way to an Irish republic would be bloodless was rather dented by Lloyd George's otherwise euphoric post-Armistice speech on 12 November when he referred to Ireland: 'There are two paths that are closed – the one leading to a complete severance of Ireland from the British Empire, and the other to the forcible submission of Ulster to a Home Rule Parliament against their will.'[16] Parliamentarianism was at an impasse, as it seemed inevitably to be where Ireland was concerned.

Proscription trammelled Sinn Féin's election campaign. Its election director was arrested and removed to England, meetings were broken up by police and exhortations against voting for republicans were dropped from airplanes. It was women who did much of the electioneering. More than half of the candidates were, like Constance, in jail. She had a great advantage in standing for St Patrick's Division since it was composed of the hinterland of Liberty Hall where she was known and loved on account of her work there in 1913. The results were announced on 28 December. The Irish Party won six seats, the Unionists twenty-six, most of them in Ulster; and Sinn Féin won the remaining seventy-three. The result was a resounding protest against the status quo, and a demand for the establishment of an Irish republic.

Countess Markievicz was the only woman elected out of seventeen women candidates in the United Kingdom of Great Britain and Ireland, and thus became the first woman ever elected to the British Parliament. She defeated her principal opponent, William Field of the Irish Party, who had held the seat for twenty-six years, by 7835 votes to 3742. She would retain for many years to come the distinction of being the only woman to be elected on her own record. In the following years, women MPs were elected via what became known as the 'widows route', i.e., they succeeded to safe seats vacated by their husbands, generally on their demise. Lady Astor for instance, who was elected in the following year in a by-election, becoming the first woman to actually take her seat at Westminster, took her husband's seat when he moved to the House of Lords. Constance was quite *blasé* about her victory. In mid January she asked Eva for books on 'Imperialism and earlier Peace Conferences and anything about Empire-building and theories about internal construction of a State'. But she did not mention it directly until 6 February. 'I get such funny letters from the ends of the world and I begin to understand why MPs employ secretaries. My election was a foregone conclusion. I must know most of those who voted for me.'[17]

While this illustrious person made the best of solitude and prison life – Kathleen Clarke was at last released because of ill health in February – those of her fellow MPs at liberty constituted themselves the 'Parliament of the Republic', which had been declared in 1916. On 21 January 1919, twenty-seven members, calling themselves TDs (Teachatai Dala, meaning Deputies to the Parliament) in place of MPs met at the Mansion House to inaugurate the first Dáil Éireann – the parliament of Ireland. Thirty-four members, including Countess Markievicz, were absent because they were in jail. As the roll was called, the answer Fe Glas ag Gallaibh (imprisoned abroad) was made thirty-four times. The proceedings were opened by Fr Michael O'Flanagan, the priest who was removed by his bishop from his curacy in Roscommon because of his political prominence. Deputies stood to listen to the Declaration of Independence:

> We, the elected Representatives of the ancient Irish people in national Parliament assembled, do, in the name of the Irish nation, ratify the establishment of the Irish Republic and pledge ourselves and our people to make this declaration effective by every means at our command.

The Dáil issued a demand for representation at the peace conference to be held shortly. To have an independent representative of the Irish nation at the peace conference to be held when the war – fought ostensibly for 'the rights of small nations' – was over was always a major ambition of the revolutionaries. Connolly had believed the Rising would make this possible, and Constance added it to her election manifesto. It was clearly the best method of legitimizing worldwide Irish aspirations, of finally emerging in the eyes of other nations from under the cloak of the United Kingdom. Then the Democratic Programme of Dáil Éireann was read by Piaras Beaslai and adopted unanimously. This was a reaffirmation of the Proclamation of 1916 and contained equally idealistic but concrete propositions for the creation of a welfare state:

> It shall be the first duty of the Government of the Republic ... to secure that no child shall suffer hunger or cold from lack of food or clothing or shelter, but that all shall be provided with the means and facilities requisite for their proper education and training as citizens of a free and Gaelic Ireland.

The Dáil would 'abolish the present odious, degrading and foreign law system, substituting therefrom a sympathetic native scheme for the nation's aged and infirm ...' Industries would be developed on 'the most beneficial and progressive co-operative lines'. The government undertook to 'seek the co-operation of other countries in determining a standard of social and industrial improvements in the conditions under which the working classes live and labour'. While Labour was not represented in Dáil Éireann, the programme adopted by the assembly was a Labour document, prepared by the Labour leaders Johnson and O'Brien. It had been diluted, however, by some outraged Sinn Féin leaders, including Michael Collins, who thought it communistic. This resulted in the deletion of the article providing for the 'organisation of people into trade unions and co-operative societies with a view to the control and administration of the industries by the workers engaged in the industries'.

The entire proceedings of the first meeting of the First Dáil lasted just two hours; this, and its adoption of a high-minded, and to many eyes, ludicrously unrealistic programme and the way in which it was conducted in Irish – a sometimes halting Irish perhaps – allowed many people to think it all mere mumbo-jumbo and a charade. But it was utterly serious. It marked definitively the constitutional seizure of independent status and the accession to nationhood on the part of Ireland. The Irish people had given them a mandate, democratically, to do so. The elected representatives of these people would never attend the parliament at Westminster again.

In March the Government became alarmed at the prospect of the deadly influenza epidemic invading the prisons and decided to release the political prisoners. In a kind of bilateral amnesty, Captain Bowen-Colthurst who had murdered Francis Sheehy-Skeffington and others was also released from Broadmoor. Con, released on 10 March, paid a visit to the House of Commons for a gratifying look at her name over the peg allotted to her in the cloakroom, and returned to Ireland to a welcome even more tumultuous than before. She was met by

> deputations of everybody ... We motored into Dublin to Liberty Hall. Last time was nothing to it. The crowd had no beginning or end. I made a speech and we then formed up in a torchlight procession and went to St Patrick's. Every window had a flag or candle or both. You never saw such excitement.[18]

She returned too, to find a guerilla war in its first bloody stages. Back in 1910 *Bean na h-Éireann* formulated in one of its more militant statements what the military policy of republicans

should be: 'We want nothing less than a campaign of extermi-
nating the police ... As matters stand the first line of English occupation to be struck at must be the police.' It was an invidious
policy since members of the Royal Irish Constabulary (RIC) were
fellow Irishmen. But they were also a paramilitary force; armed,
living in barracks, and by tradition, zealous upholders of British
rule in Ireland. They were justly regarded, in their local areas, as
spies and informers for the authorities. To young men and boys
who had witnessed the debacle and the glory of the Easter Rising
a few years before and who since then had organized themselves
into the Irish Republican Army via the Volunteers or the IRB or
Sinn Féin – by now a seamless web of revolution – the RIC was the
visible enemy and the obvious target.

On 21 January, the day on which the Dáil convened, a
party of policemen escorting a load of explosives to a quarry
at Soloheadbeag in Co. Tipperary was ambushed by a group of
Volunteers that included Dan Breen, who would achieve fame as a
crack guerilla fighter. Two policemen were killed and the explosives
were seized as material for bombs. This action, like many similar
actions in the following months, received no imprimatur from
the Dáil; but it had, nonetheless, the assembly's tacit approval.
Sinn Féin's election programme, after all, had as a policy that of
'making use of any and every means available to render impotent
the power of England to hold Ireland in subjection by military
force or otherwise'. The failure of the Dáil representative, Sean T.
O'Kelly, to gain admittance, despite his best efforts, to the peace
conference in Paris seemed to prove that the only means available
were, inevitably, the means of violence.

Éamon de Valera had not waited to be released from Lincoln
Jail, but escaped in February with the aid of Michael Collins. On 1
April the Dáil reconvened. De Valera was elected President of the
Republic and named his ministers. They included Arthur Griffith
(Home Affairs), Eoin MacNeill (Industry), Michael Collins
(Finance); and Countess Markievicz (Labour). Constance was the
only woman member of the cabinet and for several years to come
she would be the only woman to sit in any government. Only in
the USSR, which also had a revolutionary government, did she
have a counterpart in Alexandra Kollontai, Commissar for Social

Welfare. This was not the only link between Ireland in 1919 and Soviet Russia. The government of the USSR was the only national government to recognize the Irish Republic in 1919.

De Valera may have felt obliged to form a Labour ministry to maintain Labour support for his revolutionary government. Constance herself told Kathleen Clarke that she had to threaten to go over to Labour in order to be appointed. And her appointment did of course win approval from Labour. The Irish Women Workers Union, under Helena Molony, expressed this: 'We rejoice that the first woman elected to Parliament in Ireland is one to whom the workers can always confidently look to uphold their rights and just claims.'[19] But de Valera had few thoughts or feelings to spare for the interests of Labour, not now anyway when there were more urgent and simpler problems to solve. He emerged from prison to find the Democratic Programme, in which he had no hand or part, adopted by the Assembly over which he presided. He immediately repudiated it, declaring that he was withdrawing from the programme 'because while the enemy was within their gates, the immediate question was to gain possession of their country'. He found it a burden and a 'straitjacket'. It was certainly not a feasible or practicable programme for a country bristling with enemy guns.

Con's position as the sole intermediary between the marginal socialist tendencies and the burgeoning bourgeois tendencies of the revolution would be a source of frustration for her. But for now, she was able to concern herself with tasks that were somewhat less intractable. She sat on the committee, for instance, set up to consider the welfare of prisoners of war and the disturbing cases of children taken into custody by the police for questioning and kept for days or even months before being charged with offences. In May she was engaged with the American Commission on Irish Independence, the three members of which went on to testify before the Congressional Committee on Foreign Relations. They were shocked to find the high military profile everywhere in Ireland, the curtailment of the movement of individuals, and that the Countess was under constant surveillance. Constance's influence is very evident in their testimony, in their emphasis on the high rate of infant mortality, the attacks on women and children and the importance of the labour movement – including the hint, cannily inserted for American ears, that there was a danger of a turn to Sovietism if their country 'is not freed of foreign control and exploitation'.

The labour movement had an ambiguous attitude towards Sinn Féin. But during the war of independence, or the Anglo-Irish War as the current conflict came to be called, both worked in tandem, in practice if not officially. The Irish Citizen Army involved itself in gathering information and smuggling arms and ammunition. In May, Constance spoke at Newmarket, Co. Limerick, under the auspices of the Citizen Army, on the subject of the Dáil policy of boycotting the police: 'They must be shown and made to feel how base are the functions they perform,' said de Valera in the Dáil, 'and how vile is the position they occupy.' The meeting was proscribed and when it went on anyhow, the police moved in. Constance got away by using another woman, dressed in her hat, coat and her blue Liberty scarf (given her by Eva years before) as a decoy. A month later, she was arrested for this seditious speech and sentenced to four months in Cork's female prison. At her trial she conducted a strenuously argued defence, but did not deny saying 'Burn everything British except its coal'. Friends thought she looked tired and ill at her trial, held in Mallow, Co. Cork. But she presented as usual her valiant and most cheerful self in her letters to Eva.

Cork Jail was the 'most comfortable jail' she was yet in, with a nice garden 'full of pinks, and you can hear the birds sing'. Friends sent in all her meals; and roses, and 'heaps of strawberries and cream'. 'Have you done any more horoscopes lately?' she asked Eva, 'and can you tell me how often I get to jail? And shall I be hung in the end?'[20] Eva was developing, side by side with her political work, the youthful interest of the Gore-Booths in esoteric and arcane philosophies such as Buddhism and theosophy. Her nature was increasingly ecstatic. The onset of middle age and illness brought her a keener spirituality – then, she wrote, the soul 'awakes from her long acquiescence. She feels within herself the pent-up spiritual energies'.[21] Eva was someone who, a few years later, could write to a friend *apropos* the physical pain she was suffering: 'It's dreadful of course, but frightfully interesting.'[22] Constance too had this most gallant quality, an astounding and courageous nonchalance in the face of life's trials, a readiness to consider the innate interest of an experience, however terrible, worth its accompanying discomforts.

The casting and interpretation of horoscopes was a major interest among the theosophically inclined such as Yeats and Maud Gonne. The horoscope Eva cast for Constance survives, though her interpretation of it does not. Con may have been gratified to learn that while the number of her jail terms or her ultimate fate could not be read in her stars, her problematic character could. Present-day astrologers can see in her horoscope, as Eva must have, clear indications of her destiny.[23]

Uranus on the Descendant and Pluto at the Nadir show, they say, that she had an irresistible impulse to transform the world; that she was born, literally, a rebel, and would seek to effect this transformation through annihilation of the existing order. Capricorn on the Ascendant meant she was torn between this impulse and a contrary urge to conformity, discipline and the observance of societal forms and modes of behaviour. She was therefore that rather paradoxical creature, a traditional revolutionary, drawn to uniforms, organizations and hierarchies. Membership of revolutionary groups allowed her to both conform and rebel, while the aspects of Mars meant she was a natural leader within them. The relative absence of earth in her horoscope meant she lacked roots and a sense of belonging, which might suggest why she had such a passionate attachment to Ireland as an abstract idea. Her unconventional marriage, they claim, could be foretold from the position of Mars in the 8th House; and that while she sought to be the dominant partner, she was easily hurt by any hint of rejection. And Jupiter in the sign of Pisces apparently gives compassion, a strong impulse to self-sacrifice and the probability of a change in religious belief.

Whatever the sense of fatalism this kind of information may have induced in Constance, she was full of a robust and curious scepticism while in jail, brought on by her extensive reading. She was reading Lenin and John Mitchel, Haverty's *History of Ireland* and Chesterton's *History of England*, the novel *Knocknagow* by Kickham, and others by Thackeray. Her letters ranged in discursive style over subjects suggested by these works. While she liked

Chesterton's iconoclasm, she preferred Mitchel's rhetorical style: 'We rather like adjectives and symbolic things over here.'[24]

Maeve had, at this point, ambitions about being a professional violinist and her mother wondered what Eva thought of 'Maeve's music'. 'Is there a spark in it? I never care for mere technique. I suppose she is in a state of being wildly amused and interested in life.'[25] She assured Eva that she was 'very interested in family gossip, always'. Despite appearances – Nora Connolly visited more than once and was struck by how lonely she seemed – she was quite buoyant. She loved the moths that fluttered through the bars at night, 'all splotched over with orange and red' and 'opalescent and shimmering, moonlight colours'. It was very hot during August, 'too hot to think, except about you, darling'. In October, she was overjoyed to hear news of Stasko who, it seems, was anxious to return to Ireland:

> If you only knew what a joy it was to hear about Staskow. I feel as if I never know from day to day whether he is alive or not. What on earth does he want over here? He wouldn't like it if he got here. Of course if it's true that he has married a rich wife, he'd be alright, but if not I don't know what he'd do.[26]

Stasko, working in Archangel as a translator for the White Russian Army and the British Expeditionary force, had married a Russian girl, Alexandra Ivanova Zimina. Her father managed a timber mill and she may have had some wealth. But the marriage would end when she could not or would not follow him to Poland after the Polish-Russian war.

Constance wondered too on which side Casimir was in Russia and hoped 'Lenin will win through after all'. It was in this year that the house at Zywotowka was burnt down as the Bolsheviks took control in the Ukraine and that Casimir's mother and older brother, Jan, died of typhus. Now the titular head of the family but with his patrimony and the family lost or split up, Casimir escaped to Poland among the exodus of refugees. In Warsaw he began to make his way again as an artist and playwright.

As for Ireland and its nascent republic, Constance was confident – even if Stasko wouldn't like it – about its future: 'Directly we get the Republic into working order we shall do a lot.'[27]

NOTES

1. *Unmanageable Revolutionaries*, Ward, p. 123.
2. Letter in National Museum, Dublin.
3. *Ireland Since the Famine*, Lyons, p. 387.
4. *Tomorrow Is Another Day*, Seamus O'Connor (ROC publications, Dublin, 1987) pp. 43–4.
5. *Prison Letters*, Roper, p. 181.
6. *Ibid.*, p. 180.
7. Letter to Stasko, 14 August 1951, now in private collection.
8. Kathleen Clarke cited in *Maud Gonne – Lucky Eyes and a High Heart*, Cardozo p. 327.
9. *Daughters of Erin*, Coxhead, p. 103.
10. *Prison Letters*, Roper, p. 187.
11. *Prison Letters*, Roper, p. 187.
12. In the National Museum, Dublin.
13. *Constance Markievicz*, Van Voris, p. 251.
14. Ibid.
15. *The Damnable Question*, Dangerfield, p. 299.
16. *Prison Letters*, Roper, p. 193.
17. *Ibid.*, p. 297.
18. *Unmanageable Revolutionaries*, Ward, p. 136.
19. *Prison Letters*, Roper, p. 225.
20. *Poems of Eva Gore-Booth*, ed. E. Roper, p. 61.
21. *Ibid.*, p. 88.
22. Interpretation provided by the Irish Astrological Society.
23. *Prison Letters*, Roper, p. 229.
24. *Ibid.*, p. 231.
25. *Ibid.*, p. 245.
26. *Ibid.*, p. 235.
27. *Ibid.*

THIRTEEN

STATESWOMAN ON THE RUN

IN OCTOBER Constance was released. Once again she found that events had moved fast in her absence. The Dáil had been declared illegal in September and Sinn Féin, Cumann na mBan and the Gaelic League were proscribed. On the revolutionary side, the policy of war against the police was rapidly developing into a full-scale conflict. Isolated police barracks were subject to harassment and attack from IRA 'flying columns'. These were small groups of guerilla fighters who moved in, opened fire and then disappeared into the surrounding countryside. As a result, there were whole-sale resignations from the RIC. Their intelligence network was breaking down and the besieged police force was retreating into the larger barracks in towns and villages.

Flying columns were composed of local 'active service units' – young single men for the most part, younger sons having no responsibility for farms or families, who found the life of a fugitive, yet heroic, desperado exhilarating and personally liberating. They cadged food from farmers, slept in fields, barns and in the homes of often unwilling sympathizers. For, while the local people might not actively support the war they were conducting, it was almost unknown for them to be refused shelter or sustenance. By the end of 1919, twenty-one policemen had been killed.

Constance too went on the run – as a member of the illegal Dáil, if for no other reason, she was under constant threat of re-arrest. When at Christmas she had a hamper sent to Eva's household in Fitzroy Square, she got someone else to choose the contents: 'I was taking no risks before Christmas as I did so want to have one at liberty. I told them to put in a turkey for Esther and other carnivorous friends.'[1] The new hardline militancy was largely due to the influence of Michael Collins, member of the Supreme Council of the IRB and a man of administrative brilliance, of coldness of purpose and of warm-blooded vitality. The more political-minded de Valera had left Ireland for America in June to seek support, recognition and funds for the republic, leaving a vacuum into which Collins, temperamentally a latter-day Fenian, stepped.

Collins was regarded then, and still is, as a figure of almost mythical proportions. He was known popularly and affectionately as the Big Fellow. He was handsome, boyish, steely, laconic, abrasive, charming ... And he inspired both antagonism and loyalty in his men. He was given, for instance, like a Lawrentian protagonist, to challenging them to wrestling matches. In the eyes of the enemy, he was a gangster; and it is not difficult, indeed, to see him in that light. In Dublin, he operated his own private 'execution squad' who posed as builders' labourers and went on missions wearing guns under their aprons. Like Constance, Collins was 'on the run' and they both shared the sense of excitement engendered by this perilous status and both had a reputation for a miraculous capacity for invisibility as they went brazenly about.

'It's so awfully funny being on the run,' Constance wrote, 'I don't know which I resemble most, the timid hare, the wily fox or a fierce wild animal of the jungle.' Like Collins, she flaunted her position in a tantalizing manner by whizzing around on a bicycle – his had a chain that whined in a particular and dangerously recognizable manner. 'There are very few women on bikes in the winter,' Con wrote gleefully, 'so a hunted beast on a bike is very remarkable.'[2] Collins's most brilliant and deadly weapon was his control of the intelligence network he himself devised. He had spies everywhere: in the Special Branch, in Dublin Castle, even among the officers of the British army.

In December there was an attempted assassination of the Viceroy, Lord French, the brother of feminist and supporter of republicanism Charlotte Despard. A few days later the Government of Ireland Act was presented to the House of Commons, an Act guaranteed to cause escalation of the conflict. Providing for the establishment of two parliaments, one in Belfast and one in Dublin, it was designed to pacify the northern unionists and to indulge their wish for hegemony. In thus creating a divided nation, it seemed designed too to antagonize the nationalists who were the overwhelming majority everywhere except in Ulster. In early 1920 there were continuing raids and reprisals on both sides. In April the war intensified when the IRA raided tax offices throughout the country, destroying all records and disrupting the collection of revenues, and burnt 300 empty police barracks in the west of the country. In an attempt to subdue the inflammable situation the government next decided to send to the assistance of the RIC a supplementary force from Britain. This force was recruited from the ranks of demobilized soldiers. There were not enough RIC uniforms available to properly fit them out so the new recruits wore khaki coats with the dark-green RIC trousers and cap. The Irish called them Black and Tans, after the well-known pack of Scarteen hounds. Psychologically scarred from the battlefields of Europe and the post-war depression in England they were now set upon by civilians – as far as they could tell – with guns, who ambushed them and attacked them and then melted back into a hostile landscape. The Black and Tans were inclined as a result to see all civilians as the enemy and behaved towards them with a terrible brutality.

In September the Black and Tans were supplemented with a second emergency force, the Auxiliary Division. The Auxiliaries were ex-officers, were paid £1 a day to the 10 shillings paid to the Black and Tans, wore blue uniforms and glengarry caps – and quickly achieved a reputation for even greater brutality than the Black and Tans. The unarmed civilian population was increasingly victim to reprisals for acts committed by the IRA. Both the Auxiliaries and the Black and Tans were badly disciplined and largely autonomous and by mid 1920 it became the policy of some units to shoot civilians on sight, to raid dwelling houses and terrorize the inhabitants, to burn creameries and homesteads suspected of sheltering guerillas. At the height of the conflict the entire populations of small towns and villages were reduced to sleeping in the fields at night when a member of one of these forces was killed in the area.

The RIC found themselves in a wretched position. Many of them could not condone the methods of the emergency forces. Yet, they were marooned in barracks and forced to commandeer their food from people among whom they had lived before in relative harmony. Many resigned. One constable who was outraged by the advice of his superior officer that 'the more you shoot the better I will like you' and who defected to the other side, was Constable Jeremiah Mee from Co. Kerry. Mee came to work as an assistant in Constance's Department of Labour. He was impressed by her 'dignified bearing and direct business-like manner'.[3] She, in contrast to Michael Collins, recognized almost at once that he was not a spy and invited him to come and work for her.

While terror raged, the Dáil, underground though it was, tried to present an appearance of order and stability. It was the democratic face of revolution. Michael Collins, as Minister of Finance, floated a national loan, which was generously subscribed, to finance its activities. In contrast to the grimy desperation of the guerilla fighters, the Dáil members had a bureaucratic image. They wore suits, carried briefcases and were paid a salary. Constance, for instance, received a salary of £250 p.a. as Minister for Labour. Their clandestine meetings, whether as an assembly or as individual departments, took place in offices or private houses. Their role was to establish the semblance of an independent Irish government and as time went on, they did succeed, in several domains, in appropriating the functions of the British administration. Since so many of the men were in prison, or fighting elsewhere, or on the run, it was women who carried out much of this work.

Women were instrumental in producing and circulating the *Irish Bulletin*, the weekly republican news-sheet, which brought to the outside world news of what was going on. Constance always encouraged women to seek a more active role in public life. 'She tried to have us all taught elocution,' said Sighle Humphreys. 'She did teach us herself actually, she had classes. She was like that, she wanted to bring younger women on – we'd say we can't speak and she'd say there is no such thing as you can't speak.'[4] When local government elections were held in January 1920, Con wrote dolefully to Eva that she 'could not get any women to stand in either of the wards of St Patrick's'.[5] Nonetheless, forty-three women were elected to the Sinn Féin-dominated local councils, which pledged allegiance to the Dáil.

The judicial system collapsed, its courts deserted for the republican courts held in creameries, barns and outhouses. Republican justices were called 'Brehons' like their ancient Gaelic counterparts, and they were often women. Hanna Sheehy-Skeffington was President of the Court of Conscience of Dublin Corporation and Aine Ceannt and Aine Heron often presided together as justices for the Rathmines-Pembroke area of Dublin. But otherwise they mostly copied the British system. Courts were attended by professional lawyers who could now get no other work. Since offenders, however, could not be sent to jail they tended to get off lightly. They might, as a punishment, be held in a remote location until the following Sunday when they would be paraded publicly after Mass. The infrastructures of normalcy and social amenities – the cleaning of streets, the mending of roads – broke down. Big houses were raided for guns and sometimes set on fire. Shooting parties were ambushed and relieved of their guns. Dan Breen's marriage took place in a field while he was on the run. Both the groom and the priest who officiated wore guns, while the bride, Cumann na mBan member Brighid Malone, wore a 'Celtic' *bawneen* dress. Martial law came to be applied in some areas.

Much of the Dáil work was merely propaganda. Constance's department was among the more effective in its practice. It was her Department of Labour, which initiated the Labour courts to resolve trade disputes. On one occasion, Con presided over a meeting between the employer and union representatives of the rosary bead factory. The employer's reluctance to come to terms was hastened wonderfully by her regular reminders that a military raid was expected shortly. During the negotiations, she would cut in with 'twenty minutes', 'fifteen minutes', then 'ten minutes'. At this point, the employer's representative agreed to all demands and fled. The existence of the Department doubtless helped to harmonize the activities of Labour and Sinn Féin at this time. Between May and December of 1920 for instance, transport workers refused to run trains carrying the military forces or their stores.

Masquerading as a bureau for the letting of apartments, the Department of Labour in Frederick Street was the only Dáil department not raided by the police – due, according to Jeremiah Mee, to Con's rigorous attitude to security. In addition to the 'Apartments to Let' sign, her offices also contained a number of pianos so that the women among the staff could pretend to be teachers of music. And there were planks arranged against the back windows to enable them to get away with due speed in the event of a raid. Con got great amusement from devising these stratagems. Once, when a raid seemed imminent, she packed all the departmental papers in a trunk and she and Maire O'Brien, who worked with her, set off with it in a taxi through in search of a hiding place. The taxi-driver drove round and round for some time while Constance racked her brains. Finally she hit upon the idea of placing the trunk in the window of a second-hand shop belonging to a sympathizer, with a high price tag attached to it to discourage possible purchasers. The trunk was literally under the noses of the enemy, as the shop in which it sat for weeks was situated directly opposite the headquarters of the Black and Tans. In the Dáil however, she was almost alone in her commitment to Labour interests and could not depend on support from her cabinet colleagues. Try as she might, she had little power to develop the more radical tendencies of the revolution.

In the general ferment of the time, social conflicts were coming to a head. Landless labourers and smallholders were again taking over large estates, usually of absentee landlords. In Munster some workers went so far as to take over mills and factories, and formed themselves into what they called 'Soviets'. Constance tried to persuade the cabinet that non-support of the workers could 'disrupt the Republican cause' and tried to get the Dáil to adopt a policy of establishing co-ops and the 'commandeering' of the Irish Packing Company 'to show the workers we have their interests at heart'. This, her colleagues refused to do. Neither did they respond to her proposal that the Dáil pledge itself to a 'fair and full re-distribution of the vacant lands and ranches of Ireland among the uneconomic holders and landless men'. Instead, land courts were set up as a means of arbitration, which, by and large, were more than sympathetic to the claims of large landowners. As the IRA was used to implement the decisions of the land courts, the polarities within it between the radical elements and the merely nationalistic became apparent. In some places, the IRA acted as a counter-revolutionary force by restoring the land to the landlords. In others, it implemented the division of large estates.

In late September 1920 Constance took a French journalist and clandestine adviser on Irish affairs to the French government Maurice Bourgeois, accompanied by Maud Gonne MacBride's young son Sean MacBride, on a tour of Wicklow. On their return journey, the car, driven by Sean, was stopped by police, whose attentions were attracted by the car's 'engine, horn and lamps all being out of order'. When they saw that the greatly sought Countess Markievicz was a passenger, 'all the King's horses and all the King's men arrived with great pomp'.[6] She was taken off to Mountjoy and remanded in custody until some crime could be found with which to charge her. Just then Eva and Esther Roper were on holiday in Italy. Constance had always encouraged Eva in whatever she was doing but now, back once more in prison, she was quite wistful in her comments about Florence and about the Italian heat and sunshine. She declared stoutly however that 'I am more useful where I am'.

Con's main activities during this term of confinement in Mountjoy were learning Irish and gardening. Her attitude towards Irish varied from exasperation at the stupidities of the grammar – O'Growney's – she was using, to lyricism about the 'soft', 'subtle' and 'gentle' nuances of the language. 'The real difficulties – (i.e. the verbal noun and prepositional and adverbial phrases) are never tackled or systematized … Flails are things they are very keen about in grammars; cows and rye, mice and cats are favourite subjects.'[7] By the following June she was setting herself nightly exercises in composition. Throughout the spring, she was able to work in the prison garden; she dug it out – 'I don't believe it had been honestly dug' – and tended her patch so enthusiastically that she made what had been a desert, when she began, into a garden where sweet peas and eating peas, pansies and carnations flourished. Next she started work on the construction of a rock garden.

For once Constance was not the only felon in the Gore-Booth family. Stasko was in jail in Russia. And Lady Mary Gore-Booth, Josslyn's wife, had a brother serving six months in Pentonville over this same winter. He was Colonel Cecil L'Estrange Malone, a Liberal MP who became unexpectedly radicalized when he visited Russia in 1918. He met leading Bolsheviks and as part of Trotsky's entourage journeyed to Tula by train and reviewed with the Red Army chief his army's troops. On his return L'Estrange Malone was a founding member of the British Communist Party and became the first Communist MP. He had got his sentence after speaking at a meeting opposed to the British expedition to Archangel. What really got him charged with sedition and landed him in jail was his remark *inter alia* at the meeting about the legitimacy of executing bourgeois opponents in a revolution. 'What' he asked, 'are a few Churchills or Curzons on lamp-posts compared to the massacre of thousands of human beings?' Later he would join the Labour Party and by the end of the decade was a Labour MP.

Throughout the winter of 1920–21 the world outside the prison gates became ever more dark and bleak as a bellicose and authorized anarchy held sway. In February 1921 Major-General Sir Nevil Macready, Commander in Chief of the Irish Administration, who, as a soldier, disapproved of the unruly emergency forces, remarked, 'They treat the martial law areas as a special game preserve for their amusement.'[8] Attacks from either side resulted in reprisals and counter-reprisals. Parts of the countryside came to resemble a wasteland as mansions, houses, bridges and roads were destroyed. Corpses were found in fields and on city streets. Terrible things happened. Perhaps the most cold-blooded example of all such operations took place on 21 November. On the morning of that day, eleven officers of the British army, believed by Michael Collins to be active in intelligence work, were shot dead, many of them in their beds, by Collins's execution squad. Four others were wounded. That afternoon, in retaliation, the RIC and Auxiliaries opened fire on the crowd gathered in Croke Park for a football match between Dublin and Tipperary. Twelve people were killed and sixty wounded.

It was a 'miracle that so few were killed' Constance wrote to Eva. She heard the guns in Croke Park from her prison cell. 'You are quite right when you say that things are lurid here. The Croke Park affair lasted twenty minutes by my watch and there were machine-guns going. It felt like being back in the middle of Easter week ...'⁹ She went on to say she hadn't 'given up the Bolshies yet ... The French Revolution gave France new life, though all the fine ideas ended in horrors and bloodshed and wars. The world too gained. Nothing else would have given courage to the underdog and put fear into the heart of the oppressors in the way it did.' She was reading lives of Tolstoi and Danton – 'I rather love the latter'¹⁰ – and, later, the poet Austin Clarke, whose 'long yarns about kings and historical magnificence [she found] very original in this country where the poet wanders in dim twilight mixed with turf-smoke, peopled with peasants and mystic beings with pale hands'.¹¹

In early December after more than two months on remand, she was court-martialled on a charge of conspiracy: of conspiring to 'promote a certain organisation (Fianna Éireann) for the purpose of committing murders of military and police, the drilling of men, the carrying and using of arms'.¹²

The authorities had at last caught up with those nefarious and seditious weekends under canvas in the hills that began eleven years before. In her usual spirited self-defence, Constance took issue with the witness's report of her arrest. She pointed out that the Fianna was never a proclaimed organization, even now, and frankly told the court: 'I started the Fianna because it came to me that it was the duty God gave to me to teach the boys of Ireland to be like the Fianna of old, to ... make them feel it was their duty to give their lives for Ireland if she stood in danger.' Her sentence was two years' hard labour.

In May 1921 the elections to the two new parliaments created by the Government of Ireland Act of 1920 were held. In the twenty-six counties to be governed by the new Dublin parliament, the Sinn Féin candidates were returned unopposed. 'They are,' said Macready, 'practically all gunmen.'¹³ These, the members of the First Dáil, regarded the Act of 1920 as a travesty of their republican aspirations and did not recognize it. Yet they now declared themselves members of the Second Dáil. In the six counties of

Ulster, the majority of members elected to the government of Northern Ireland were unionist. While they for their part would have preferred to sit at Westminster as before, they accepted this parliament of their own as the next best option.

Éamon de Valera had returned from America in December 1920. Because he was absent for much of the conflict, he was regarded by the authorities as an unsullied and respectable figure in comparison to the gunman Michael Collins who was Acting President of the Dáil while he was away. De Valera was also an enthusiastic diplomat. In June Lloyd George changed the government's intention of declaring martial law throughout the twenty-six counties and sending further reinforcements. Instead, he sent word to de Valera that he wished 'to explore to the utmost the possibility of a settlement'. De Valera agreed to go to London to meet the prime minister on the condition that a truce should come into force before he left. Hostilities ceased on 11 July. That month, Con's rock garden in Mountjoy was getting to be 'quite interesting, with little stairs up and down and paths and a sort of obelisk at the top ...' Her plans for it were quite long-term: 'Unluckily the weather is too dry for anything to be planted. Once it begins to rain, I shall make heaps of cuttings and cover it with things.'[14] On 24 July she was informed that she was free to leave. It was the last time for a while that she would be rudely, if in this case, not regrettably, snatched away from the business in hand.

She emerged into an atmosphere of subdued jubilation and expectancy. The republic had virtually achieved recognition, it was felt, with the truce, and with the enemy's willingness to treat with its representatives as equals. The truce has since been regarded by some as a ploy by the British to slow down the revolutionary impetus and to weaken discipline and morale in the republican army. But at the time, it was an enormous relief to both sides to lay down arms and return to the normalcy of life in barracks or on the farm, and an even greater relief to the population to be free at last of terror-ridden nights and days. A letter Con wrote to Eva reflects, to some degree, the country's mood: 'Life is so wonderful. One just wanders round and enjoys it. The children and the trees and cows and all common things are so heavenly after nothing but walls and uniformed people. It is so funny, suddenly to be a

Government and supposed to be respectable. One has to laugh.'[15]

Her position in the government was, in fact, ambiguous. In her absence, the substitute Minister for Labour, Joseph McDonagh, had organized an effective boycott of goods made in Belfast as a protest against the pogroms and discriminations practised there towards Catholics. Protestant – or unionist – hegemonists in that city had felt increasingly threatened by the political developments and were conducting a vendetta against those whom they regarded as republican. The cabinet approved of McDonagh's work and, on Con's return, created a new post for him as Director of the Boycott. She, as Minister for Labour, would continue with her work on labour relations, but was removed from the cabinet. The Dáil's President, de Valera, wanted a smaller executive and therefore made what he termed certain 'unnecessary ministries' extra-cabinet. These included the Labour ministry. Constance clearly saw her consent to accept demotion as a concession to the effective running of a war cabinet – it seems that de Valera explained to her privately why it was necessary, for Ireland's sake, that she should agree. Two women members of the Dáil, Kate O'Callaghan and Mary MacSwiney, rose to express their regret that the only woman member of the cabinet was to be deprived of cabinet rank. Nobody was eager however, to make it a red-line issue at this crucial point in their nation's history.

De Valera was now sending carefully wrought missives across the Irish Sea – in duplicate, since he sent the Irish as well as the English version – to David Lloyd George, or Daithi Uasal Leod Seoirse, setting out the terms on which he would agree to negotiate. Constance described one of these letters as 'a magnificent document'. Another of her contributions in the Dáil was concerned with the teaching of Irish in the schools. Remembering her recent struggles with O'Growney's *Grammar*, she rose to say she hoped something would be done 'towards getting out a really competent Irish grammar'.

But much of the Dáil's time was devoted to the question of what powers the assembly should grant to its representatives who would go to London to treat with the Prime Minister, what their demands should be and who should go. Most of the deputies were united in their determination that the bottom line should be nothing less than recognition of the Republic. De Valera, who had met Lloyd George, knew this was highly unlikely, and had thought up an alternative, which he felt might be acceptable to both sides. This he described as a form of external association with the empire. For Constance and others he drew a series of diagrams consisting of a large circle, representing the empire, and a small circle tangential to it, representing Ireland, to show what he meant. De Valera and all who grasped the subtleties of his wordplay were confident that this at least might be achieved.

In October Constance was re-elected President of Cumann na mBan. Cumann na mBan had played an active part in the war, or the 'Terror' as Constance called it, and was rejuvenated by a number of young, decisive women becoming new members. It was a body similar in its identity to the Inini of more than a decade before. She was now living in Frankfort House in Rathgar, the home of a nationalist family, the Coghlans. Her own house in Rathgar, St Mary's on Frankfort Avenue, was long sold. There were several Coghlan children whom their mother had prepared for Con's arrival by announcing that a Miss Murray was coming to stay. May, the eldest, had worked in the offices of the Department of Labour and knew who Miss Murray really was. But the younger children always regarded her as Auntie Murray and developed a happy relationship with her in the following years.

It was around this time that she received a letter from Casimir, the first since 1916. This letter was destroyed with her other papers so it is difficult to say why, in her reply, she was at such a loss as to what to say to him. It may be that his letter was not very intimate – since they had not seen each other for eight years, this is understandable. He was living in Warsaw and working for the American Consulate General in the city as a Legal Adviser and Commercial Counsellor. Both he and Stasko had suffered at the hands of the Bolsheviks – the house at Zywotowka having been burnt down and the family dispersed. The baby Stasko had with Alexandra had died of typhus and he was now in prison, enduring terrible privations, after serving in the Imperial Marine Guards. Casi may have railed against the Bolsheviks or made remarks with which Constance, given her own politics, could not in conscience sympathize – although remarks she would make in a letter to Stasko show she under no illusions about them. Anyway, her muted and rather stilted reply betrays a studied attempt to be friendly and conciliatory without committing herself in any way. Much of her letter is devoted to news of people he knew in Dublin and assurances that he was much missed – by them, at least.

My dear Casi,

I was very glad to see your writing on an envelope. I don't suppose I should have got your letter except that it arrived in the time of the Truce … You ask me 'what are my plans?' Well, I have none, in fact it's quite impossible to make any at a time like this. Everybody here remembers you. I have come across a great many of the old acting crowd lately and everyone besieges me with questions … Poor Nesbit is shut up in a camp. I'm sure I don't know why. He always used to ask after you. I never go anywhere that someone does not want to know have I heard from you. 'Sink' is always wishing for you back…

I am so glad that you have been successful with plays, and only hope that you are fairly comfortable. I've often been very unhappy thinking of all you and your people must have suffered. Did they lose everything at Zywotowka? Is Babshia alive still? … I'm so sorry about Stas. I wonder why anybody considers it wrong to marry the girl you love. Surely it was not political, he hated politics so. Do write and tell me.

Most of the pictures and some of the furniture are safe up to this. Lots of things were stolen and destroyed in 1916.

A one-act play of mine was played last night with great success … If this Truce goes on you ought to come over for a bit. I know a lot of Irish now, you will be surprised to hear. Now goodbye for the present. Do write to me again soon.

Constance de Markievicz[16]

Casi obviously told her about Stasko's difficulties, and his own. She tells him nothing of what she has been doing, nothing of the harrowing and momentous events she – and his adopted country – have experienced. She even affects a disinterest in them as if anticipating his disapproval. It is the letter of one old friend to another who share acquaintances and cultural interests but who are divided not only by political allegiances but also by the wastage, through time and distance, of old emotions. A few years before, she had pressed Eva to get news of Casi. She had written to Josslyn, at least once from the Department of Labour, requesting Casi's address and asking him to send him some money, and had sent him money herself. She says nothing of this. His long silence and perhaps a disappointing coldness or criticism in the letter he eventually did write perhaps explain her temperate response. She was very proud and would not seek to justify herself in his eyes any more than she sought to justify herself to her family.

NOTES

1. *Prison Letters*, Roper, p. 217.
2. *Ibid.*, p. 217.
3. *The Rebel Countess*, Marreco, p. 255.
4. Speaking on Radio Éireann broadcast, 13 November 1982.
5. *Prison Letters*, Roper, p. 218.
6. *Ibid.*, p. 251.
7. *Ibid.*, p. 269.
8. *The Damnable Question*, Dangerfield, pp. 325–6.
9. *Prison Letters*, Roper, p. 255.
10. *Ibid.*, p. 259.
11. *Ibid.*, p. 269.
12. From a report of the trial in *The Irish Independent*, 4 December 1920.
13. *The Damnable Question*, Dangerfield, p. 327.
14. *Prison Letters*, Roper, p. 275.
15. *Ibid.*, p. 300.
16. Letter in the National Museum, Dublin.

FOURTEEN

THE BITTER SPLIT

ON 11 OCTOBER 1921 the Conference between the Dáil representatives and representatives of Westminster opened in London. They met, according to Lloyd George's formula, to consider how 'the association of Ireland with the community of nations known as the British Empire can best be reconciled with Irish national aspirations'. The Irish representatives were Arthur Griffith, Michael Collins, Robert Barton, E.J. Duggan and George Gavan Duffy. The English representatives made a formidable grouping – they included Lloyd George, Winston Churchill, Lord Birkenhead and Sir Gordon Hewart, the Attorney-General. The Irish delegates were sent as plenipotentiaries – that is, they were given full powers to 'negotiate and conclude' a treaty, although they were supposed to submit any agreement to the cabinet for approval before signing. They had been told they might compromise on the question of status – the title 'Free State' could replace that of 'Republic'. But they were not on any account to accept the principle of allegiance to the crown; only the word 'recognition' of the king as head of the commonwealth was acceptable. This was where de Valera's formula of external association with the commonwealth was to come into play. It was agreed that some form of autonomy might be granted to the six northern counties that sought to remain within the United Kingdom; but only as long as they remained within the aegis of the Dublin parliament and not Westminster.

For two months the delegates were locked in confrontation. It was the Irish who finally climbed down; and they did so without referring to the Dáil cabinet in the draft of the treaty. In the early hours of the morning of 6 December, after a day of gruelling and desperate negotiations, they signed the Articles of Agreement, coerced into compromise in the end by Lloyd George's threat of immediate war if they did not. The document they signed gave to Ireland more autonomy than she had known for several hundred years. But it dis-established the republic that had gallantly asserted its existence since 1916. In its place it established the Irish Free State, an entity that would have the same status within the empire as Canada and Australia. As a symbol of this status, members of the parliament of the Free State would be required to take an oath of allegiance to the Crown:

> I ... do solemnly swear true faith and allegiance to the Constitution of the Irish Free State as by law established and that I will be faithful to H.M. King George V, his heirs and successors at law in virtue of the common citizenship of Ireland with Great Britain and her adherence to and membership of the group of nations known as the British Commonwealth.

To republicans like Constance, other unacceptable provisions were those conditioned by Ireland's proximity to Britain. His Majesty's Imperial Forces were to remain in control of certain ports – at Berehaven and Cobh in the South and Belfast Lough and Lough Swilly in the North – and, at times of war or strained relations with another power, any other facilities the British government might consider useful. Britain would also control Irish airports and airspace.

The Irish response to the treaty was divided. To de Valera, Constance, and almost half of the Dáil, the signing of the treaty was a grievous and terrible mistake, a betrayal of all that had been achieved, at such a price, in the preceding years. Redmond and the Irish Party, they felt, could have won that much. Among the other half, a kind of Thermidorean reaction had set in with the truce.

They considered dominion status, the right to fiscal autonomy and an Irish army and police force sufficient gains, for the time being. Their view was ably expressed by Michael Collins when he said the treaty gave 'not the ultimate freedom that all nations aspire and develop to, but the freedom to achieve it'.[1] Only the British side was jubilant. It had kept the empire intact. It had avoided setting a precedent of submission, which trouble spots like India and Egypt would seek to exploit. It had not lost its power where it perhaps mattered most, i.e., militarily. And it had mollified the unionists.

As far as de Valera was concerned, his intricate designs had brought about a wretched outcome. Then – and often since – it was felt that if de Valera himself had headed the delegation, negotiations would have fared better for republican aspirations. He had given several different reasons, when pressed, why he should not go, though it was clear that he was the most able negotiator available. Basically, it seems, de Valera's statesmanlike ambitions demanded that he remain outside the fray, unsullied by accusations of either intransigence or of failure to achieve all that had been hoped for and expected. Also, his choice of delegates seemed wise at the time, but with hindsight, he might have chosen better. Arthur Griffith was never resolute in his opposition to the oath of allegiance and the British quickly exploited him as the weak link on the Irish side. Michael Collins had little time for de Valera's subtleties of distinction. Robert Barton, an Anglo-Irish gentleman (brother of Constance's – and Poppet's – friend Dulcibella) did not impress Lloyd George. E.J. Duggan, picked because he was a lawyer, was among those who, in the eyes of more intransigent people such as the guerilla leader, Tom Barry, were already being suspected of a certain 'shoneeism' or over-deference to British forms and protocols.

To the republican confreres however, all was not yet lost. The treaty, before it could come into force, would have to be ratified by the Dáil. On 14 December the Dáil convened. The protracted, emotive and in many ways, agonizing debate lasted into the New year, with an adjournment on 22 December for Christmas. The republicans, now referred to increasingly as the 'diehards' evoked the recent dead and how they would be betrayed by a retreat from the living, tangible reality of the republic. To this argument, Collins countered with a reminder that while deputies had 'spoken about whether dead men would approve of it' and 'whether children unborn will approve of it', few had spoken 'as to whether the living approve of it'. Collins was perhaps more compromised than anyone by the treaty. He had been extremely reluctant to go to London, seeing, just as de Valera did, the dangers inherent in compromise. He had signed it only because he genuinely did believe in Lloyd George's threat to make war 'within three days' if he did not. And he knew, as head of the IRB and Director of Intelligence, the vulnerable state of the republican army at the time of the truce, and that the republic could not be defended in the event of war.

Ironically it was Constance who may have unwittingly weakened anti-treaty support when she seconded, despite de Valera's opposition, the motion for adjournment until after Christmas. In that countrywide peaceful, domestic hiatus, the spectre of war and continuing struggle seemed more and more unpalatable. On 3 January, she rose, dressed in her green Cumann na mBan uniform, to give an impassioned, wide-ranging and substantial speech. She began in Irish, a language in which she was now quite competent, and then went on: 'I rise today to oppose with all the force of my will, with all the force of my whole existence, this so-called Treaty – this Home Rule Bill covered over with the sugar of a Treaty.' In a firm rejection of the class to which she belonged by birth, she opposed the granting of special privileges of representation in the proposed upper chamber to southern unionists, implied in an overture Griffith made to them:

> Now why are these men to be given something special? ... The people who, in Southern Ireland, have been the English garrison against Ireland and the rights of Ireland ... that class of capitalists who have been more crushing, cruel and grinding on the people of the nation than any class of capitalists of whom I ever read in any country... . They are the people who have combined together against the workers of Ireland, who have used ... every institution in the country to ruin the farmer, and more especially the small farmer, and to send the people of Ireland to drift in the emigrant ships and to die of terrible disease or to sink to the bottom of the Atlantic.

She was looking, she said, 'for the prosperity of the many, for the happiness and content of the workers, for what I stand, James

Connolly's ideal of a Workers Republic'. At this, the deputy interrupted her: 'A Soviet Republic.' 'A co-operative commonwealth,'
Constance replied.

She presented a dissertation on what the oath actually signi-
fied, emphasizing the dishonour inherent in taking an oath one did
not believe in:

> Now personally, I being an honourable woman, would sooner die than
> give a declaration of fidelity to King George and the British Empire
> [because] if we pledge ourselves to this oath we pledge our allegiance
> to this thing, whether you call it the Empire or the Commonwealth
> of Nations, that is treading down the people of Egypt and of India.

England, she said, was now being more dishonourable and
'acting in a cleverer way than she ever did before':

> Now you all know me, you know that my people came over here in
> Henry VIII's time and by that bad black drop of English blood in me,
> I know the English – that's the truth. I say it is because of that black
> drop in me that I know the English personally better perhaps than the
> people who went over on the delegation.

This aroused laughter from the benches and a call – 'Why
didn't you go over?' 'Why didn't you send me?' asked Constance,
rather pertinently. She appealed to the assembly to remain true to
their ideals, to walk on

> the stony road that Leads to ultimate freedom and the regeneration
> of Ireland; the road that so many of our heroes walked ... I fear
> dishonour; I don't fear death, and I feel at all events that death is
> preferable to dishonour ... I have seen the stars and I am not going to
> follow a flickering will o' the wisp, and I am not going to follow any
> person juggling with constitutions and introducing petty tricky ways
> into this Republican movement which we built up – you and not I –
> because I have been in jail.

The five other women members of the Dáil unanimously
echoed her stand. Because all of them had had menfolk, husbands,
brothers or sons who had died in the years since 1916, this stand
was categorized by Deputy McCabe of Sligo as a 'craving for
vengeance'. They denied this charge. But in the unhappy years to
come, this image of intransigence and fury was imposed on all
republican women and reached the level of caricature.

Con's socialist arguments were upheld at this juncture only by Liam Mellowes. He also expressed the rather paradoxical readiness of the republicans to put aside practical considerations for the sake of their ideals:

> We do not seek to make this country a materially great country at the expense of its honour ... We would rather have this country poor and indigent, we would rather have the people of Ireland eking out a poor subsistence on the soil; as long as they possessed their souls, their minds and their honour.

The debate came to an end on 7 January. It ended with tears and a split. When the vote was taken, sixty-four deputies were in favour of approval of the treaty; fifty-seven were against. de Valera spoke of the 'glorious record' of the Dáil for the previous four years. 'It has been four years of magnificent discipline in our nation. The world is looking at us now.' Here he broke down in tears, unable to continue. On 10 January de Valera and his supporters walked out of the chamber in a hail of vituperation from both sides – 'Deserters', 'Oath-breakers' etc. Constance had the last word, flinging back as she left the epithet 'Lloyd Georgites'. The truncated assembly then proceeded to elect Arthur Griffith as president. The republic was no more. There would be elections within a few months in which the republicans hoped to rally the country to their standard but this hope was faint. A provisional government was appointed to rule in the interregnum.

The egalitarian spirit of the republic was further betrayed when, in March, the Dáil refused to allow the vote to women between 21 and 30; partly because it was thought that Cumann na mBan, which had been the first body to overwhelmingly reject the treaty reflected the views of women generally; partly because in the preparation of a new electoral register, the franchise would be also extended to young militant men who were not at present on the register. Constance in her Dáil speech described how equality for women was her 'first bite, you may say, at the apple of freedom':

> And soon I got on to the other freedom, freedom to the nation, freedom to the workers ... I would work for it anywhere, as one of the crying wrongs of the world, that women because of their sex, should be debarred from any position or any right that their brains entitle them to hold ... Today I would appeal ... to see that justice is

done to those young women and young girls who took a man's part in the Terror.

She was not left to brood, however, on the probable debacle of republican hopes in the coming election. In January she was a delegate at the Race Congress in Paris, a conference that had been planned since the year before with the well-meaning aim of establishing Irish identity in the eyes of the world. W.B. Yeats, his brother Jack Yeats, and the artist Evelyn Gleeson were among those who read papers. But the Congress predictably became a hotbed of intrigue between pro- and anti-treaty factions. And Con and Maud Gonne MacBride were put out by the almost monarchical status bestowed on the Duke of Tetuan who came from Madrid to preside over the proceedings – the Duke also bore the title 'The O'Donnell' as the descendent of Hugh O'Donnell, one of the so-called 'Wild Geese', the native Irish aristocracy who fled to the Continent after the defeat of 1601. The Duke, wrote Madame MacBride, knew nothing of Ireland except its horses.

On 1 April Constance left for America on the *Aquitania* with the task of swaying public opinion in favour of the republican side. Both the republicans and 'Free Staters' sent rival delegations to persuade Americans of the rightness of their respective causes. Of the four republican delegates, two were women, Con – who aroused enormous interest in America because of her colourful history and plucky, charming personality – and Miss Kathleen Barry, a young Cumann na mBan woman, and sister of the executed boy-hero, Kevin Barry, already famed in song.

The two women often travelled and addressed meetings independently of the men and were everywhere hosted and feted as Hollywood stars would be a decade or two later. There were roses, roses all the way, and brass bands, scrambling photographers and decorated cars. Reporters across the continent devoted much space to painstaking descriptions of their appearance, clothes and personalities. Con was, 'despite her martial achievements', not a martial-looking person – 'frail rather, and almost deprecatory except when she is talking about the Irish Republic ...' 'Very tall and slender she has the stoop characteristic of so many women of her height ...' 'Quixotic and shrewd, mystical and wayward, a figure to kindle the imagination ...' 'She is rather sharp-featured, clear and yet some[what] tanned of complexion, and a person of much nervous energy ...'² Kathleen Barry was presented as the winsome and classic version of the Irish colleen.

For two months they travelled the length and breadth of the United States, addressing meetings in small towns and large cities, at which subscriptions and pledges were given, worth in all about £20,000. They attended receptions and banquets, gave interviews to reporters and politicians and visited sources of local pride. As was then customary in the west, they were shown over several prisons. In Butte, Montana, on an official visit to a copper mine, Constance, who had been 'put up to things by wicked friends in the IWW' asked 'awkward questions': 'I insisted on going into hot places and seeing men working with a pick and drill. I insisted on climbing into a stoop ... ' She was horrified by the sight of men 'breathing in copper dust eight mortal hours a day'. 'Few men,' she told Eva, 'live to be old in Butte, Montana.'³

She loved the clean, modern, spacious feel of American domestic architecture:

> The bathrooms are a joy and even the small houses have them; walls and all of shining white tiles and cupboards built into the walls, so convenient. Akron especially took my fancy. We drove out to the suburbs, and even the poor houses stood alone, among greenery.⁴

She described graphically the different landscapes and vegetation and climates she passed through, wondering, since Eva had journeyed across America as a young girl with their father, whether she 'passed the same way long ago and loved the same beautiful length of river, rock or group of trees'.⁵ She saw things with an incisive artist's eye – in the orange groves of Los Angeles, 'great piles of golden balls on the brown earth, ready to be packed and shipped away'.⁶ And in Montana:

> weird unwholesome-looking mountains, slimy rocks and hollows and slimy brown earth with patches of dead grass or sage bush, looking as if the Deluge had just drained off it, and as if each hammock might hide a scaly, prehistoric monster and each stagnant pool a water-snake.⁷

Impressed by the apparent contentment of gum-chewing members of the audience in different auditoriums, she put aside her cigarettes and took up the irritating habit of chewing gum until she was requested to desist by her companions.

On an interminable train journey through Minnesota, she wrote a loving and solicitous letter to Stasko, which largely concerned his welfare and his wife's, 'my daughter-in-law'. Jim Larkin, she told him, had promised to use his influence with the Bolsheviks on his behalf. She herself had been shut up for three and a half years, she told him, 'and some of it was awful'.

'Also dear Casi,' she wrote, 'I hate to think of him having to work on a job.' She reproved him a little for railing against the Bolsheviks:

> I know little about them but one thing I do know that our people suffered far worse from the English; and what I begin to believe is that all governments are the same, and that men in power use that power for themselves and are absolutely unscrupulous in their deal-ings with those who disagree with them. I am finishing this letter in the train ... The scenery is beautiful, wild and rugged with patches of snow everywhere, and real cowboys rounding up cattle in the fields.[8]

On their travels, Con often spoke to Kathleen Barry of 'my little daughter' and bought presents for Maeve, including Hudson Bay furs in Seattle. Kathleen imagined Maeve to be a young girl, a child really. She was very surprised when, on their arrival in London, a tall, well-built young woman came to her hotel room, introduced herself as Maeve Markievicz and asked for her mother. Constance was somewhere about the hotel and when Kathleen suggested that she look for her downstairs, Maeve confessed that as it was some time since she had seen her mother (their previous meeting seems to have taken place in Cork Jail about three years before), she could not be sure she would recognize her. When Maeve did go downstairs, she came back once more to Kathleen to have it confirmed that the lady having coffee with two friends was indeed Constance.

On her return from America she went straight into the crucial election campaign, to take place in June 1922. The Labour Party too put up candidates, displaying its conservative character in supporting the treaty. The treaty split had exposed the deeper divi-sions in Irish society. As the historian T.A. Jackson wrote:

> The line-up was between the actually or potentially land-hungry, supported by Republican intellectuals and urban revolutionaries on

one side, and the urban bourgeoisie, the state-functionaries, the land-owners and the upper strata of the peasantry on the other.[9]

The electorate was confused by an election pact between pro-treatyites and anti-treatyites, which broke down shortly before the election. It was also a problem that the constitution on which the people were to vote became available only on the day the election was held. The pro-treatyites, or 'Free Staters', won 56 seats; the anti-treatyites, or republicans, won 36. Labour won 17, Farmers 7 and Independents 6. Constance lost her seat. She had had little time to campaign after her hurried return from America. But the result was decisive. The people had rejected the Republic and given a mandate to govern to the Free State.

During Con's absence in America, some republicans seized and occupied the Four Courts. This was the elegant Georgian building upriver from O'Connell Bridge that housed valuable archives and had been a scene of action in 1916. After the election, Michael Collins very reluctantly bowed to intense pressure from the British to clear them out. On 28 June the 'Free Staters' opened fire on the Four Courts using 18-pounders loaned to them by their former enemy, General Macready. As the siege continued, republicans converged on the city centre to take up the defence, mainly using buildings in and around O'Connell Street. Hotels were requisitioned and the street echoed to the sound of gunfire and was palled in smoke and dust. It was like 1916 all over again. But a bitter twist of fate had determined that people who fought side by side in 1916 were intent on killing one another now.

In Frankfort House, Constance knew from the first heavy boom to the north that the Four Courts was under attack and rushed to its defence. In the following days as the battle intensified around them, she moved from garrison to garrison along with her fellow-fighters. One of them described her expertise as a sniper from her precarious position on the parapet of the roof of the Hammam Hotel on O'Connell Street:

> Coming on towards evening the fighting was mostly a snipers' battle. There was a sniping post on the roof-tops at the top of Henry Street. It was a well-placed, well-manned post. The snipers in it – there were two or three of them, taking over from one another so that their fire

was continuous – made my position in the shelter of the cornice as dangerous a one as you could find.

I was due for relief and I wasn't sorry for that. But when my relief came, who was it but Madame. Played-out as I was after two or three hours up there under continuous fire, I didn't like the idea of a woman taking over that position. But Madame just waved me to one side with that imperious air she could put on when she wanted to have her own way. She slipped into what little shelter there was, carrying with her an automatic Parabellum pistol – the kind we used to call a Peter the Painter.

I couldn't rightly say how long she was up there, for I was so tired that I drowsed off to sleep. But when I woke up, the first thing I noticed was something different in the sound of the firing. The steady, continuous rattle of fire that I had learned to pick out from the sound of rifle and machine gun fire up and down the street had ceased; the snipers' post in Henry Street was silent.[10]

On 6 July after – just as in 1916 – a week of battle, the republican forces surrendered their posts in central Dublin. Constance was in one of the last outposts under the command of Cathal Brugha, a 1916 man. Kathleen Barry remembered how Brugha went up to her and said 'Madame, I order you as a soldier to hand over your rifle' and how Constance did what he asked after only a very momentary hesitation and then marched off towards the back door. Brugha himself then went out the front door into the broad daylight of O'Connell Street with a gun blazing in each hand. He was immediately mown down. Churchill sent a fraternal telegram of congratulations on the Government's success to Michael Collins, a recipient for whom it must have been a bitter pill. The fight however moved to the country and the methods learned in the Anglo-Irish War – of ambush, reprisal and counter-reprisal – were now applied to the new enemy of erstwhile comrades. Sometimes they were applied literally by brother to brother.

Within a few months many regarded as the bravest and the best of both sides were dead. Michael Collins died in August, ambushed on a country road in County Cork. Liam Mellowes and Erskine Childers were executed. Arthur Griffith, whom Con had come to regard with some admiration, died in hospital that summer, his death perhaps induced by stress. Country towns – Kinsale, Bandon, Carrick-on-Suir, Cork – were taken by republicans and retaken by 'Free Staters'. In these fraught times, events that a year or two before would have been symbolic of glorious victory now seemed of little account to Constance and to people like her: the vacating of barracks by British troops, barracks, which were promptly taken over by one side or the other; the British trucks and armoured cars rumbling out of the gates of Dublin Castle for the last time. Brighid Lyons at least found consolation in this sight:

> I remember going down to Dame Street the day the British left the Castle. Now that was always the mythical symbol of the British Empire to us, and here they were leaving it and Collins was taking it over. We were very pleased and proud to see it, and I thought the Treaty was at least a great measure of freedom and we could build on it and go in the future.[11]

To Constance, this would have seemed a milk-and-water, even ignominious, response. She was now on the run, moving from safe house to safe house, and writing articles for the republican *Poblacht na h-Éireann,* with the strong clear propagandist voice of uncompromising conviction. To her the Free State was adopting the coloration of that recent enemy and the Castle was seeing out one repressive regime only to be inhabited by another.

It is true that in its repressive measures, the Free State was rivalling its recent enemy. For the moment, its sole *raison d'être* was the suppression of republicanism. In September it brought in a Special Powers Act and in October, a measure, which made the carrying of an unauthorized weapon a capital offence. As a result, there were wholesale executions: in January 1923 there were thirty-four. Morale and discipline disintegrated and killings become vindictive and ugly. In December for instance, the government executed four prisoners in retaliation for the shooting of a Dáil Deputy; one of them was Rory O'Connor who had been best man the year before at the wedding of Kevin O'Higgins. Now O'Higgins was among the government ministers who gave the order for the execution of his friend. The revolution, like Saturn, had begun to eat its own children. In May 1923 de Valera ordered his soldiers to dump arms: 'The Republic can no longer be successfully defended by your arms. Further sacrifice of life would now be in vain ...' But with the firm determination that was to become a hallmark of republicans, he implied that this was not really a surrender. The people, he said, were 'weary, and need a rest ... A little time and you will see them recover and rally again to the standard?'[12]

From the previous January Constance was absent, mainly in Scotland and northern England, and later for several weeks in London, acting as a kind of public relations person for the republic. She wrote articles for *Eire*, the successor to *Poblacht na h-Éireann*, and spoke at numerous meetings, many of them well-attended and fervent. Her speeches, it was reported in *Eire*, were ably convincing: 'the Irish people of the English capital of the appalling treachery and tragedy of the so-called Treaty and the brutal warfare of King George's Ministers in Ireland and the Republic'.[13] In July she was back in Ireland, recalled by de Valera to campaign for the general election in August. With this election the government was seeking to confirm its mandate to rule. Still the repression continued. Thousands of republicans were now interned without trial in prisons and camps where they were subject to punishment by flogging. Many more were on the run. De Valera was arrested in Ennis in July as he made an election speech and was imprisoned for over a year.

Although their election campaign was harried and disorganized – so many of them being interned or on the run – the republicans, standing as Sinn Féin, won a small increase in their representation. But so too did 'free staters', now forming the party called Cumann na nGael. Constance won back her old seat. But of course she, like the other Sinn Féin deputies, would not be taking their seats because of the Oath of Allegiance. For the next four years, and the first years of the Free State's existence, the Dáil functioned without the benefit of an adequate opposition. For some months to come, Con's opposition to the regime continued to be expressed through the old decisive tactics of street-protest and hunger strike. These were tactics that in the harsh Ireland of the 1920s came to seem outdated and histrionic.

During the autumn of 1923 the republicans interned in prisons and camps resorted to the weapon of the hunger strike. By early November over 8000 internees were refusing to eat. Constance, still at freedom, spent her days holding meetings, organizing petitions for the release of the internees. She was 'getting on splendidly' at this, she wrote to Eva. But on 20 November she was arrested while she was speaking from a dray parked in Dublin's Kevin Street. With the cheerful manner she used to assume, and sometimes affected, for Eva's benefit, she wrote:

> I went on hunger strike directly I was taken. They offered me tea in the Police Station and I just decided right off. I only did three days and I was quite happy and did not suffer at all. I slept most of the time and had lovely dreams and the time went by quite quickly. I think I would have slipped out quite soon.[14]

She was obliged to fast for only three days. On the day of her arrest, a young man died after not eating for thirty-four days, provoking a decision among the leaders to call off the hunger strike so as to save further loss of life.

She was imprisoned for over a month in the North Dublin Union, a former workhouse – 'a vast and gloomy place, haunted by the ghosts of broken-hearted paupers'[15] – where the women were confined communally in great dormitories. Constance behaved with the same staunchness that she had shown in Holloway. She sketched and did watercolours of 'the girls', insisted on scrubbing floors, with her skirt tucked inside her bloomers, while most of the others read or knitted; and took over the care of a girl called Baby Bohon from Co Sligo who was very ill from refusing food for thirty days. She cooked the girl meals, cushioned her starvation-ridden body with her own to ease her backache and gave her her own pair of mittens to protect her from the cold. 'We are really a very cheerful little party,' she wrote to Eva. On Christmas Eve Constance was released from her last incarceration. On that winter's day she emerged to face the bleak reality of life in the Free State.

NOTES

1. Dáil Éireann, Private Sessions, vol. 2.
2. *The Rebel Countess*, Marreco, pp. 274–5.
3. *Prison Letters*, Roper, p. 289.
4. *Ibid.*, p. 287.
5. *Ibid.*, p. 286.
6. *Ibid.*, p. 289.
7. *Ibid.*, p. 289.
8. Letter in the National Museum, Dublin.

9. *Nationalism and Socialism in Twentieth Century Ireland* (E. Rumpf and A.C. Hepburn, Liverpool University Press, 1977).
10. *Constance Markievicz*, Van Voris, p. 325.
11. *Curious Journey*, Griffith and O'Grady, pp. 263–4.
12. Message to the republican forces, 24 May 1923.
13. *Eire*, 17 March 1923.
14. *Prison Letters*, Roper, p. 281.
15. *Ibid.*, p. 281.

FIFTEEN

LIFE IN THE FREE STATE

THOSE FIRST years in the Free State and the last years of Constance Markievicz's life were extremely bleak for radicals and romantics like her. It was a state conceived in a spirit of grand quasi-mystical hope and optimism. When it was finally born, it was a stunted and twisted creature, already grown and hardened and wearing the features of the old enemy. Those who kept the faith with the short-lived republic could be said to have been, by and large, the dreamers, the idealistic and visionary. It was the hard-headed men who took over – the supposedly practical and moderate – who had seen in turmoil and change a threat to property and well-established values and who now proceeded to govern in the interests of the business community, the larger farmers and the professional classes.

Constance, an idealist first and last, had long repudiated what they now sought – status, wealth, privilege and security. In this sense, those lines of Yeats's, which depict her as one who 'Drags out lonely years/Conspiring among the ignorant'[1] are true in part. She was lonely in the new dispensation both by temperament and in fact since her republican soulmates were scattered and isolated. Some remained in prison until the summer of 1924. After that, many of them were forced to emigrate, unable to comply with the new regulation obliging employees of the state to take an Oath of Allegiance. The Free State government was determined to stamp out what they saw as the anarchy of republicanism and this regulation was one of several measures devised to do just that. Jobs to which they might have gravitated, as teachers, members of the new police force (the Garda Síochána), the Army and the Civil Service were thus closed to them. Maire Comerford, 'tired and brokenhearted', spent the 1920s eking out a living on a remote chicken farm and gradually lost contact with her old friends.

Constance hated the Free State's appropriation of the symbols of the republic – the tricolour, the green uniform of the Volunteers for its soldiers, the Dáil – and how they were co-opted into the machinery of a government that was merely 'business as usual but under new management'. The phrase 'green post-box politics' was coined to express what was regarded as no more than lip service to the old aspirations. The machinery of state was organized quickly and competently – an unarmed police force, local authorities, courts of justice – but they mirrored the British system they replaced, not the old Gaelic order the Dáil of pre–1921 had attempted to recreate. In its social philosophy, the Free State was as far as could be imagined from Constance's ideal of Connolly's worker's republic or a cooperative commonwealth. The Democratic Programme of the First Dáil was rejected, Kevin O'Higgins, Minister for Home Affairs, describing contemptuously its policy on natural resources as 'largely communistic'. Its economic policy, aiming at fiscal rectitude and deflation, was negative rather than expansionist.

Ireland, always the poorest section of the British Isles, was to remain so for many decades to come. The first Free State government cut pensions, salaries and stopped payment to the uninsured unemployed. It lowered the rate of income tax and recommended cuts in wages. 'There are certain limited funds at our disposal,' said the Minister for Industry and Commerce, 'and people may die in this country and may have to die through starvation.'[2] Emigration continued to increase. One aspect of republicanism the Free State did retain though was the policy of Gaelicization. This was carried out grimly and in a way that seemed repressive and sectarian to later generations. It became mandatory for Irish to be taught in schools for at least one hour a day. To English-speaking children and sometimes-unwilling teachers, this often felt like coercion. Films and books considered 'subversive of public morality' or liable to impose the 'standardization' of Anglo-American culture were censored or discouraged. Divorce was made impossible.

In much of this at least, some people of both sides found common ground. There is nothing that suggests Constance disapproved of Gaelicization in this form – apart from her exasperation with O'Growney's *Grammar* – although as an egalitarian, she would not have wanted Gaelicization to become synonymous with Catholicism. It is significant that she was not in the party of republican women that included Madame MacBride, Mrs Pearse, Kathleen Clarke and Hanna Sheehy-Skeffington and who caused pandemonium at the Abbey Theatre during a performance of Sean O'Casey's *The Plough and the Stars*. This was because they considered it amoral and a slur on the manhood of 1916 – a view that was shared by several of the players and production people. Of what good was compulsory Irish, she may well have thought, when the heroes of 1916 had to be defended by reaction; when the King lived at the Viceregal Lodge in the shape of his Governor-General, Tim Healy; and when the Minister for Home Affairs and Vice-President, Kevin O'Higgins, could seriously propose that the King himself be brought to the Phoenix Park to be crowned King of Ireland? To her, it seemed that the movement she had discovered with such zest years before and to which she had given much of her life, had to start over again. She was too old and weary to be able to contemplate that with much heart.

Yet, she tried. She succeeded in inspiring Cumann na mBan to keep up their uncompromising identity. She re-marshalled the Fianna, although their martial character was toned down. Within a few years she had been elected to Rathmines Urban District Council. As a Councillor she championed the interests of the working class on committees concerned with housing, public health, child welfare and so on, and campaigned for facilities like public swimming baths. She had not lost her imperious manner. Maud Long, then a young girl in Cumann na mBan, regarded her with distant awe because of her past and her reputation and remembered her 'shouting like a man – she would call "ahoy there" or "you there" if she wanted you'. Maud also remembered her never sitting down at meetings but always standing restlessly by the wall. It was obvious, however, to those who had known her before that her vitality, something like the wellspring of her being, had snapped.

Jeremiah Mee, the RIC man she had brought into her Labour ministry, said that when he first knew her she was 'handsome … athletic, bright-eyed and keen'. Four years later, at a meeting in Sligo, he found her 'a careworn woman, broken, dispirited and sad'.[3] People who were in sympathy with her attitudes saw her as a hero, a veteran, but to others she had come to seem *passé*, beached in an age that had moved beyond the heroic times she belonged to. A small boy, brought by his parents to see this famous figure speak at a meeting, saw only an old woman with an unpleasant voice shouting from the trailer of a tractor in a field. The writer, Mary Colum, who always remembered Con's comment in her heyday – 'I am not interested in men, because I have had the pick of too many men' – was saddened to see her at Æ's in the mid 1920s, much changed:

> No trace of beauty remained; she was like an extinct volcano, her former violent self reduced to something burnt out … It made me sad to see how little attention was paid to Constance Gore-Booth by those in the room; perhaps the habitués of Æ's had become accustomed to seeing her sitting exhausted there in the corner, the brown poodle at her feet.

To Mary Colum, she was

> haggard and old, dressed in ancient demoded clothes; the outline of the face was the same, but the expression was different; the familiar eyes that blinked at me from behind glasses were bereft of the old fire and eagerness. She gave me a limp hand and barely spoke to me … She was obviously a dying woman, sunk in dejection resulting either from imprisonment or from the loss of her hopes. What she had fought for had not come into being; maybe nothing on earth could have brought it into being, so romantic and heroic was it.[4]

But the decline depicted by Mary Colum was gradual and Con's dispiritedness only episodic. Her will to fight and to hope remained indomitable. She acquired an old car, which required a lot of nursing and attention and led to her being nicknamed Lizzie after it. 'She understood cars,' said the writer, Francis Stuart, who saw her on at least one occasion in Grafton Street under the bonnet of that car. Francis Stuart was then married to Maud Gonne MacBride's daughter, Iseult, and Constance used to visit them in their cottage at Glencree in Co. Wicklow. Francis was, if somewhat desultorily, a republican, and he kept always a note of introduction Con gave him to be presented to Mary MacSwiney in Cork, saying simply, 'This is Francis Stuart. Please help him.' He found her much more likeable than other republican women who rather intimidated him: 'She was warm-hearted, natural, very interested in practical things like how were we living and how we were managing, if we had a car ... So it was very easy to talk and get along with her. Unlike Maud Gonne who always put herself at a distance.'[5]

Maud Long remembered her wearing a motoring hat, one of those saucer-shaped hats with a veil that were very popular around 1910 and were advertised in *Bean na h-Éireann*.

She used to allow the Coughlan children to accompany her and the dog on drives and while they piled enthusiastically into the car for these excursions, her eccentricity made them squirm with embarrassment. When the car broke down, and it generally did, she had a habit of removing her skirt so she could crawl unhindered under and around it in her bloomers. When she brought them into Grafton Street, they would be disgorged from the car at the door of Woolworths; and summoned when it was time to go home by an imperious voice yelling 'Children, children', from the direction of the street, for all the shop to hear.

In 1924 she wrote a pamphlet called *James Connolly's Policy and Catholic Doctrine* in which she reiterated for herself as much as for her readers all that Connolly believed in. She quoted extensively from his writings and from *Rerum Novarum*, Pope Leo XIII's encyclical on social justice, to illustrate to the faithful and to reassure them that Connolly's ideals were not contrary to Catholic teaching, despite the Church's tolerance of the Free State and its condemnations of republicanism. Maud Long's parish priest for example refused to allow her to receive communion when she was wearing her Cumann na mBan uniform.

That summer, Casimir, in London as part of a delegation from Poland, came over to Dublin and stayed for a month. The reunion seems to have been a complicated pleasure for both him and for Constance – a previous biographer says he hung around the watering holes of the city for several days before going to see her and that he came, in fact, to ask for a divorce.[6] But when they did meet, he made no such request, his intentions, if they existed, evaporating perhaps in the face of his renewed memories and her gladness at seeing him. He may have put off meeting her in those first days because he was reluctant to find her changed – as Dublin was changed, the bright certainties of its Edwardian past tarnished. Together they took a tram out to Fairview, to visit Kathleen Clarke and inspect the paintings and trunks she had in her keeping since the dispersal of Surrey House. He found his portrait of Jadwiga, his first wife, and took it back to Warsaw as a keepsake for Stasko who had never known his birth mother. He also took a photograph of Constance, taken for publicity purposes before she went to America. He kept it on his desk for the rest of his life.

They must have talked about plays and the theatre. By September, Constance had set up the Republican Players Dramatic Society. The Society produced several plays including two of hers. In the following spring she became completely absorbed in writing a three-act play set in the Black-and-Tan period. 'I simply could not stop,' she wrote to Eva. (She was electioneering at the time.) 'One day I got my car out at 7 and never stopped driving round until weary and sleepy I rang up a house at 2.30 to beg for a bed. But every minute I had to wait for someone outside a house – out with my old book and anyhow the play is finished at last.'[7]

The play, *Broken Dreams*, is written in the mode and idiom of the 'peasant' or 'national' plays made popular by the Abbey some years before. Its theme is the dishonour and treachery of those who took up Ireland's cause only out of egotism or a desire to exploit it for their own advantage. Her heroine, Eileen, is clearly an idealized self-projection:

> Tall, slim and good-looking … Her face is refined and inclined to be ascetic. There is little suggestion of sex in her, she is more like a young boy in her manner. Even with the men who love her, she is so

simple and frank. She wears a well-made short tweed skirt and coat
... and good strong country walking-shoes with low heels. She does
not affect either marcel wave and manicured hands, nor does her face
give the effect of being powdered.[8]

The villain, Seamus, is 'pleasure-loving and sensual'. He has
a low forehead, and is 'rather smartly-dressed in foreign clothes
but wears a trench coat and Trilby hat like the other boys'. The
hero, Eamonn, has 'a good brow ... a man who feels deeply but
has great powers of self-control. His clothes are of Irish material
and make. He wears a trench coat and Trilby hat.' *Broken Dreams*
shows that her imagination was still fired by the old, dear, simple
verities of nationalism. She felt its theme intensely. Mary Colum
thought it poignant that Constance talked about her play as if 'it
were her one interest in life'.

It is not surprising that when Éamon de Valera formed a
new party from the more moderate elements in Sinn Féin early
in 1926, she left Cumann na mBan to join it. De Valera, together
with Constance, was now one of the few survivors of 1916 and
the only one to embody and formulate its myth. He seemed to
share with her the clarity and nobility and unity of the old, not
merely rational, nationalism. But he was also pragmatic. His
party, Fianna Fáil (meaning Soldiers of Destiny) was founded with
the aim of having the Oath of Allegiance removed and re-entering
the Dáil. It offered a viable way out of the vacuum of disillusion
and marginalization of the 1920s and thus appealed to Constance
who could not bear inaction. She wrote to Eva that 'some unlog-
ical persons are howling' at de Valera's proposal to enter the Free
State parliament: 'They stand for the principle and for the honour
of the Republic and prefer to do nothing but shout continually
"The Republic lives".'[9] She remarked that it was likely to be a long
time before the oath was removed. But 'anyhow it is something to
go for with a chance of success'. It was Constance who presided
at the meeting to launch the Fianna Fáil party in April 1926 at
the La Scala Theatre. Cumann na mBan hated to lose her but she
could not remain in both organizations since Cumann na mBan
was committed to working with the IRA. In joining Fianna Fáil,
Constance was forsaking the old nationalist tradition of physical
force in favour of constitutional methods.

She was seeing quite a bit of Maeve who used to 'blow in' on her way to Sligo and 'commandeer' the car. Maeve had done the London Season to please her grandmother but liked it as little as her mother had. 'I love the queer little musical instrument she has,' Con told Eva, 'and the way she has of lilting to it all sorts of silly little songs without any pretension at all but very attractive.'[10] Maeve 'loved machinery' and helped her mother 'pull the car to pieces'. She was like Constance too in being a keen gardener and would later take a B.Sc. in Horticulture at Swanley Agricultural College for Women. But she and her mother, perhaps because they were too alike, still seemed to lack the sympathy that comes from mutual trust. Some months earlier, Con had written to Stasko that Eva 'is the only relation I have left. She is a wonderful old darling.'[11] Otherwise, Con felt alienated, however unnecessarily, from her family: 'Joss I never see and never want to see,' she said, and chose to think that 'Gaga' (her mother) saw her whenever she came to Dublin only because 'I am useful to her':

> The rest of them live in England ... I don't mind. I never worried, I only tell you so that you know, if I blow across them I shall be quite amenable to any of them. They are no worse than anyone else, and I suppose it's very embarrassing to have a relation that gets into jail and fights in revolutions that you are not in sympathy with.

Her characteristic impulse to be modern asserted itself. She had her hair, which she used to wear knotted on top, cropped into a bob: 'I have it quite short at the back and parted at the side, covering my ears. It is quite smooth and straight as a rule, for I seldom curl it.' She told Stasko that the red Russian boots the Markieviczes had had made for her when she was staying at Zywotowka were fashionable again and they were 'the smartest boots in Dublin'. Then, just as she was finding an equanimity, even an optimism about the future, she lost Eva. In June 1926 her 'only relation' died suddenly of an internal cancer she had suffered from for some time. When Constance got the telegram from Esther, 'everything seemed to go from under' her. She did not attend the funeral in London because, she told Eithne Coyle, she 'simply couldn't face the family'.[12] But in September she went over to stay with Esther for a while. She sat for long periods in Eva's room and began to commune in meditation with her as she had done when she was imprisoned in Aylesbury. At odd moments, especially at moments of crisis, she would feel her presence. She could not relinquish, even when Eva was dead, the sense of protection and approval that the living Eva had always given her.

That winter, a friend entered her room unexpectedly and found her crying quietly to herself. 'I was always dreaming and planning to take you both along to some beautiful places in the car,' she wrote to Esther. 'I was writing a play and doing a copy to send her ... And then everything seemed to be cut off all at once.'[13] During that winter of 1926–7, there was a serious coal shortage due to a strike. Day after day Constance drove out to the mountain bogs, piled her car with turf and hauled it in heavy bags up countless stairs to the old people of her constituency. Many of her friends could not understand why she did this. Why would she not at least let others haul the bags up those stairs when there were so many 'who would be only too happy to do it'?

But for Constance, it was a very womanly thing to do. Men, typically, would hold endless meetings to discuss the problem while the people froze. Although she was an indefatigable attender of meetings because they were the only form of politics available to her, she disliked them and was inclined to sketch and doodle and write letters when they grew tedious. Meetings were politics as practised by men and to which she had decided to conform. But what she really believed in was immediate alleviative action. Carrying bags of turfs directly to those who needed it was an act of protest, that perhaps she didn't articulate to herself, against that pervasive version of politics, which had, time and again, failed to effect the changes she worked for.

Fianna Fáil's programme for the elections of June 1927 included Irish self-sufficiency. This meant that tariff barriers would protect national economic development. This policy appealed to Constance and she may have helped to formulate it because she and de Valera sometimes met to discuss such issues. During the campaign she broke an arm while cranking the car and is reputed to have said 'Glory be. It's only my arm, I can still talk.'[14] She continued to go electioneering with her arm in a sling. And she was still wearing it when, after a successful election for Fianna Fáil

– the party won 44 seats to its rival Cumann na nGael's 46, and Constance easily kept her seat – the Fianna Fáil deputies walked to the Dáil chamber. They had decided to attempt to gain entrance without taking 'the oath' – the Oath of Allegiance to the King. In a picture taken on this occasion, Constance looks, although she was tall, very frail and alone beside the men around her – strong, burly, younger – striding confidently into the future. When they refused to take the oath, the door was barred against them and they retired to take up again their stance of abstention.

In the following October the Fianna Fáil party did enter the Dáil, or the Free State parliament, as Constance called it, refusing to bestow on it that hallowed title. To do so, de Valera both did and did not take the oath. In Irish, he told the Clerk of the Dáil – whose own knowledge of Irish may not have been quite up to understanding what he was saying – that he was merely putting 'his name down in this book in order to get permission to go into the Dáil, but it has no other significance'. While he took the testament, he covered it and said 'You must remember I am taking no Oath'. To ask whether Constance would consider this sleight-of-hand dishonourable or acceptable is academic because by then, she was dead.

Early in July during a meeting of the Fianna Fáil executive, Constance became ill and was brought to Sir Patrick Dun's Hospital. She was placed, at her own insistence, in a public ward. She was operated on for appendicitis and seemed to recover, but later had to have a second operation for peritonitis. It was now evident that she was gravely ill. The hospital was besieged with old friends. Esther Roper arrived from London and she and Helena Molony, Maire Perolz, May Coughlan and some others undertook a night vigil in the hospital's boardroom to pray for her recovery. Éamon de Valera came and found her in great pain but independent and vivacious as ever. He suggested that she might like to be moved to a private ward. 'She was angry with me because she felt that I was suggesting that what was good enough for the ordinary poor was not good enough for her. She had always helped the workers and the needy and she wanted to be identified with them.'[15]

Then, to Constance's enormous joy, Casimir and Stasko arrived from Warsaw, summoned by a radiogram from Esther, which was broadcast on the BBC World Service. They had a bouquet of roses sent ahead and as her trembling fingers opened the packaging she said proudly, 'Look. Don't they know how to do things.' At sight of them she announced 'This is the happiest day of my life.' Casimir sketched a deathbed portrait; a faded and attenuated figure, it is a deeply saddening image of a woman, prematurely aged, who was once so vital. And yet she could speak with her old verve. Stasko teased her about refusing an admirer who became a diplomat and would have made her an 'Excellency', and wanted to know why she had married Casimir instead: '"Because I liked your father better" she rejoined in that quaint quizzical way of hers. "I liked your father best", those were her last words to me on this earth...'[16]

Maeve too was often by her bedside. The four members of the Irish branch of the Markieviczes were assembled together for the last time. In the streets outside, groups of the poor people whose love she had won sang and prayed and begged for news. She, who had been heard to say wryly, 'I sometimes long for the peace of the Republican Plot', declared happily now, 'But it is so beautiful to have had all this love and kindness before I go.'[17] In the early hours of 15 July 1927 she died, surrounded by her family and friends. Her mother had died the January before and in the Bible Con had by her bed, she had written: 'To Mother and Eva 1927 – They are not dead, they do not sleep; / They have awakened from the dream of life.'

Casi sent a telegram to Josslyn. 'Constance passed away peacefully this morning 1 a.m. Markievicz.'

Her funeral was one of those huge public funerals, which Dublin gives to her champions, and perhaps to those she feels she has failed. It also reflected the divisions in Irish society. The government refused her body the honour of lying-in-state in a civic building. Instead, after a night reposing in St Andrew's Church in Westland Row, the coffin was brought to the Pillar Room of the Rotunda Hospital. This classically imposing hall was a venue for entertainments such as dances and Christmas fairs but it was also where Constance had attended her first Sinn Féin meeting. The myriad organizations she had influenced and had influenced her in the past two decades turned out – the Citizen Army, Cumann na mBan, Sinn Féin, Fianna Fáil, The Workers Union ... Fianna boys stood to attention and the populace filed past to pay their respects to she whom they knew as Madame. Many were in tears.

The funeral procession was watched by thousands of citizens. On the way to Glasnevin it took a detour to St Stephen's Green for the traditional re-visit of places dear to the deceased. Coming back it took two hours to pass the length of O'Connell Street. Eight tenders were required to carry the wreaths and flowers. Sir Josslyn and Lady Mary travelled with the Markieviczes behind the carriage bearing her coffin, wrapped in the tricolour and covered in flowers. Behind them came the Fianna Fáil TDs headed by Éamon de Valera and behind them, Cumann na mBan, Sinn Féin, the Fianna and it seemed, the whole trade-union movement led by Jim Larkin wearing a red rosette in his lapel. There was a banner from the USSR with Russian script, though this did not please Casimir and Stasko. At Glasnevin, Free State soldiers stood by to prevent a volley being fired over her grave. De Valera delivered a moving oration:

> Madame Markievicz is gone from us, Madame, the friend of the toiler, the lover of the poor. Ease and station she put aside ... Sacrifice, misunderstanding and scorn lay on the road she adopted, but she trod it unflinchingly ... We knew the kindliness, the great woman's heart of her, the great Irish soul of her, and we know the loss we have suffered is not to be repaired. It is sadly we take our leave, but we pray high heaven that all she longed for may one day be achieved.

That same week children got a day off school to mourn the death of the Vice-President, Kevin O'Higgins, shot the Sunday before by republicans. O'Higgins' coffin was also wrapped in the tricolour. He was given a full military funeral and government ministers walked behind the cortege.

Constance Markievicz's last journey, lacking official pomp but replete with spontaneous love, was in keeping with her life. As ever, she was on the people's side, and they on hers, that side, which often looks at the time like the wrong side, but somehow always seems the right side in the end.

NOTES

1. From 'In Memory of Eva Gore-Booth and Con Markievicz', in *Collected Poems, W.B. Yeats*, p. 263.
2. *Labour in Irish Politics*, Mitchell, p. 197.
3. *The Rebel Countess*, Marreco, p. 284.
4. *Life and the Dream*, Colum, pp. 278–81.
5. Francis Stuart in conversation with the author.
6. Cited in *Constance Markievicz*, O'Faolain.
7. *Prison Letters*, Roper, p. 306.
8. Ms in the National Museum, Dublin.
9. *Prison Letters*, Roper, p. 307.
10. *Ibid.*, p. 308.
11. Letter in National Museum, Dublin.
12. *The Rebel Countess*, Marreco, p. 298.
13. *Prison Letters*, Roper, p. 312.
14. *The Rebel Countess*, Marreco, p. 298.
15. De Valera, *The Irish Independent*, 10 July 1967.
16. *The Polish Irishman*, Patrick Quigley (Liffey Press, Dublin, 2012).
17. *Prison Letters*, Roper, pp. 109–10.

BIBLIOGRAPHY

BOOKS

Bashkirtseff, Marie, *Journal* (London: Virago, 1985).

Beckett, J.C., *The Anglo-Irish Tradition* (Belfast: Blackstaff, 1977).

Beckett, J.C., *The Making of Modern Ireland* (London: Faber, 1981).

Beresford Ellis, Peter, *A History of the Irish Working Class* (London and Sydney: Pluto, 1985).

Borzello, Frances, *The Artist's Model* (London: Junction Books, 1983).

Cardozo, Nancy, *Maud Gonne, Lucky Eyes and a High Heart* (London: Gollancz, 1979).

Catty, James, *Ireland 1851–1921, a Documentary Record* (Dublin: Fallon, 1986).

Casey, Daniel J. & Rhodes, Robert E., *Views of the Irish Peasantry 1800–1916* (Hamden, Connecticut: Anchor, 1977).

Caulfield, Max, *The Easter Rebellion* (London: Muller, 1964).

Colum, Mary, *Life and the Dream* (New York: Doubleday, 1947).

Connolly, Sean, *Religion and Society in Nineteenth Century Ireland* (Dundalk: Dundalgan Press, 1985).

Coxhead, Elizabeth, *Daughters of Erin* (London: Secker and Warburg, 1965).

Cronin, Anthony, *Heritage Now: Irish Literature in the English Language* (Dingle: Brandon, 1982).

Cronin, Sean, *Irish Nationalism* (Dublin: Academy, 1980).

Denson, Alan (ed.), *Letters from Æ* (London: Abelard Schuman, 1961).

Digby, Margaret, *Horace Plunkett* (Oxford: Basil Blackwell, 1948).

Domville, Eric and Kelly, John, *The Collected Letters of W.B. Yeats* (Oxford: Clarendon Press, 1986).

Drudy, P.J. (ed.), *Ireland: Land, Politics and People* (Cambridge: Cambridge University Press, 1982).

Edwards, Ruth Dudley, *Life of Patrick Pearse – The Triumph of Failure* (London: Gollancz, 1977).

Ferriter, Diarmaid, *A Nation and Not a Rabble* (London: Profile, 2015).

Fingall, Elizabeth, Countess of, *Seventy Years Young* (London: Collins, 1937).

Finnegan, T.A., *Sinbad's Yellow Shore* (Keohane, Sligo: Dolmen, 1977).

Foster, R.F., *Vivid Faces* (London: Allen Lane, 2014).

Fitzpatrick, David, *Politics and Irish Life 1913–1921* (Dublin: Gill & Macmillan, 1977).

Fitzpatrick, David (ed.), *Ireland and the First World War* (Dublin: Trinity History Workshop, 1986).

Fogarty, L. (ed.), *James Fintan Lawlor, Collected Writings* (Dublin: The Talbot Press, 1947).

Fox, R.M., *Rebel Irishwomen* (Dublin and Cork: Talbot Press, 1935).

Foy, Michael and Barton, Brian, *The Easter Rising* (Stroud, 1999).

Gillis, Liz, *Women of the Revolution* (Cork: Mercier, 2014).

Gore-Booth, Eva, *Collected Poems* (London: Longmans Green, 1929).

Gore-Booth, Eva, *The Death of Fionavar*, illustrated by Constance de Markievicz, (London: MacDonald, 1916).

Gregory, Lady, *Our Irish Theatre* (New York: Putnam's, 1915).

Griffith, Kenneth and O'Grady, Timothy E., *Curious Journey* (London: Hutchinson, 1982).

Hone, Joseph, *J.B. Yeats: Letters to his Son and Others* (London: Faber & Faber, 1944).

Hone, Joseph, *The Life of Henry Tonks* (London: Heinemann, 1934).

Hunt, Hugh, *The Abbey, Ireland's National Theatre* (Dublin: Gill & Macmillan, 1979).

Larkin, Emmet, *James Larkin: Irish Labour Leader 1876–1947* (Massachusetts: Routledge & Kegan Paul, 1965).

Levenson, Sam, *Maud Gonne* (London: Cassell, 1977).

Lyons, F.S.L., *Ireland Since the Famine* (London: Fontana, 1978).

Lyons, F.S.L., *Culture and Anarchy in Ireland 1890–1939* (Oxford: Clarendon Press, 1979).

MacBride, Maud Gonne, *A Servant of the Queen* (Dublin: Gollancz, 1974).

McCoole, Sinead, *Easter Widows* (Dublin: Doubleday Ireland, 2014).

MacEoin, Uinseann, *Survivors* (Dublin: Argenta, 1980).

McGarry, Fearghal, *Voices From the Easter Rising* (Dublin, Penguin Ireland, 2011).

Magnus, Sir Phillip, *Gladstone* (London: Murray, 1954).

Markievicz, Casimir Dunin, *The Memory of the Dead* (Dublin: Tower, 1910).

Markievicz, Constance de, *Women, Ideals and the Nation* (Dublin: Inighnidhe na h-Éireann, 1907).

Marreco, Anne, *The Rebel Countess* (London: Weidenfeld & Nicholson, 1967).

Martin, F.X., *Leaders and Men of the Easter 'Rising, Dublin 1916* (London: Methuen, 1967).

Matthews, Ann, *Renegades* (Cork: Mercier Press, 2010).

Mitchell, Arthur, *Labour in Irish Politics* (Dublin: Irish University Press, 1974).

Murphy, William M., *Prodigal Father, The Life of John Butler Yeats* (Ithaca: Cornell University Press, 1978).

Neely, W.G., *Kilcooley* (Belfast: Universities Press, 1983).

Neligan, David, *The Spy in the Castle* (London: MacGibbon & Kee, 1968).

Nowlan, Kevin B., *The Making of 1916* (Dublin: Stationery Office, 1969).

O'Brien, Nora Connolly, *Portrait of a Rebel Father* (Dublin: Four Masters, 1975).

O'Broin, Leon, *Dublin Castle and the 1916 Rising* (Dublin: Gill & Macmillan, 1966).

O'Casey, Sean, *Drums Under the Windows* (London: Pan, 1972).

O'Casey, Sean, *The Story of the Irish Citizen Army* (Dublin: Maunsel, 1919).

O'Connor, Seamus, *Tomorrow Was Another Day* (Dublin: ROC, 1987).

O'Day, Alan (ed.), *Reactions to Irish Nationalism* (Dublin: Gill & Macmillan, 1987).

O'Faolain, Sean, *Constance Markievicz or the Average Revolutionary* (London: Jonathan Cape, 1934).

O'Ruairc, Padraig Og, *Revolution* (Cork: Mercier Press, 2014)

Plunkett, Horace, *Ireland in the New Century* (London: John Murray, 1905).

Quigley, Patrick, *The Polish Irishman* (Dublin: Liffey Press, 2012).

Roper, Esther (ed.), *Prison Letters of Countess Markievicz* (London–New York–Toronto: Longmans Green & Co, 1934).

Rumpf, E. and Hepburn, A.C., *Nationalism and Socialism in Twentieth-Century Ireland* (Liverpool: Liverpool University Press, 1977).

Ryan, Desmond, *Remembering Sion* (London: Arthur Barker, 1934).

Shiubhlaigh, Maire ni, *The Splendid Years* (Dublin: Duffy, 1955).

Singleton-Gates, Peter and Girodias, Maurice, *The Black Diaries of Roger Casement* (New York: Grove Press, 1959).

Skinnider, Margaret, *Doing My Bit for Ireland* (New York: Century, 1917).

Stephens, James, *The Insurrection in Dublin* (Dublin: Scepter, 1965).

Thomson, David, *Woodbrook* (London: Penguin, 1976).

Thornton, Alfred, *The Diary of an Art Student in the Nineties* (London: Sir Isaac Pitman, 1938).

Torchiana, Donald T., *W.B. Yeats and Georgian Ireland* (Evanston: Northwestern University Press, 1966).

Townshend, Charles, *Easter 1916* (London: Penguin, 2005)

Townshend, Charles, *The Republic: Fight for Irish Independence* (London: Penguin, 2013).

Van Voris, Jacqueline, *Constance Markievicz in the Cause of Ireland* (Boston: University of Massachusetts Press, 1967).

Ward, Margaret, *Unmanageable Revolutionaries* (Dingle: Brandon, 1983).

Wynne, Maud, *An Irishman and His Family* (London: John Murray, 1937).

Yeats, W.B., *Collected Poems* (London: Macmillan, 1982).

Yeats, W.B., *Autobiography* (London: Doubleday Anchor, 1958).

NEWSPAPERS, PERIODICALS, PAMPHLETS ETC.

'James Connolly's Policy and Catholic Doctrine' by Constance de Markievicz, Dublin 1924, *Bean na h-Éireann, Eire, Fianna, Freeman's Journal, An Phoblacht, Sinn Féin, The Peasant, The Irish Worker, Worker's Republic, Irish Bulletin, Spark, The Irish Citizen, The Nation, New Ireland, The Sligo Champion, The Sligo Independent, The Times, The Irish Times, The Irish Press, The Irish Independent, The Word, The Literary Digest.*

OTHER SOURCES

Dáil Éireann: Private Sessions vol. 1, August to September 1921; vol. 2, December 1921 to January 1922. Dáil Éireann: Official Report, Debate on the Treaty, Dublin 1922. The Griffith Valuation. Archives of the Bureau of Military History.

INDEX